Rethinking Tribe in Indian Context

Rethinking Tribe in Indian Context

Realities, Issues and Challenges

Editors

BIDHAN KANTI DAS
RAJAT KANTI DAS

RAWAT PUBLICATIONS
Jaipur • New Delhi • Bangalore • Guwahati • Kolkata

ISBN 978-81-316-0817-3

Published by
Prem Rawat for **Rawat Publications**
Satyam Apts, Sector 3, Jawahar Nagar, Jaipur 302 004 (India)
Phone: 0141 265 1748 / 7006 Fax: 0141 265 1748
E-mail: info@rawatbooks.com
Website: www.rawatbooks.com

New Delhi Office
4858/24, Ansari Road, Daryaganj, New Delhi 110 002
Phone: 011 2326 3290

Also at *Bangalore, Guwahati* and *Kolkata*

Typeset by Rawat Computers, Jaipur
Printed and bound in India

Contents

Part III
Mainstream Development and Tribals

Part IV
Forest and Tribals

Part V
Governance and Tribals

Part VI
Emerging Areas of Tribal Studies

List of Tables and Figures

Tables

Figures

Preface

It cannot be denied that the general understanding about tribes is somewhat hazy, confusing and at times biased. It lacks clarity and takes things for granted. A sincere effort should be made to critically examine the conceptual process fraught with cross-current of ideas that goes with tribal formation. In order to see them in proper perspective, tribes are to be contextualised. Admittedly, issues and problems associated with tribes are not always their own making. In a country like India marked by pluralism, cultural and physical diversity, political ambiguity and growing intolerance, tribal rights need to be reassessed, though not in the way the top-heavy administrators or theoretically overburdened academicians would like to see them. What is needed is practical and positivist thinking without taking recourse to imposing ideas of one's own making. One should have a clear understanding about the present realities, issues and challenges confronting tribes in various contexts in contemporary India before making any attempt to conceptualise tribes as a distinct category. The proposed book will cover multi-disciplinary areas including anthropology, sociology, political science, history, tribal studies, social work and natural resource management.

We hope this volume will be a substantial contribution to tribal studies in India, looking beyond mere inclusion and exclusion perspective.

Bidhan Kanti Das
Rajat Kanti Das

a

Acknowledgements

At the very beginning, we would like to express our gratitude to all our contributors, whose expertise and knowledge in tribal studies from diverse academic backgrounds have contributed enormously to the initiative that has resulted in the production of this book. This book came to light after some unintended delay and we appreciate all our contributors for their patience and continuous support extended during this period.

Most of the chapters that feature in this book were presented at a three-day national conference on 'Conceptualising and Contextualising Tribes in Contemporary India' in February 2014. It was organised by the Institute of Development Studies Kolkata (IDSK) in collaboration with Indian Anthropological Society, Kolkata. This conference was a highly stimulating event driven not only by the excellent set of presentations from our speakers but also equally by the discussions and comments from the participants. This energetic, enthusiastic and critical group of people ranged from doctoral students and young researchers to reputed researchers from various academic disciplines. This book would be incomplete without an acknowledgement of the valuable contribution of all the participants of the conference.

We are grateful to Professor Achin Chakraborty, Director of the Institute of Development Studies Kolkata (IDSK) for constant inspiration and logistic support. We acknowledge with thanks, the constant support and inspiration of our colleagues at the Institute of Development Studies Kolkata (IDSK) for organising the conference. We express our warm thanks to Dr Gorky Chakraborty at IDSK who continuously enquired about the progress of the book. We are grateful to the Indian Council Social Science Research, New Delhi and Institute of Development Studies Kolkata (IDSK) for providing financial assistance in this endeavour.

We would like to thank those who have helped in and supported the process of producing both the conference itself and this book. We recall with gratitude the excellent support we received from our library personnel, particularly Ms Madhusri Ghosh, Ashok Patra and Biswanath Ghosh who helped us to procure relevant literature whenever required. We express our thanks to Ms Sanchari Guha for editorial assistance. We are also grateful to the entire staff of IDSK for helping generously whenever such help was needed.

Again, many thanks to the contributors for the trust they reposed in us despite some delay. Finally, we take the opportunity to express our gratitude to Mr Pranit Rawat of Rawat Publications for undertaking the publication of the volume. Our thanks are due to the editorial team at Rawat Publications, Jaipur, for adding value to this manuscript.

Contributors

Abhijit Guha, Professor, Department of Anthropology, Vidyasagar University, West Medinipur, West Bengal.

Arun D. Paul, Research Scholar, Department of Social Work, Delhi School of Social Work, University of Delhi, New Delhi.

Bidhan Kanti Das, Associate Professor of Anthropology, Institute of Development Studies Kolkata (IDSK).

Dayabati Roy, Guest Faculty, Department of Sociology, University of Burdawn, Bardhaman, West Bengal.

Dipannita Chakraborty, Principal, Dasaratha Deb Memorial College, Khowai, Government of Tripura, Tripura.

Jayanta Madhab Tamuly, Research Scholar, Department of Peace and Conflict Studies and Management, Sikkim University, Gangtok, Sikkim.

Pradeep Kumar Mishra, Assistant Professor, School of Rural Management, Xavier University, Bhubaneswar, Odisha.

Rajanita Das Purkayastha, Researcher, Social Solidarity Economy (SSE), ASEC–Malaysia and India.

Rajat Kanti Das, former Professor and UGC Emeritus Fellow, Department of Anthropology, Vidyasagar University, Medinipur, West Bengal.

Rajatsubhra Mukhopadhyay, Professor of Sociology, Department of Sociology, North Bengal University, Siliguri, West Bengal.

Samir Kumar Das, Professor of Political Science, Dean of Arts, University of Calcutta; Former Vice Chancellor, North Bengal University, Siliguri, West Bengal.

Santanu Panda, ICSSR Post Doctoral Fellow, Department of Anthropology, Vidyasagar University, West Medinipur, West Bengal.

Subir Rana, Associate Research Fellow, Institute of Chinese Studies, New Delhi.

Swatasiddha Sarkar, Assistant Professor, Department of Sociology, North Bengal University, Siliguri, West Bengal.

CHAPTER 1

Introduction

Contemporary Relevance of Tribal Studies in India

RAJAT KANTI DAS AND BIDHAN KANTI DAS

From the anthropological perspective, a tribe used to be seen as a self-reproducing 'life world' of stable organisations and shared histories. Such a group needed to be territorially bound and culturally distinct. But territorial integrity, which used to be associated with a tribe almost in an absolute sense, can no longer be applied in all situations. Not only are tribes placed in different situations, the situation itself has changed much to the disadvantage of a tribe, which can no longer keep aloft its ideal character. Again, from tribe's own point of view, it is not easy to maintain its ideal form without being affected by various extrinsic and intrinsic factors. Conventional economic categories associated with tribes have given rise to new functional categories in terms of new technology-oriented activities. Increasing contact with the outside world has led to changes of far-reaching consequences in the tribal society. Among the changes, one is extension of exchange nexus to the tribal economy resulting in unequal exchange in respect of both goods and inputs, which sometimes act as an instrument of exploitation. This could be one reason why tribals are almost invariably equated with marginalised, deprived or disadvantaged groups. But the strength and weakness of tribe cannot simply be explained only by seeing how the relations are getting commercialised and how the negative inputs are finding easy access into the tribal system. To identify the areas where tribal's internal social and environmental needs have come into direct conflict with the profit-raising activities encouraged by the state and other business organisations would probably be a more useful exercise. What is of particular importance is the fact that this conflict has become an inseparable component of tribal existence at present.

Today the tribals find themselves entrenched into 'state based' models of the political. The impact of the broader political framework operating in the domains of tribal culture and society was never so strongly felt as it is today. Still, the tribals as social actors respond to their cultural, social and even political exigencies and expectations of their members in a way that bears the stamp of distinctiveness and often decisiveness. This is not always a smooth affair. They sometimes take resort to extremist activities to retain or reaffirm their distinctive character. Though territorially bounded localities as represented by tribes are getting rarer and more complex, they need to be distinguished from 'de-territorialised localities', which gives rise to a new form of articulation with the global process. But there are also tribal localities which function as sites of resistance to greater political forces striking at their socio-cultural autonomy. The papers included in this volume, though varied in nature, have one common concern: to see tribes in the context of politico-historical, economic and social pressures emanated from external sources and view them from regional, national and even global perspective. The mood is one of manifesting tensions between change and pursuance of cultural integrity, between resistance to development as it is perpetuated by the state and selective adoption of measures to claim the benefits, between occupational mobility and reproduction of traditional values, between adherence to locally bounded systems and opting for regional, national and in few cases international alliances. Tribal studies no doubt concentrate more on locals, small regional groups, disadvantaged communities, but it cannot be denied that more often local values, customs and practices are raised to a level of absolute principle from which all deviances are judged and even analysed. In such a representation the dissenting voice(s) do not always mean violation, deviance and are therefore immoral. It is possible to create meaning out of those experiences.

Clearly there is a need for rethinking the rather one-sided view of tribes in terms of social exclusion and inclusion propagated by those who are primarily engaged in academic theorising and by those who in the name of governance use it rather mechanically as a set pattern. A predetermined analysis and assessment of tribes leaves much to be desired. It sometimes creates confusion and even gives a distorted, if not totally wrong picture. The tribal question has to be treated more nationally, which means that it should be more nuanced, balanced and would focus more on their own perspective. The type of development prescribed by the government for tribes is primarily aimed at concentrating on their backwardness and poverty and speaking rather loudly about the measures to be taken to cure them or implement those measures to ameliorate their poor material conditions of life. Conventional development strategies devised by the government have reduced the tribals to mere objects of study and experimentation to provide a framework for attribution of government responsibility. But who does really benefit from such exercises? Moreover, do the beneficiaries strengthen the case of tribes as compact and coordinated groups for their inclusion as a special category? The enlightened sections of the community are caught between national/local connections and have become entangled with the practice of pursuing divisive hegemonies that operate within the regional, national or even international structures of power. That is probably the reason why our own search for congruence of political identity – operating locally or regionally – and national identity has become increasingly problematic. To put it another way, our understanding of tribes as a socio-political unit with a shared culture and possession of common material, non-material or institutional structure identifiable at the local level is problematic. If tribes exemplify a form of collective self-representation, the representation today is far from a uniform, unconditional and smooth affair.

In other words, any attempt to define tribal groups in contemporary India is problematic. At the same time, there is a growing realisation that the universalist definition of 'Tribe' adopted by national policy-makers needs to be revised. So, there is a need for closer scrutiny of the concept of tribe and determine its contextualisation process. Ideally, this should involve examining processual nature behind tribal phenomenon, its perspectival and plural quality and part played by it in constitution and reconstitution of state and non-state organisations. The inner dynamics of tribal system should be looked into. Contemporary anthropologists try to understand tribe in the dual framework 'self in the other and other in the self' connotation. In this context it becomes imperative to take a relook at the conceptual basis of treating tribe as a distinct category.

Tribe and Tribal Related Issues as Projected by Contributors

An attempt has been made in this book to get a clear picture of the different facets of tribal existence with reference to its encounter with modern forces operating in the field of political economy. Each individual case has its own merit and may be taken as a test case in any concept-building exercise. Put together, the contributions will be able to give a comprehensive picture of tribal existence in contemporary India.

Rajat Kanti Das in his paper '*Contextualising Indian Tribes: Some Common Attributes*', contends that far from a homogeneous category, Indian tribes reveal a wide range of diversity. Such a categorisation may be a more meaningful exercise if tribes are seen from a 'regional' perspective. Admittedly, they are the product of a regional history and the territorial integrity they manifest has a regional reference. It has to be conceded that the traditional definition of 'tribe' adopted by anthropologists does not reflect the correct situation confronting tribes in the Indian context. So far as tribes are concerned, culture and occupation may not automatically be linked together. The author argues that changes in occupation may not signify changes in cultural capacity. Again, tribe's entry into the modern state is a recent phenomenon compared to other societies. That does not mean they had no association with any form of state-organised system. Some of the Chota Nagpur tribes were directly involved in the process of state formation. For him, if the tribes manifest a type of 'traditionalism', it is because through this they try to glorify their cultural tradition. The ideologies of glorifying cultural traditions tend to take the form of ethnic ideologies. Though such traditions are consciously developed and constructed, these have relevance for the peoples in question. With materialistic values of 'commercial cultures' entering into the tribal system, traditional culture seems to have lost its grip over the people so long grounded in traditional practices and behaviours. 'Econocentric' and 'techno centric' emphasis of developmental intervention have shaken the very base of culture (Cernea 1995). In this situation, author argues that a special endeavour on the part of tribals is needed so that they could 'self-locate' themselves. Politics, revolving around group interests, have now engaged tribes to a greater extent and in the process they have become entangled more and more with conflict-ridden activities. Their involvement with extremist activities under the garb of Maoists could be a political strategy aimed at demolishing the officially dictated policies concerning their development.

In his paper *'Conceptualising the Context: "Tribes" of North Bengal'*, Samir Kumar Das reflects not so much on tribes as such – but on certain groups and communities whose identity as *tribes* is, to say the least, problematic. Problematic, for him, not because their desire of being scheduled as tribes remains unfulfilled – although that is the most commonplace trajectory of research hitherto conducted on tribes in India – but because they find it difficult to articulate their desire in the first place, refuse to express it in case they are able to articulate their desire in the face of repeated denials and rejections by the so-called mainstream society; and finally if they are ever successful in expressing it, the desire itself eventually turns out to be disastrous for the community leading to its disorganisation. These are the consequences they are pre-required to face.

In his article *'Application and Distortion of Indigeneity as an Expression of Tribe'*, Rajat Kanti Das argues that 'indigeneity' in its present form may not be conceived as a typically anthropologically concept because it is now heavily loaded with the question of political and legal representation. Admittedly, the composition and distribution of populations, inter-ethnic relations and power structure always remained region specific. The political history of an indigenous people has been shaped by other populations in the region, whom it was regularly in contact with. For him, the tribal character of indigenous groups may be suggestive of the fact that they have always been dominated over by the non-tribals who have assumed the position of mainstream population through the state structure, thereby perpetuating a system of domination and suppression. According to Das, there is a need to redefine indigeneity according to local requirements, particularly for attainment of political goals by the indigenous peoples. Indigenous peoples need to be recognised within wider comparative contexts of anthropological depiction of such peoples with the help of solid historical ethnography. Here the present day anthropology has a specific role to play, he concluded.

Rajat Subhra Mukhopadhyay in his paper *'On the Question of Inequality of Tribal Social Formation'* opines that the concept of 'tribe' as an 'ideal' form of homogeneous social organisation is in crisis now. There is a need to re-examine the meaning of the word 'tribe', which is firmly rooted in the lexicon, both contextually and empirically. Tribe is often perceived as a 'distinct' type of society which is socially or structurally undifferentiated, un-stratified and egalitarian in its social formation. Author's experience shows that at present the 'tribe' representing an anthropologist's 'ideal type' can rarely be found as they have been absorbed, in varying degrees, in the wider society. The tribes in contemporary India, both in its 'traditional' and 'transitional' settings, are hardly egalitarian in their social formation. Some endemic and emerging forms of social inequality are well present among many of them. Mukhopadhyay lays emphasis on examining the concept of 'tribe' from the perspective of social inequality. The forms of inequality and stratification that have been observed among some tribes in India can be cited here for ready reference. These have, for him, considerable relevance while conceptualising and contextualising tribes in contemporary India.

The paper *'Politics of Identity and Growing Tribalism in the Darjeeling Hills'*, by Swatasiddha Sarkar has the moot point that the idea of identity from being a matter primarily of personal belongingness has transcended itself towards community filiations. There is no gainsaying the truth that in plural societies like ours the bases of identification have been many and multifarious. The trajectory of mapping up one's own identity has made myriad manifestations – ethnic, religious, regional, national appellations are being the most prominent ones. Sarkar contends that it is rather non-problematic to argue that modern individuals have multiple identities but the areas of concern for the social scientists is the issue that when and how one particular base of identification (among many) becomes overpowering than others. What seem important are not merely the bases of identification but their context with varying meanings. For him, the moot point is that the identity formations and identification are transitory, temporal. These are at best social constructs. And as social constructs they underlie relations of power and questions of dominance. The growing body of literature has amply confirmed that these issues of identity are never unified and are increasingly fragmented and fractured, never singular but multiple; constructed across different, often contradictory, channels of cultural practices and positions. Moreover, the issues of identity and identification are rolled in the 'historical pasts' or 'cultural givens' of a community life but they use them more as necessary resources to compete the process of 'becoming' rather than of 'being'. Sarkar seeks to situate the issues of ethnic revivalism and growing tribalism in Darjeeling hills within the above-posed conceptual framework. The analysis of tribal situation in Darjeeling hills is a pointer. Besides being the historical site of a durable ethnic conflict, Darjeeling hills have acquired political prominence in recent times for being the playground of ethnic revivalism and tribalism. Besides the Bhutias, Lepchas and Sherpas – the three designated tribes of Darjeeling hills since India's independence – majority of the hill population are of Nepali ethnic stock. Sarkar further seeks to examine this crucial issue of politicisation of tribal identity for which a handful of hill communities are undergoing ethnic revivalism in a programmatic manner in the present-day context. Growing tribalism in Darjeeling hills, according to him, has appeared as a live current of hill politics at that period of time when ethnic revivalism took place in a big way in the neighbouring country of Nepal. The gravity of the problem under study becomes even more palpable when one takes into account the governmental step to create separate development board for the already designated tribes (viz. Lepchas) as a measure to protect their interests. Whether the current spell of identity politics and the consequent tribalism and ethnic revivalism thereof in the Darjeeling hills approximate the processes of *'desanskritisation'* or a new mode of *'kiratisation'*, is indeed a matter of discussion and debate. Again, whether the exclusiveness of Gorkha identity gets diluted out of all these and, consequently, whether it can sustain itself as a hold-all category irrespective of the fate of ethnic revivalism and tribalism in the hills, are questions which need further exploration.

Jayanta Madhab Tamuly in his paper *'The Teesta Warriors: A Study on the Cultural Dimensions of the Emerging Lepcha Identity in the Backdrop of the Anti-Dam Movement in Sikkim'*, closely examines how anti-dam movement turns out to be a mechanism to protect cultural existence and identity. The anti-dam movement, led by the Lepchas of the hilly state of Sikkim, has been transcending its boundary from mere geo-technical issues and appears to be an identity movement of the indigenous Himalayan tribe. Lepchas of Sikkim, centrally habited in the reserved forest of Dzongu, claim the hydro-power projects and the dams over the river Teesta to be the serious threats for their living and identity. Hence, this movement against the dams turns out to be a mechanism to protect their existence and identity which has already attracted worldwide attention. In this process, Lepchas have been carefully deploying their cultural instruments ranging from their traditional dress codes to songs and religious symbols. The author tries to look into the cultural dimension of the identity movement of the Lepchas. The use of culture in collective mobilisation, formation of identity and coordination of diversified ideological groups for the sustenance and protection of the ethnic identity characterise a small Himalayan tribe like the Lepchas. In the present case the thrust is on anti-dam movement as a protest movement and how it actually helps in protecting their identity.

Arun D. Paul in his article *'The Need for Promoting Indigenous Indicators to Tribal Development: A Case Study of the Paniyan Tribe from Kerala'* raises question on the abysmal status of tribal in India despite affirmative policies and programmes. At the same time, he pointed that these measures focusing upon improving human development indicators (HDI) largely problematise the nature of tribal communities leaving out the approach itself. Employing a case study of tribal in Kerala, such HDI-focused development paradigm for tribal development is problemetised in this paper. According to him, though Kerala has the highest HDI in India comparable to most developed nations, it has been observed that the debates largely miss the abominable status of the tribals in Kerala, which is an irony to Kerala's 'Development Experience'. The paper is based on the field work conducted with Paniyan tribal community, the most deprived of thirty-five notified tribal communities, in the Wyanad district of Kerala. Using historical and narrative analysis in the process of research, five historical phases of dispossession that Paniyan had gone through is identified. Each phase is demarcated by the arrival of an outsider community with superior livelihood practices or technologies engaging with tribal and later developing exploitative production relations with tribals. Based on historical analysis, Paul has shown how a common pattern of servility of tribals to different outsider communities emerges. He pleads for new development variables for policy-making based on sociological and anthropological studies, especially when the tribal development programmes have not yielded the expected results since Independence.

In their paper *'Towards Demarginalisation of the Lodhas of West Bengal: A Study in the Assessment of the Impact of Development Efforts by the State'*, Santanu Panda and Abhijit Guha closely examine the development scenario of the Lodha-tribal community in the context of particularly vulnerable tribal groups (PTGs) in West Bengal. The Lodhas carry with them a long history of injustice and have been able to draw the attention of the administrators, anthropologists, social activists and the media as well. During colonial times this community was designated as a 'criminal tribe' and carried the social stigma during the post-colonial period, although the government created category after category (e.g. 'Denotified' and 'Primitive Tribal Group') to designate this marginalised community. Being on the margins of the mainstream, this forest dependent community suffered economic and social injustice despite governmental funding towards their development. The anthropologists have studied the Lodha society and culture in the traditional ethnographic fashion and at the same time suggested developmental measures for the improvement in their living conditions. The social workers on the other hand, were found to be more engaged and quite justifiably, to fight against social injustice and human rights violations among the Lodhas by the state and the dominant groups of the society. The grassroot-level reality, which emerged from the media reports, anthropologists, accounts and activists literature, revealed that the marginalisation of the Lodhas continued long after Independence. The authors in this case made a location-based empirical assessment of the field realities of Lodha development by the state and found that from the beginning till today most, if not all, of the governmental attempts towards development of the Lodhas were misplaced, and as a result the funds remained unutilised, wasted and did not work at all, although variations in terms of utilisation were also observed. They argued that a more systematic and down-to-earth approach, which is sensitive towards the needs of the community should be undertaken to demarginalise the Lodhas of West Bengal.

Pradeep Kumar Mishra's paper *'Forest Policies and Tribal Livelihoods: An Organisational Perspective'* deals with various aspects of implementation of forest policies from organisational perspective. Forest policies in India have invariably influenced tribal livelihoods. Till 1970s forest policies favoured commercial exploitation that led to continuous depletion of forests which in turn eroded the livelihood base of tribal population. In 1980s the conservation focus was brought in, resulting in reduction of deforestation but tribal livelihoods still remained unaddressed. Only after the National Forest Policy of 1988 the tribal livelihoods were recognised, which received a further push after the forest rights act was passed in 2006. Though forest policies vis-à-vis tribal livelihoods have been studied from political economy, socio-cultural and ecological perspectives, but the organisational perspective has not received adequate attention. The author has given particular attention on the roles and stakes of various organisational stakeholders in changes in forest policies and implementation of related programmes. He argued that organisations (particularly forest department) have played key roles in converting the informal tribal economy vis-à-vis forest to a formal shape that increases the hardship of tribals including dispossession of land. Further, there are various procedural matters that influence proper implementation of policies, which confirm that bureaucracy is not a neutral entity. The interest of organisation and bureaucracy often comes before the policy objectives. According to Mishra, tribal identity as perceived by the organisational actor matters in implementation of policies. But very often the identity-based organisation as opposed to the tribal identity structure takes the front seat.

Bidhan Kanti Das in his paper *'Making Forest Dwellers Deprived: Examining Implementation Process of Forest Rights Act, 2006 in India'*, closely examines how far the historical Forest Rights Act, 2006, could benefit the forest dwelling communities, particularly the tribal communities in concrete terms. The Forest Rights Act, 2006, represents a seminal moment in India's contested forest politics. For the first time, the state has acknowledged that the expropriation was a 'historical injustice'. The author highlights how state agencies subverted the rights provided in the act from rule framing to implementation at ground level. In most cases, the act becomes mere individual land rights distribution process, diluting larger rights issue, community forest rights in governing forest resources. So, the author argued that whatever rights are provided in the Act should be properly reflected during 'rule framing' which is principally done by primary stakeholder, i.e. forest bureaucracy. It cannot be denied that there is a scope for violation of rights provided in the Act during implementation level as revealed in earlier legislation like PESA 1996 that empowered tribal communities. The violations of this sort affecting directly the tribal communities should be taken care of. The author questions the intention of forest bureaucracy who believe that forest can only be preserved without human interference with the help of an analytical model. The experience of the author suggests that such a western model of conservation, though academically sound, has little practical bearing, more so when the matter concerns tribal communities in India.

Drawing upon the findings of field work conducted a village of Hooghly in West Bengal in the period 2006–07, Dayabati Roy in her paper *'Tribe, Political Party and Local Self-Government: An Ethnography on the Santal in Rural West Bengal'*, tries to re-examine and reconceptualise the tribe in the context of contemporary socio political transformation. The general pattern of the village based societies in India is that they are uneven and are marked by inequity and assertion of identity. But the question is whether or how these features are (re)constructed, obscured and/or becoming prominent against the backdrop of recent policy reforms. The focus should be particularly on socio-political processes by which tribe as a social category is taking a new shape and recreating a new pattern of politics in consequence of implementation of local self-government or the Panchayati Raj Institutions (PRIs) in the rural setting of West Bengal. Panchayati Raj Institutions have been contemplated and constituted as the most effective tool to implement the concept of decentralisation at the village level in India. To further decentralise the power to the so-called weaker sections of Indian society, including the women, the 73rd amendment to the Constitution of India made the mandatory provisions of reservation of one third panchayat seats for women, and a share of seats to the Scheduled Caste/Scheduled Tribe people equal to their proportion in the local population. The effects of the panchayats and a state-centric political party on the life-world of the Santal people are significant enough to suggest that the administrative definition of tribe is to a great extent inapt. So tribe as a category needs to be redefined. From the national perspective, the hierarchical division between the ruling elites (the dominant castes and classes) and the marginal social categories like the tribes still remains as a barrier in the functioning of grassroot democracy in India.

Dipannita Chakraborty in her paper *'Conceptualising Tribal Autonomous Rule in Tripura: A Study with Reference to Tripura Tribal Area Autonomous District Council from Historical Perspective'*, examines the working of the Tripura Tribal Areas Autonomous District Council (TTAADC) and seeks answers to the questions whether the socio-economic disparities still persist, whether tribes could avail of the opportunities, and whether land scarcity problem could be satisfactorily tackled. The TTAADC was set up emphasising on self-rule, empowering the tribes of the state with greater opportunities and making them capable of dealing with the changing world. Tripura was at the receiving end in the aftermath of the partition, population pressure grew by leaps and bounds along with a mad rush for land acquisition among the immigrants. A long cherished dream of the indigenous people was believed to have been fulfilled, certain administrative and legal authority was handed over to the Council which aimed at working towards safeguarding the tribes' rights in respect to land acquisition, use of forest land, social customs, economic development, primary education. Chakraborty examines the working of the TTAADC during all these years, focussing on such questions whether the tribes have actually availed the opportunities, whether the socio-economic disparities still exist, whether land scarcity problem is dealt with. Tripura being a border state with an equally large marginalised plainlander population living in plain lands whether this self-rule has created a schism among the people. In other words, whether TTAADC has been able to satisfy the aspirations of the tribal people in Tripura and also wipe out the sense of alienation. She also attempts to find out how much the autochthons can exercise their free will in improvement of their status in the development process. To get a clear picture encompassing all these parameters, she has particularly concentrated on a case study of Padmabil Block of Tripura.

Subir Rana in his article *'Salvaging a Common Descent and Lineage between an Ex-Criminal Tribes of India and the Present-Day Gypsies of Europe: weaving History and present day tales on the boundaries of 'Civilisation''*, dwells at length on the background of the Criminal Tribes Act XXVII of 1871 to check movement and ambulation by marginal communities and historically with respect to a specific tribal community called Nats. Mobility by ambulatory communities like nomads, gypsies and vagabonds especially on the periphery of ancient kingdoms and empires was not supposedly a preferred way of life by the ruling elite during ancient times, but it was never construed as law and order problem for imperial administrations. However, with the onset of medieval ages in Europe and elsewhere in the world, non-sedentary lifestyle began to be associated with the 'myth of the nomad' 'aimless wandering,' 'vagrancy,' 'wanderlust' and even 'sexual excess.' This 'othering' and discriminatory attitude of the metropole towards the fringe population affected India too in the 18th and 19th centuries. Itinerant communities in India which included many mobile trading communities, street entertainers, eunuchs, prostitutes, beggars and mendicants increasingly began to be viewed as rebels and spies especially after the Sepoy Mutiny of 1857 and therefore a major concern for the Empire. A looming threat of law and order breakdown ran across the already weakening spine of colonial governance as a result of which the Criminal Tribes Act XXVII (CTA) of 1871 was introduced. According to the CTA, mobility was seen as a criminal activity and all tribal and forest communities were labelled as 'hereditary criminals' or 'predatory castes',[1] thereby linking crime with genetics. The CTA at best was an effort to impose 'governmentality' by restricting 'regimes of circulation,' controlling and regulating native bodies and producing 'bipower.'There were reasons as to why movement and ambulation by marginal communities became a criminal act and encouraged the colonial state to impose the CTA. The Nats which was labelled as a 'criminal tribe' according to this Act has come for special investigation by Rana. Nat was an occupational term for a community of tramping entertainers that included conmen, conjurers, charlatans, tattooists, herbalists, cattle herders, bards and genealogists. There is linguistic similitude between the Nats, Jats, Sansis, Kanjars and Doms. He argued that the oft-debated issue of a common lineage and descent between the peregrinatory communities in the form of 'untouchable castes' and 'criminal tribes' of India and the present-day Gypsies of Europe demands special attention.

The paper *'Tribal Entrepreneurial Growth: Drawing Comparative Inferences from Malaysia and India'* by Rajanita Das Purukayastha has focussed on tribal entrepreneurship in the context of Malaysia and to an extent India. Entrepreneurial studies have always been considered as a means of wealth-making process, despite the fact that entrepreneurship is necessarily a context-dependent social process. Rural development, through enterprise formation and entrepreneurship, is a pre-requisite for inclusive development, especially for middle-income countries aspiring to join the league of high-income nations by 2020. A primary constituent of rural areas and villages across different developing nations of South Asia are the tribal or indigenous population. Through their variegated socio-cultural, linguistic practices and ecological interactions, the ethnic groups build a distinct demographic, economic and communicative identity of their own. Interestingly, tribal populations in different developing countries of South and South-Eastern Asia have been subjected to innumerable hardships, mainly socio-economic, which have left them undeveloped and poverty-stricken. In the Indian scenario, tribal enterprises are seriously under-represented and chronically ailing business units, with a special relevance to private firms owned by Scheduled Tribes (STs). Using economic census reports, the study has been able to investigate the present-day problems of these ST enterprises. It is interesting to note that owing to their dependency on forests, tribal or indigenous form of entrepreneurship is conspicuously distinct from other forms of entrepreneurship in their built-in socio-cultural dynamics as a process of entrepreneurship. Mere economic return or business value is not the only motto of such enterprises. On the other hand, the scenario in the neighbouring country of Malaysia provides evidence of gauging the entrepreneurial growth among indigenous minorities which have recorded a steady growth over time. Using a thorough analysis of relevant literature, the author makes an attempt to draw comparative inferences of the problems and the prospects of selective tribal and indigenous forms of entrepreneurship, represented by the aboriginal and tribal communities of Malaysia and India, respectively.

Emerging Issues and Need for Reorientation of Tribal Studies

Tribes in India obviously are not a homogenous category. They are at different levels of socio-economic transformation and also have their own customary practices and world views. They differ widely among themselves in terms of regions they live in, languages they speak, physical features they display, ecological conditions they inhabit, size of community they represent, stages of social formation and level of acculturation and levels of development in which they are placed (Xaxa 2005). This is not due to the forces operating from within but rather from outside. For example, the differentiation in terms of access to land is more due to land alienation arising out of fraud, deceit, indebtedness and state-sponsored activities leading to large scale displacement of tribes from their land and resources (Singh 2002; Fernanades and Paranjpye 1997). On the other hand, social differentiation has caused considerable fragmentation of tribal society. Social solidarity that tribes once enjoyed has come under severe stress due to differentiation in religious sphere, political participation, economic activities and social composition (Xaxa 2005). The nature and degree of differentiation within a tribal group and/or between tribal group also varies. At the ideal level, Santal as a tribal group, are characterised by specific norms, values and customary tradition. But, in reality, Santals today function more like a 'truncated' or fragmented group category. For example, Santals of Chota Nagpur region or Santals of Midnapore or Santals of tea garden areas of Jalpaiguri or Assam cannot be equated in the form of one homogenous tribal group. How far they remain closer to traditionally defined socio-economic status with the change in social, ecological and economic conditions needs to be investigated. Moreover, different sections of Santals reveal differential access to resources available in the region. The whole question of Santal existence has to be understood in the context of regional particularities. Again, there may be confusion about the reference group level representation. For example, in a scheme where Santals of Chota Nagpur region are treated as a reference group, Santals of Midnapore, or Santals of Tea garden areas of Jalpaiguri or Assam could at best be considered as regional categories. But this may lead to further debate and discourses. In some cases the reference group may include the non-tribes as well. Generally speaking, there may not be any differentiation between the Santals of different regions particularly at the ideal level, which means whatever differentiation occurs is in the sphere of material life. Broadly, the differentiation process may be envisaged as a conflict between transformation at the material and the retention of the ideal structure. These are the important areas that may be explored in detail. Moreover, in contemporary India, both in its 'traditional' and 'transitional' settings, tribes are hardly egalitarian in their social formation. Some endemic and emerging forms of social inequality are well present among many of them, which have considerable relevance while conceptualising and contextualising tribes.

In multicultural India, tribes contribute immensely to the realm of diversity. Ideally speaking, social ties and cultural practices are restricted to the level of community. But in the present situation, since economic and political activities are no longer confined within the bounded system of a community, the community factor has considerably been diluted and as a result, social ties and cultural practices are imperfectly connected. Sometimes these are given new meanings depending on the constraints, compulsions and opportunities available at the regional level. Tribal orientation and consolidation of interests find expression in the way such communities 'locate' themselves in such a specific situation. Contemporary tribal societies need to be looked at from a regional perspective, which means there cannot be a single universal category to be in the case of a large and regionally dispersed tribal group.

On the other hand, certain groups and communities are trying to identify themselves as a tribe purely for material benefits to be procured from the state, which makes the tribal question problematic at the conceptual level. Sometimes, they take resort to protest movements for their recognition as a tribe. One of the interesting areas of research might be the nature of evidences and arguments put forward for claiming the status of a tribe. The basic problem lies with identification of a tribe at the administrative level, which has little to do with the concept of tribe as such. Some researchers argue that there is practically no valid concept to define a tribe. But concept building exercise in the case of tribes is not going to be an easy affair.

Another important issue is the power relations existing within as well as between the different tribal and non tribal communities in an area. In a democratic set up, benefits of developmental programmes may be controlled and cornered by demographically dominant tribal groups leaving behind the smaller tribal groups at a disadvantaged position. It seems that the size of the community matters, particularly in the context of development. This has far-reaching consequences in the political field. Understanding the distribution of public goods and services and the changing power dynamics within the different tribal groups and non tribal communities will throw light on inter-community relations taking the form of power relations.

Tribals of India differ from one another not only in terms of their ecology, cultural identity, economic organisation and social and religious practices but also in terms of nature of their relationship to national political and economic systems (ILO 1994). Poverty, social exclusion, susceptibility to exploitation and poor health are almost constant companions of a sizeable section of tribals. The high forest land of the tribals is also known for valuable mining resources. Ironically, these areas also report a very high incidence of poverty (Poffenberger et al., 1996). Over the past two centuries, in central India, where more than half of the total tribal population live, tribal people have been increasingly subjugated by state agencies, landlords and money lenders (Xaxa 2011). It is argued that the loss of their agricultural lands through privatisation, industrialisation, and degradation of forests have made them poorer, left them alienated, disempowered and vulnerable to exploitation. The all-India experiences have suggested that economic growth, in fact, leads to disproportionately higher cost for tribal communities in terms of resources alienation, socio cultural intrusion and dismantling traditional institutions (Shah and Pathak 2014). That they suffer from exclusion, neglect and under-development may be attributed to their geographical isolation and separation from the mainstream. One of the reasons why tribes are recognised as a distinct category is cultural specifity. Politically speaking, it makes the tribal group function like a uni-directional society and in such a society culture shapes individual attitudes and, in turn, is continued by the actions, beliefs and behaviours of individuals. There is scope for examining this aspect.

In the present context, cultural distinctiveness has been linked with ethnic identity or group identity, which finds expression through ethnic organisation or politics. But at the basic level, one is confronted with the nature and formation of the group. The group taking the form of an ethnic group is small, territorially and culturally distinct. Such a group very often assumes a minority character which makes it vulnerable to the extent it suffers at the hands of the majority groups. It often leads to encounter between the powerful and powerless, the dominated and the dominators. It is worth examining to what extent contemporary tribal communities, particularly in eastern and north-eastern India, manifest minority character and politically subordinate position to the dominant groups. More important perhaps is the way they manifest it. Is it passive submission or protest, which sometimes takes the form of a violent movement or a combination of factors that lead to the formation of minority groups as a mark of segmentation of interests or fragmentation of rights?

At the social level, one may raise the question as to how the tribal societies of today should be viewed. One way of looking at the problem is to determine the mode of sharing of institutions that may be classified as compulsory, alternative and exclusive. On the basis of sharing of these institutions, it may be possible to ascertain how far a society is homogenous, heterogenous or plural. In the last category the incorporation of elements is regarded as basically a political act. It cannot be denied that every society, particularly a tribal society, assumes a societal culture that is reflected in the way of life of its members. This is the centripetal force that is binding on each member whose various components signify the magnitude and direction of various responses to a set of stimuli that may be traced back to the level of consciousness. It is, however, difficult to establish a single universal pattern. Instead, each society (tribal) may be viewed as developing a cultural orientation, that is, descriptive of attitudes of most of its people most of the time. There is an intimate relationship between social ties and cultural practices.

The Government of India has undertaken policies and programmes since Independence to enable the tribal communities to join the mainstream of national life. After six decades of implementation of affirmative policies and programmes, HDI of the tribals continue to be the lowest compared to other sections of society in terms of all parameters like health, education and income. The situation is further aggravated if we consider the disaggregated data on different tribal groups. Moreover, these communities also suffer from geographical and cultural exclusion, which are not reflected in the HDI. Further, policies and programmes for the welfare and development of tribals ignore the social realities and consider them as homogenous groups for applying common policies and programmes for their development. But the question remains, why the tribals are not performing well in terms of key human development indicators despite intervention of affirmative policies and programmes since Independence? For policy-makers and bureaucrats, factors like traditional social structure and culture are often cited as the major constraints behind this bleak situation. However, inadequate fund allocation, poor implementation programmes or delivery mechanisms are also cited as factors particularly by social researchers for this shoddy state of affairs. In fact, there is a dearth of systematic study on how far the traditional social structure and culture put a brake on adopting the so-called modern approach of developmental interventions (Xaxa 2011). In what way the ineffective implementation of developmental programmes or bureaucratic apathy contributes to the sorry state of affairs? Do these factors vary from one tribal group to other? The Eleventh Plan period of Planning Commission, Government of India laid stress on active participation and management of development initiative by tribals on their own. But the expected results are still to be achieved.

Historically, tribal communities have undergone various processes of deprivation leading to marginalisation in both pre- and post-colonial periods. One important step was the introduction of private property rights and regulation of revenue received from agriculture during colonial regime. As a result, large tracts of land including forest areas where tribal communities lived for generations were brought under settled agriculture. By this process, tribal customary rights to land used by them for centuries to sustain their livelihood were not given due consideration. Another important step towards marginalisation was the centralisation of forests and forest produces with promulgation of Indian Forest Act, 1865, with several amendments of the Act leading to Indian Forest Act, 1927, which is still effective. Further, post-Independence India has introduced more and more legislations like Wildlife Protection Act 1972, Forest Conservation Act 1980, curtailing access to forest resources. To implement several policies and legislations, forest administration established its own technical and cultural knowledge system through which it controls the production of and access to forest knowledge (Blaikie and Springate-Baginski 2007). During the last 150 years Indian Forest Service (IFS) has produced a distinctive internal culture and knowledge system of reproducing forestry management objectives and activities like survey and reserve of forest tracts, forest management plans, silvicultural operations, etc. for continuous flow of timber and actual field management of forest resources. Forest managers believe this knowledge system as 'modern', scientific and authoritative. 'Scientific forestry' has become the mantra of forest administration. Issues of local people's socio-economic needs, biodiversity and wildlife protection have historically been ignored in training courses. The process of working with local people in managing forest resources has been ignored too. So, the organisational structure in formulation of forest policies and delivery of programmes in India needs to be studied as it has implications for shaping tribal livelihood pattern.

So far as tribals are concerned, land and forests have significant bearing on their livelihood, culture and identity. Dispossession and lack of these resources lead to adverse consequences in their social and cultural life. They find it hard to retain their self-esteem, confidence and even legitimate political space, an essential prerequisite for claiming their rightful inclusion. Many scholars argue, whatever achieved through policies and programmes is some kind of 'adverse incorporation' into mainstream (Hickey and Toit 2007). The forest resources, as the basic productive resources for tribals, should therefore be treated as the core of tribal development and poverty amelioration. Incidentally, two landmark legislations directly challenged the undisputed authority of the state in connection with restoration of tribal self-rule and rights over natural resources like Panchayats (Extension to Scheduled Areas) Act 1996 and Forest Rights Act 2006. Since then, there has been a great deal of research on PESA and FRA and their implications relating to institutions such as joint forest management committees and panchayat raj institutions aimed at restoring the rights of tribal communities and affected individuals. Researches have now been directed to ascertain the effectiveness and challenges lying ahead to restore power and control over resources by the tribals. It sometimes means going against state agencies as well as local powerful 'elite' and other agencies who work more for their own interest rather than the interest of the tribal communities. It is often claimed that the positive legislation like FRA 2006 did not actually benefit the forest-dwelling tribal communities in terms various rights particularly land rights across India with some successful stories. In fact, forest bureaucracy is not prepared to lose their hegemony over forest resources.

The impact of large-scale development projects and policy of denial of access to forest resources is greater in terms of magnitude and scale compared to the ameliorative measures like reservation in various spheres and other affirmative action programmes for the welfare of tribal people (Xaxa 2011). These interventions severely affect the economic as well as social and cultural life of tribal communities. The magnitude and scale of those interventions are much greater, which has increased further with liberalisation causing severe dislocation in the life of the tribals. This often leads to protest and resistance among the tribals. It is argued that social, economic and political deprivation of the tribals has led to the emergence of tribal identity with the help of historical and contemporary evidences. Scholars further argue that affirmative action programmes are incapable of elevating them from the given social base in which they were traditionally located. Rather, affirmative action has further distorted the existing social base and exposed them to vulnerability. Despite India's policy of affirmative action and self-determination for marginalised people, structural differences in income generation perpetuate poverty (Kijima 2006). Autonomy over resources and self-governance will enhance social base. To enable self-governance, it is argued that basic structures affecting local people's access to land, forest, water and other rights must be changed and prior access be restored (Sundar 2005; Saravanan 2009).

It seems obvious that inequity and identity are the inherent features of socially uneven societies. But the question is whether or how these features are (re)constructed, obscured and/or becoming marked against the backdrop of recent policy reforms. Exploring the socio-political processes by which tribe as a social category is taking new shape and recreating a new pattern of politics in consequence of implementation of local self-government in village India deserves closer attention. On the other hand, independence and autonomy are the two complementary concepts which need to be expanded to all spheres of life in order to enjoy freedom without sacrificing the essentials of meaningful tradition. In regions where diversities exist in the form of racial, ethnic, linguistic, cultural differences, the concept of self-rule within a constitutional framework enables a community to take its own decisions regarding administration without being 'guided' or 'pressurised' by any other community. This principle of democratic decentralisation ensures more community participation as the latter is institutionally and statutorily involved in managing their own affairs and decision-making processes. Here the claims of the tribals come to the force.

The Government of India on its part has adopted several constitutional measures to safeguard the tribal people ranging from protection of tribal traditions and belief systems, autonomy, protection from exploitation by moneylenders, prevention of alienation of tribal land, reservations in education, employment and political representation. The Fifth Schedule and Sixth Schedule laid down certain special provisions for tribal areas and recognised the importance of traditional tribal councils to control their own affairs and protection of their land and customs. Despite these constitutional provisions, they are at the bottom of society: they are the poorest, most marginalised, oppressed and deprived population in the country (Nathan 2004; Rath 2006). Studies are available on the evaluation of implementation of those provisions in improving livelihood and preservation of cultural rights citing loopholes of implementation (Yadav and Misra 1980; Vyas 1989; Roy Burman 1989; Shah and Pathak 2014).

Still the very approach of the government in dealing with tribes is not above question. There is an impression that the government has deliberately diluted the question of tribal identity because it undermines nation as a cohesive unit. It gives scope to those among the tribals who are not in agreement with government's administrative position to express their grievances. The emergence of hardliners has to be seen from this angle. Again government's inadequate handling of tribes is clearly noticeable in the case of 'criminal tribes'. One of the new areas of research in contemporary India is re-examining the historical accounts, socio-economic status of tribes and interaction with mainstream population who are declared as criminal tribes under 'Criminal Tribes Act XXVII' of 1871 by colonial government. Following the denotification order passed by the Government of India after Independence, about 150 tribes were denotified in 1952. At present, these denotified and ex-criminals comprise 126 tribes and castes, with a population of about 20 million spread all over India (Rath 2006). Their source of livelihood are threatened with drastic disappearance of grazing and forest lands, gradual loss of traditional method of entertainments. In addition, they do not have domiciliary status due to nomadic nature. As a result, they are included neither in the national statistics nor in the planning process. Some of them are not even included in the ST category and thereby deprived from various benefits from state agencies. These denotified tribes are most adversely affected by cultural hegemony and prejudice, economic marginalisation and political exclusion. This raises fundamental question of social equality, economic equity, ecological sustainability and people's participation, cultural autonomy and democratic integration. Many scholars are now engaged in re-examining those tribes, their history of criminality and the reasons behind those acts and compare those with other parts of world.

A primary constituent of rural areas and villages across different developing nations of South Asia are tribes or indigenous population. Through their variegated socio-cultural, linguistic practices and ecological interactions, the ethnic groups built a distinct demographic, economic and communicative identity of their own. In the Indian scenario, tribal enterprises are seriously under-represented and chronically ailing business units, with a special relevance to private firms owned by STs. Tribal or indigenous entrepreneurship is conspicuously distinctive from other forms of entrepreneurship through their in-built socio-cultural dynamics which play a prominent part in building the solid foundation to such cultural entities. Mere economic return or business value is not the only motto of such enterprises. Scholarly attempts are on to examine the pattern of entrepreneurship among ethnic groups in different parts of the world including South Asia.

Note

1. It was W.W. Hunter, a Senior Civil Servent whom the British Government sent to take a stock-taking after a century of British rule in India and who referred to these tribal communities as 'predatory castes'.

References

Burman, B.K.R. 1989. 'Tribal Development in Perspectives', In *Tribal Development: Past Effort and New Challenges.* Edited by J.P. Singh and N.N. Vyas. Udaipur: Himanshu Publications.

Cernea, M. 1995, 'Social Organisation and Development Anthropology', *Human Organization,* 54: 340–352.

Fernandes, W., and V. Paranjpye. 1997. *Rehabilitation Policy and Law in India: A Right to Livelihood.* New Delhi: Indian Social Institute.

Hickey, Sam, and Andries du Toit. 2007. 'Adverse Incorporation, Social Exclusion and Chronic Poverty.' CPRC working paper 81. Chronic Poverty Research Center, University of Manchester, Manchester.

International Labor Organization (ILO). 1994. *Indigenous and Tribal Peoples and the ILO.* Geneva, Switzerland.

Nathan, D., and Virginius Xaxa (eds). 2012. *Social Exclusion and Adverse Inclusion: Development and Deprivation of Adivasis in India.* Oxford, UK: Oxford University Press.

Poffenberger, Mark, Betsy McGean, and Arvind Khare. 1996. 'Communities Sustaining India's Forests in the Twenty-first Century.' In *Village Voices, Forest Choices.* Edited by M. Poffenberger and B. McGean. Oxford: Oxford University Press.

Rath, G.C. (ed). 2006. *Tribal Development in India: The Contemporary Debate.* New Delhi: Sage Publications.

Saravanan, V. 2009. 'Political Economy of the Recognition of Forest Rights Act 2006', *South Asia Research,* 29, No. 3: pp. 199–221.

Shah, A., and J. Pathak (eds). 2014. *Tribal Development in Western India.* London: Routledge.

Singh, K.S. 2002. *Birsa Munda and His Movement, 1872–1901: A Study of a Millenarian Movement in Chotanagpur.* Kolkata: Seagull Books.

Vyas, N.N. 1989. 'Tribal Development: Between Primordiality and Change'. In *Tribal Development: Past Effort and New Challenges.* Edited by J.P. Singh and N.N. Vyas. Udaipur: Himanshu Publications.

Xaxa, V. 2011. 'Tribes and Social Exclusion'. Occasional paper, No. 2. CSSSC-UNICEF, Social Inclusion cell. CSSSC, Kolkata.

Xaxa, V., 2005. Politics of Language, Religion and Identity: The Tribes in India, *Economic and Political Weekly*, Xl, No. 13: pp. 1363–70.

Yadav, H., and C.S. Misra. 1980. 'Impact of the Tribal Development Programmes on Employment, Income and Asset Formation in Bastar District of Madhya Pradesh', *Indian Journal Agricultural Economics,* 35: pp. 69–73.

PART I

Conceptualising and Contextualising Tribes in the Indian Situation

CHAPTER 2

Contextualising Indian Tribes

Some Common Attributes

RAJAT KANTI DAS

There is a common understanding about tribe that it is environmentally circumscribed, which is the outcome of its prolonged association and intimate contact with the natural environment. It also creates a social boundary system and cultural specificity. Historians would argue that tribe or, for that matter, tribal identity is a colonial construct. This also remains true for tribes in the Indian context. Tribes were territorially organised and the territorial claims made by such communities today bear with them the British colonial legacy. The whole question of original settlers concerning tribes was given a political twist by the colonial government. Colonial government's area-based approach in dealing with tribes of specific areas was aimed at keeping the tribal issue alive and making them succumb to the pressure of hegemonic control. From the social point of view, tribes could be treated more like a corporate group and the governing order of such corporate groups is understood to be some type of territorial validity, which may be imposed or developed from within. During the colonial rule, the government hardly looked into the validity of the territorial claims made by tribes, but followed a policy of differential treatment and purposeful, selective interference into their affairs with a view to arouse in-group feelings in them together with out-group alienation as a safeguard against any form of external intrusion. The administration sought to have a smooth sailing by pitting groups against one another. Identity politics involving tribes made a beginning since them. In the post-colonial situation, a regional identity having communal margins is considered in some quarters to be more meaningful than a purely state-defined identity. By stressing on 'regional' reference, a sense of 'otherness' is created within a common conceptual grid. Earlier, tribes were organised as the orderly system of territorial units. It is too much to expect that in the post-colonial situation tribes would continue to remain so, closeted to their territory. Actually, the tribal system came under severe stress during the colonial rule itself. The Oraons, Mundas and other tribes could lead a relatively undisturbed life in Chota Nagpur plateau for centuries before the British annexed the area from the Nagabansi Maharaj of Chota Nagpur in 1765 (*The Imperial Gazetteers of India*, Vol. 21: 200). Obviously the focus here is on the regional history and important events that have shaped it. What is apparent is territorial adjustment or adaptation has a regional basis. In that case, there is difficulty is treating tribes as a general category. Territoriality has another dimension that assumes significance with the change of political scenario. The Nagas provide an important example of such a dimension being put to action. As was well known, territoriality was the hallmark of Naga Society. The importance of a Naga Village was recognised as a territorially organised resource base and as a bastion of traditional values and symbols with its emphasis on reproduction and repetition of those, and not their transformation. With the induction of Nagas into the national mainstream, territoriality as a principle carries a somewhat different meaning to them. Today, the recurrent armed struggles launched by the extremist sections of the Nagas have one moot point: to restore territorial integrity of the Nagas as a whole with sovereign control. The whole process gives an impression that perceptions not only keep on changing but those perceptions held in earlier times, which are now considered appropriate, reappear with a renewed thrust and prove their validity even today. The appropriateness of those perceptions lie in the fact that restoration of territorial integrity having a traditional base would strengthen their cause by arousing a strong national consciousness in them, where non-nationals, in this case, non-tribals, representing the larger section of the mainstream population of India would be excluded. As a region North-East India has both tribal and non-tribal representation but a 'Third Element' in the form of 'outsider' or 'foreigner' finds a place at the perception level of both sections of the population. The meaning of the term 'foreigner' is, however, more area-specific and community-specific. In Assam, immigrants from across the international border are suspected as foreigners; in Mizoram all non-Mizos are called *Vai*, while non-hillmen are described as *Udkhars* in Meghalaya. In Bodo areas, non-Bodos are called *Hasha,* while in Manipur non-Manipuris are termed as *Mayang* – meaning 'foreigners'. In Arunachal Pradesh, the Chakmas and Hajongs, even those who have stayed there for more than two to three decades, are termed as foreigners. From the tribe's point of view, the connotation of the term 'foreigner' has a special meaning. The 'foreigner' is deliberately projected as one who, for all practical purposes, is a cultural non-entity. He is to be kept out of the contact situation and, even if that is not possible, pressure must be put on him so that he does not succeed in establishing close contact with local inhabitants through which he can claim membership. He is the one who interferes with the homogeneity of indigenous culture. An impression is created that even in extreme culture contact situation the foreigner does not fit in any role relevant to indigenous cultures. His continuous presence involves a sort of deliberate violence to the local people's personality structure. The threat of encroachment posed by 'outsiders', have been projected as a real threat to the indigenous peoples who have a natural claim over the territory. Does it mean that tribe as an indigenous category should be treated in a different way? Probably it makes sense as it tries to locate tribe in its original natural habitat.

Admittedly, our understanding of tribe as a special kind of social formation still remains problematic. In the Wink's *Dictionary of Anthropology*, 'tribe' has been defined as a 'social group, usually with definite area, dialect, cultural homogeneity and unifying social organisation' In the present context, the definition appears to be inadequate. First of all, 'cultural homogeneity' is something that remains ever elusive. It is difficult to assign any fixed criteria to any form of cultural expression, particularly when culture is seen in the context of evolutionary advances made by tribal groups at different stages. Such advances signify changes in occupation, but no or little change in cultural capacity. When a hunter-gatherer tribe takes to agriculture, it is improbable that their cultural capacity which could sustain them as hunter-gatherer would automatically be enhanced. The same observation holds true for an agricultural tribe coming within the fold of industrial development. In the case of a tribe like Santal, settled cultivation provided a stable source of livelihood in a specific region. This may be explained as 'a convivial, intra-community, undifferentiated, custodial mode of livelihood' (Roy Burman 2003). When they could find a place in the city and market-linked societies, it signals a 'move towards convivial and at the same time predatory mode of livelihood with prerogative of socio-politically recognised group of individuals of accumulative approximation.' This is against the basic premises and ideals of a tribal society. Incidentally, Roy Burman (2003) has put 'all convivial, non-predatory, non-commutative societies' in the category of tribes, though he has also conceded that some amount of approximation may be involved in the present situation. Frankly speaking, linking tribes directly with occupation or occupation–based culture has little relevance today. If Santals have succeeded in establishing themselves as a tribe, it is not because they could successfully continue an occupation linked culture but because they could demonstrate in unequivocal terms that in a given ecological and cultural zone they have to be counted. They could also successfully perform and display the socio-cultural prerequisites attributed to a tribal society in a specific region. Their indispensability to an extent is their own creation.

It has almost become customary to see tribes in the context of political and economic pressures exerted from outside. According to Fried (1975), tribes are the product of specific 'political and economic pressures emanating from already existing state-organised societies'. That Chota Nagpur tribes like Santal, Oraon, Munda symbolised a type of reaction to the presence of one or more states may be too reductionist a position because some of the tribes of the region were directly involved in the process of state formation. They had long experience in dealing with colonisation and could develop strategies or tactics to co-exist with the mainstream. They are not peripheral in the ordinary sense of the term. Moreover, they do not automatically fit into the process of assimilation and gradual integration into the dominant or mainstream culture. It speaks of their capacity to sustain themselves by deriving strength from their own tribal heritage. The strength comes from their long experience of living as members of a tribal community backed by their culture. Such tribal experiences need to be historically located and described at the generic level. The whole exercise may also involve a 'time and society' discourse. Here time is expressed as the experience of time collectively or individually manifested. The process of identity formation has to be seen from this perspective. For example, Naga nationalism is not the first and foremost expression of localism. It now tries to go beyond the state-centrist formation and assumes a global dimension by becoming a sovereign nation with an agenda set in its own terms. The idea is to come out of the shackles of localism of the archaic mould and attain a bigger national identity to have a global representation. A journey from the local to national and then ultimately to the global arena will thus be accomplished in the process. In the face of growing intimacies of political process and social actors, a necessary corrective to structural accounts of power in the context of tribal society is very much on the cards. As a matter of fact, anthropologists have been trying to provide such a corrective. No longer do anthropologists limit themselves solely within state structures, most of which are still carrying the colonial legacy in some form or the other. Tribes need to be contextualised in terms of practices and codes of political power and the roles of social actors in creating or recreating them. This is quite a departure from the earlier approach of seeing a tribal phenomenon purely from a structural order. There is a line of thinking that has been gaining ground is that even 'the most local of social relations' are fundamentally political in nature (Herzfeld 1997). The focus is on 'operation of the political in all domains of society and culture'. Traditional tribal societies have been changing and the transformations are affecting 'traditional political process' necessitating change in the nature and type of representation, where representation means holding power on behalf of the members of community, kingroup, ethnic group or any other form of collective expression at the tribal level.

Clearly, traditional structures of tribal societies have proved unstable in the modern context. The same, however, cannot be said about the traditional forces of alignment. In any case, dualism in the form of modern/traditional dichotomy persists. There is an apprehension that the problems of poverty and 'backwardness' continue because of pursuing traditional structures. As Mahmood Mamdani (1976) sees it, 'the traditional was simply the not-modern, humankind's original condition, the innocence of childhood, perhaps burdened with original sin: *It was denied history'.* Only in economics, contrasting traditional and modern may be done in a clear-cut way by treating these as two sectors. In other fields, there is much overlapping and juxtaposition of meanings. Pursuance of traditionalism, at least in spirit, helps in drawing ethnic boundaries to justify the notion of exclusiveness, which has contributed to the tendency to develop ethno-political organisation at the community level. In a pluralistic situation it becomes almost impossible for a tribal group to retain its 'cultural autonomy', which has been considered to be a pre-condition to the establishment of an ethnic identity. Tribal culture is now less self-reliant and self-propelled than it was earlier. Infiltration of materialistic values of 'commercial cultures' into tribal system has shaken the very base of culture as an integration mechanism. Commercial cultures, which believe in continued economic growth and progress to be achieved through material consumption, have made a dent into the traditional tribal culture. This again raises the issue of cultural viability from a material perspective. The role of culture in the sense anthropologists have used it has been critiqued time and again. But most of these critiques suffer from econo-centric and techno-centric conceptual biases of development strategies, which Michael Cernea (1999) considered 'profoundly damaging'. Taking a cue from him, one may recognise culture as something epiphenomenal, something which eludes any form of reductionist approach. In the modern context, it may be more profitable an exercise to examine how a tribe could fit into the process of 'self-location'. The tribals are now engaged in the process of construction and de-construction of the 'self', which speaks of the fluidity of the situation they are confronted with. One may even go to the extent of recognising tribe as a true representation of an 'alternative voice', which has caught our imagination and strengthened our faith in them, It is not simply the voice of the oppressed and dominated as a class, but of a group engaged in recreating and re-establishing the 'self' in a spirit of reawakening and conscious realisation of their heritage.

The pursuance of group interests by the tribals has more and more pervaded the field of politics. They now organise themselves along ethnic lines to pursue their interests that are not only social but political in nature. In this exercise their interests very often come in conflict with those of the state. The role of ideologically surcharged extremist groups like Maoists vis-à-vis tribes also deserves close attention. It is a fact that tribals have been involved in a big way in the Maoist movement, but their representation at the top in such a movement is, if anything, insignificant. At the leadership level, they play only second fiddle to the top brass. Sometimes the local interests of the tribals come in sharp conflict with those of the protagonists of the movement. The following event narrated by Avijit Biswas on 20 February 2010 in *Hindustan Times,* Bhopal edition based on a study of the situation prevailing at a tribal settlement area Phulwaria-Korasi (Jamui) may be just one example of such clashes:

> The attack on a Birhor village on Wednesday appears to be part of a protracted battle between Maoists and the people they claim to protect local tribals. Twelve tribals were killed when Maoists stormed Korasi Village in Jamui district. Villagers belonging to Koda and Ghawar tribes said, a struggle for control over forest land had been going on with the Maoists for almost five years. Maoist control over the forest deprived the tribals of firewood, honey and other forest products, which they used to gather and sell in the market '*Maoists do not allow us to enter the forests. Life is getting difficult for us, with increased extremist hold over the area*', said Baichu Koda, a survivor of the raid. He and his family have taken shelter at the Panchayat office building. Police officers said, a small group of Koda and Ghatwar tribals have been fighting the Maoists since 2005. The group managed to snatch some arms from them. '*Since then, the extremists have not allowed local Kodas and Ghatwars to collect firewood and other forest products to earn their livelihood*' a police officer said. 'The ultras also tried to add the tribals to their cadre and use their village as a hideout during operations against the police', he said. When they failed, they dubbed the tribals as police informers and penalised them. '*Our women (who venture into the fight) also get exploited at the hands of extremists*', said refugee Kaleshwar Koda.

What happened afterwards is immaterial. Even if the tribals were forced to join the Maoist rank; theirs was probably one of the longest and protracted battles against the Maoists. If the locally grounded tribals and Maoists come together, it may be through mutual negations that they could articulate their relationship. But here the Maoists assume the dominant role projecting the other as one in need of protection and empowerment. Centrality of their 'self' lies in their tribal identity and they have been made to realise that it is this very identity which is endangered and therefore needs to be protected. Such relationships have a scale of political bearing that are contextually activated in response to strategic interests of the tribals involving their rights on resources, their own identity and preservation of their cultural distinctiveness. Rightly or wrongly, they have been convinced that the path shown by the Maoists would help them sustain their movement against the forces that have all through been trying to destabilise and exploit them. Even at the risk of sounding over simplistic, it may be said that when the government has failed miserably to protect their strategic interests, the tribals have almost been driven to a state of desperation as they intuitively take the plunge.

Their act of joining the Maoist ranks may signify taking up an extreme stand to escape frustration and degradation of life. Broadly speaking, their struggle may symbolise angry protests against economic deprivation and social injustice. But it is also true they have utilised the situation to aggrandise themselves and pose a question mark to the bureaucracy-induced official position of treating tribe purely as an administrative category. Some knowledgeable tribals are even apprehensive of the initiative taken by the extra-vigilant Supreme Court in examining excesses committed by the tribal council (for example, the recent incident of Subalpur village of Birbhum district in West Bengal caused much hype in the media. The incident surfaced the conflict between the village council and the state government. The state government through its police came down rather heavily on the village council and the brutal and merciless way of punishing the errant lovers. Even the common people reacted very strongly against the village council. A section of the tribal elite, however, become critical of the state intervention in tribal affairs). They are apprehensive because they feel that such attempts bordering on excessive sensitivity are tantamount to a direct attack on the independent functioning of the tribal council by treating it at par with the mechanism of local self-governance of the Indian political system. In that case, tribe as a self-conceived functioning system of mutual help and support will lose its meaning altogether. No doubt, there will be difficulties in finding contextual relevance of tribe in the traditional form it purports. Do the tribals seek integration at the national level with the option to negotiate in their own terms? Or do they primarily want recognition of their separate existence to add to their capacity to negotiate their own rights? Either way, things may not be that easy to be decided at the administrative level. Hope we learn from our previous experiences. The example of Maoist influence in tribal areas stands before us. In some areas of North-East India insurgency in itself has become a part of tribal life, which gives a new direction to their ethos and mentalities. We have learnt the lesson that applying coercive method may not always pay.

Sometimes, it gives rise to negative effects of unprecedented dimension. Clearly, to impose a uniform moral standard defined in our terms may be counter-productive. What is moral to them may be immoral to us and we try to justify our stand by maintaining a moral distance from them. Side by side, we initiate actions against them from a distance with the view to see their lives through lenses of our making.

Under the pretext of liberalism and disposition of fluidity, we now vouch for breaking the sharp division that exists between 'we' and 'they', otherwise a true reflection of 'self' and 'other'. In that event, the accepted rules or laws of social formation generally in use will prove to be redundant. This may be the position taken by those who call themselves 'postmodernists'. Shall we also join their ranks without even making an attempt to reassess the basic premises of tribal life? Whether the context associated with tribal is more symbolical than real is not the main issue; the two are inseparable in the sense that one cannot be delinked from the other. The problem lies at the conceptual level. There is a not a single concept but concepts dealing with translation of tribal life and each concept has its own level of generality, which may not always converge with others.

References

Biswas, Avijit. 2010. 'Phulwaria-Korasi (Jamui)', *Hindustan Times* (Bhopal edition). 20 February.

Cernea, Michael. 1999. 'Development's Painful Social Costs: Introductory Study'. In *The Development Dilemma: Displacement in India*. Edited by S. Parasuraman. London: Macmillan Publishing Co.

Fried, Mortan. 1975. *The Notion of Tribe*. Menlo Park, CA: Cummins Publishing Co.

Herzfeld, M. 1997. 'Anthropology: A Practice of Theory', *International Social Science Journal*, 49, No. 153: 301–318.

Mamdani, Mahmood. 1976. *Politics and Class Formation in Uganda.* New York: Monthly Review Press.

Roy Burman, B.K. 2003. 'Indigenous and Tribal Peoples in World System Perspective.' *Studies in Tribes and Tribals*. Volume 1. Delhi: Kamala Raj Enterprises.

CHAPTER 3

Conceptualising the Context

'Tribes' of North Bengal

SAMIR KUMAR DAS

In this paper I propose to reflect not so much on tribes – but on certain groups and communities whose identity as *tribe* is, to say the least, problematic. Problematic – not because their desire of being scheduled as tribe remains unfulfilled – although that is the most commonplace trajectory of research hitherto conducted on tribes in India – but because they find it difficult to articulate their desire in the first place, refuse to express it in case they are able to articulate their desire in the face of repeated denials and rejections by the so-called mainstream society; and finally, if they are ever successful in expressing it, the desire itself eventually turns out to be disastrous for the community leading to its disorganisation.

Most of the surveys conducted on the tribes in India seem to avoid the question of defining the concept in the first place, apparently on the assumption that someone else has already defined it somewhere in the literature and the task is to accept it as given, apply it to one's own context and work with it. A document released recently by the Ministry of Tribal Affairs, Government of India, points out:

> Despite the diversity, tribal communities do have similarities, though broad generic ones. They are known to dwell in compact areas, follow a community way of living, in harmony with nature, and have a uniqueness of culture, distinctive customs, traditions and beliefs which are simple, direct and non-acquisitive by nature. Some of these broadly similar characteristics have been used as criteria for the last few decades to identify and declare a particular community as a Scheduled Tribe. The criteria used are: primitive traits, distinctive culture, geographical isolation, shyness of contact and backwardness. But even all these broad criteria are not applicable to Scheduled Tribes today.[1]

While one wonders whether all the communities hitherto scheduled as tribes in India meet the criteria underlined here – at least to the same extent – examples of communities seeking desperately to recast and reorient them in order to meet them and qualify for being certified as 'tribe' or even to prevent others from being qualified as such are by no means rare. Thus, to cite an instance, in 2007 when the Gujjars of Rajasthan wanted to be reclassified as a Scheduled Tribe (ST) from their certification as an OBC (Other Backward Classes), they faced stiffest resistance from the neighbouring Meenas who were already enjoying ST status, resulting in violent clashes and bloodshed between them. Examples of this nature are by all means very common.

Contextualising the Concept or Conceptualising the Context?

Perhaps this was not what Max Weber understood when he was elaborating his theory of 'ideal type'. It is true that ideal-typical concepts, in his words, 'lack in fullness of concrete content', but they have a strategic value insofar as they 'both abstract from reality and at the same time help us to understand it, in that they show with what degree of approximation a concrete historical phenomenon can be subsumed under one or more of these concepts' (Weber 1978: 19–22). I read the example of Gujjars as the opposite of Weber's formulation of ideal type in that it shows how the concept instead of being an approximation created a discreet charm of its own so much so that the reality is sought to be recast and reoriented in order that it fits into the concept and meet its criteria albeit with varying degree of success.

The reason, why the charm a concept like 'tribe' has for us, is not far to seek, notwithstanding its colonial and pejorative connotations. One's identification as a tribe serves as a technology of governance in modern times first by making one part of what Errol Harris slightly rephrasing Hegel calls a 'systemic whole' (Harris 1993: 87) – within which relations amongst the groups and communities, (wo)men, animals, nature, things and so forth are conducted and secondly, by exercising control over the access to and distribution of resources. It is argued that the reclassification of the Gujjars as a Scheduled Tribe would inevitably cut into the privileges and opportunities reserved for STs and till then monopolised by the Meenas. A community's desire for certification as a Scheduled Tribe and denying the same status to others imposes on it the obligation of enumerating one's identity as tribe much in the same way as the Unique Identification Number – again a mark of identification – is a must for gaining access to subsidised cooking gas cylinders and other welfare benefits.

This, at one level, perpetually shelves the entire question of defining tribes. In India, as Andre Beteille (1992: 56–77) puts it, the problem is taken as one of their identification, not their definition. Most of the Social Science researches on tribes have been attempts at contextualising the concept of tribe, by way of assuming that there is some such definition on the basis of which identifications are made so much so that now we can talk about it without defining it. Most importantly, it is the responsibility of a sociologist or a social anthropologist to look for its close approximations in reality in the way Max Weber was prepared for viewing it with a discount through his ideal-typical concepts. Anthropological Survey of India's (ASI) mammoth 'People of India' project in that sense does not take any risk; it follows the same track by alluding to the officially documented classifications of groups and communities in India as its indisputable point of departure. While introducing the series, K. Suresh Singh, its editor, points out:

> In our compilation of the lists of communities of India under the 'People of India' project we drew upon ethnographic surveys, the lists of Scheduled Castes and Scheduled Tribes drawn up by the Government of India, the lists of Backward Classes prepared by Backward Classes Commissions set up by various state governments, and the list that exists in the Mandal Commission Report. We were able to put together about 6,748 communities at the start. This list was taken to the field, tested and checked, and finally 4,635 communities were identified and studied.[2]

There is always some sort of circular and inter-textual reference in the commonplace definition of tribe with the effect that the concept itself is never put to scrutiny. In this paper I propose to turn the table around and see how instead of contextualising the concept we can conceptualise the context, appreciate why the identity of certain groups and communities as 'tribe' is problematic (and that is why I prefer to keep the term within quotes), how the practice of making the reality fit into the concept of tribe and meeting its criteria triggers off consequences that the communities engaged in such practice find difficult or at times impossible to address and handle.

The Politics of Desire

This attempt at recasting and reorienting reality to fit into the concept, at another level, presupposes that these groups and communities suffer from what Ernesto Laclau calls 'a sense of lack' (Laclau 1994: 1–10), and they try to replenish and compensate for it by way of engaging themselves in various modes of social and political practice. What connects the lack with the practice is the desire – that is say – the desire that being induced by the 'lack' most likely prompts the practice of replenishing the 'lack'. In this paper, I propose to concentrate on the politics of desire. The uncertain and indeterminate nature of a community, as we will see in our first instance, makes it problematic for a community to articulate and express its desire in the first place. While it harbours an overpowering desire to desire, it does not know what to desire, how to prioritise the desires and work out strategies for fulfilling them. But this is not always the case. Some communities become successful in articulating and voicing the desire, although as historical records show, they find it impossible to realise it in the face of denial and resistance from other 'mainstream' groups and communities. Repeated denials and resistance, as I will argue, instead of making them mute and passive, invest them with an agency that refuses to desire and shuns the game of fitting into the concept and thus being subjected to the grids and protocols of governance. This is illustrated by our second instance. Our third instance points out how the desire that is articulated and expressed by a community may often drive a wedge within the community and eventually threaten its disorganisation and disintegration. We propose to focus on the politics of desire by referring to these three moments – of inarticulate desire, refusal (to desire) and killing desire. We define 'moment' not as a chronologically sequenced phase, but in the sense in which Hegel had used the term as a complex configuration of forces.

Inarticulate Desire: The Chains

Fringe communities such as the Chains are at a crossroads today – perched as it were on a node from which a multiplicity of pathways opens to multifarious directions. The community is yet to find out its way as there are many ways to choose from. Sonalisa Das' poem 'Rasta-to' (The Road) written in Chain language promises to find out the road some day.

The lexicographical meaning of the word *'Chain'* (also known as *Chai or Chaini*) is 'Chief' (*pradhan* in Bengali). Chains mostly have the surname of 'Mandal', which also means the 'Chief'. They are said to belong to the Mongoloid group. Chains are scattered over a wide area covering Malda and Murshidabad in West Bengal; Darbhanga, Dumka, Mungher, Purnea, Santal Parganas, Patna, Bhagalpur, Chhapra, etc. from Bihar; Ayodhya of Uttar Pradesh; Dinajpur, Rajshahi, Rangpur, Kushtia of Bangladesh and even parts of Nepal and so forth.[3] In West Bengal, they account for about 1,50,00,000 – although according to the report prepared by the Anthropological Survey of India, 'their population figure is not available' (Basu in Bandopadhyay et al., 2008: 303).

In the Foreword to Mandal's book (2001), Gupta argues that the book emphasises on the process of tribal absorption of the Chains in the great Hindu society. They have been 'sanskritised or Aryanised during the course of history' (Gupta in Mandal 2001: g). This observation seems exaggerated as the process turned out to be a difficult one in history, while it is far from being complete till today.

While most of the Chains are involved in such activities as agriculture, cattle-raising and trading in agricultural produce, their claim to Vaishya status, according to Mandal, can be supported in keeping with their occupation (Mandal in Biswas ed. 2001: 1). In 1932, a Vaishya Sammelan (or the congregation of the Vaishyas) was organised by the Chains with the objective of establishing their Vaishya-hood.[4] As a result, many amongst the Chains adopted the title 'Das' in lieu of 'Mandal'.

On the other hand, many of them also claim Kshatriya-hood on the ground that they belong to the great lunar family. The term Chain is believed to have been derived from *chand* meaning moon and accordingly they claim themselves as Chandra-Kshatriyas. They often buttress their claim by alluding to the ritual of shooting an arrow at the time of their wedding, which according to them is analogous to Arjuna's demonstration of the skill of archery in the Mahabharata (*lakshya bhed* or hitting the target by an arrow) while some others make a reference to the act of breaking the legendary Haradhanu or the Bow of Lord Shiva (*Haradhanubhanga*). They also invoke the ancient legend of Parashuram, who was the famous Brahmin sage and consecutively cleansed the planet of the Kshatriyas. Being Kshatriya, the Chains had to bear the brunt and it was at that time that they were forced to take shelter in the far-off jungles and lost their Kshatriya status. In 1942, a great Kshatriya Sammelan – *baishee* or congregation of the representatives of 22 villages – was organised in Khasmahal Jhoubona of Panchanandapur under Kaliachak Police Station in Malda at the initiative of Radhika Nath Mandal and Upendranath. About 15,000 Chains attended the congregation. Delegates from Malda, Murshidabad and Rajshahi (now in

Bangladesh) also came to take part in it while many others came from such places as Santal Parganas, Mungher, Bhagalpur and Purnea, etc. This congregation was held in a bid to establish the Chains as the Kshatriyas and retain 'the purity of their community' (*jati*) (Mandal 2010: 30). Many such *baishees* were held subsequently with the same objective in Beniagram of Farakka, in Dhuliyan, in Khidirpur of Raghunathganj, in Radhanagar of Dhanapatnagar, in Ganeshpur of Jiaganj – all located in the district of Murshidabad. In 1968–69, eminent pundits were brought in from Varanasi to determine their caste status and they recommended that they should identify themselves as Chandra-Kshatriyas (literally Kshatriyas of lunar origin) in place of Chains.

The first modern political organisation of the Chains was formed in 1963 with the name Murshidabad Zilla Chain Samaj Unnayan Samiti. Tulsi Charan Mandal attended its first meeting held in the same year. He observes that it became very difficult for the leadership to articulate their demand due to lack of political consciousness of their community (Mandal 2010: 31). The lack of political consciousness also explains why the Samiti's activities remained confined to organisation of meetings and conferences (Mandal 2010: 31). Subsequently the Samiti got registered as 'Murshidabad Zilla Chandrakshatriya Unnayan Samiti'. Many of the Chains refused to convert to Chandra-Kshatriyas. This resulted in the death of the Samiti after a while.

On the other hand, Amir Chand Mandal invoked the myth of Adisura (the demon king who once upon a time is believed to have ruled Bengal) and argued that Chains as a community are to be considered as 'Ahindu Dev Brahmin' (Non-Hindu Dev Brahmins) (Mandal 1982: 44). Their claim to non-Hindu identity has a social following too. They, as Tulsi Charan Mandal observes 'are *to some extent* adivasis' (Mandal 2012: 44, italics mine). James Wise, a British ethnographer of the nineteenth century, notes:

> It is most probable that, like other fisher castes, the Chains are remnants, or offshoots, of an aboriginal race, having no relationship with the *true Aryan* Hindus (Wise 1883: 251, italics mine).

They do not worship deities the Aryans do. They are caught in the cusp of the caste and tribal societies – located as it were on a node pointing to multifarious directions. Notwithstanding their efforts at plotting them in the existing *Varna* hierarchy, the report prepared by the Anthropological Survey of India on the Chains of West Bengal concludes: 'They are neither aware of the varna system, nor can they ascertain their position in it' (Basu in Bandopadhyay et al., 2008: 303).

The main political demand of the Chains is to be certified under Articles 340, 341 and 342 of the Constitution of India (Mandal 2012b: 28). In 1981, the Samiti held a meeting where 10,000 people from all across India took part and the demand that they be recognised as 'Most Backward Class' under the Constitutional category of 'Backward Classes' was made. A memorandum to this effect was submitted to the Mandal Commission. In the words of Mandal, such an assembly was unprecedented and was never held in the history of the Chains (Mandal 2010: 34). In 1982 a citizens' convention was held in Murshidabad and a mass petition with a demand for being certified as a Backward Class (till then the demand for Scheduled Caste status was not made) was submitted to the district magistrate for its onward transmission to the prime minister. Subsequently, a one-day fast and *dharna* was observed in Jangipur with the demand for Scheduled Caste status. It was only in 2002 that they were accorded the status in the districts of Malda, Murshidabad, Nadia and South Dinajpur.

Besides, they have such other demands as distribution of text books amongst the poor Chain students, stopping the practice of child marriage prevalent in their society, resisting river bank erosion, establishment of clubs and libraries for spreading consciousness and doing away with the superstitions that plague their society, fighting against dowry, etc. This was the first ever attempt made to elevate the Chains to the level of 'scientific and modern consciousness' (Mandal 2010: 36).

Between 1978 and 1992, Paschimbanga Samaj Unnayan Samiti under the leadership of Tulsi Charan Mandal became very prominent. In a meeting of the Paschim Banga Chain Unnayan Samiti held in 1980 in Jangipur of Murshidabad convened at the instance of Tulsi Charan Mandal, the necessity of organising the Chains was very deeply felt. Unlike the *Matuas*, it was felt that they had not been able to organise themselves. In 1980, the Samiti held a meeting in the village Nista of Murshidabad and it was unanimously decided that a journal significantly titled *Parichaya* (or identity) would be published as their mouthpiece.

Chains are by all accounts at the crossroads today. Although Sonalisa Das, poem promises to find the way, they are perched precariously on a node: part caste society, part tribal society, part that of the Dalits (Nair 1987: 5), and also part 'scientific and modern' society – all rolled into one. Their journey has not come to an end and it is impossible to predict which direction their journey might take: towards the Kshatriyas, the Vaishyas, the Dalits, their non-Hindu tribal identity or the 'scientific and modern' one. The desire is too inarticulate to be explicitly expressed. Inarticulate desire is not the absence of desire. It marks only the absence of any distinct desire.

Refusal: The Rajbanshis

In the existing literature on the subject, Rajbanshis' search for identity is viewed predominantly in a negative way and dismissed as a failure on their part in achieving the identity that they seek to establish for themselves over the years. But the so-called failure, as we will argue, has lent to their politics a mobility that prevents their community from arriving at any given station in the society. Since communities such as the Rajbanshis are constantly on the move without having successfully arrived at any social station, thus finally establishing their identity, their politics is marked by endless itineration without any final destination.

We map their metaphorical mobility along the two well-known registers of identity politics: caste and ethnicity. If the Rajbanshis have been perennially itinerant at least during the last one and half centuries, it also takes off from them any identity and reduces them albeit figuratively to their body – bare, pure and unmediated – dis-identified and unidentifiable by any of the given markers and protocols of governance circulating in the society.

Numerically the Rajbanshis are the third largest Hindu caste in West Bengal constituting 28 per cent of the total population. Although they have been reclassified as a 'Scheduled Tribe' in the neighbouring state of Assam. Rajbanshis are numerically the majority presently accounting for about 60 per cent of rural population of North Bengal and the 'earliest settlers' in the region. In 1901 when the Rajbanshis were enumerated in the census as 'the Koch' – a tribal community – there was protest against the decision by the leaders of the community who claimed Rajbanshi Kshatriya status. While in Assam they have been reclassified as the Schedules Tribe from OBC, in West Bengal they continue to be classified as a Scheduled Caste. One should also recollect that this was also the time when many other communities like the Naths (or the Jugis), Shils (the barbers), Namashudras (the most numerous peasant caste of Bengal), etc. also aspired for Kshatriyahood in North Bengal.

The Rajbanshis have been asserting their identity for more than a century through their attempts at transforming themselves into such Hindu castes as the Kshatriyas or at times the Vaishyas in order that they could secure recognition from the 'mainstream' Hindu caste society. On 27 Magh 1319 Bengali Era (BS) (1912 AD), the Rajbanshis first organised the ceremony of adopting sacred thread by the river Karatoya at Debiganj in the district of Jalpaiguri under the leadership of Thakur Panchanan Barma. The claim to Kshatriyahood continues to be as strong especially amongst a section of Rajbanshi intellectuals. One of them, Sukhobilas Barma refers to a postcard (dated 4 August 2001) which he received from one of those who had heard two or three of his addresses to the community. The writer sharply reacted against the current attempts at conferring Dalit identity on the Rajbanshis and reaffirmed their Kshatriya identity:

> I have heard your lectures in two or three meetings. Do not bring in the Dalit context – whatever opinion you express about the Kamatapuris, Rajbanshis can never be that of the Dalits. We are the ruling race of this region. We have our political history which the Bengali Bhatiyas (people from the downstream or the Southerners, the author) had never had. If we cry out identifying ourselves as Dalits, the Bhatiyas will hate us more. Do not go to any assembly of the Dalits, do not bring in the Rajbanshis to any context that will add to our indignity. The poor amongst us have been taking the advantage of reservation – let them; but do not enhance our ignominy by claiming us as Dalits (quoted in Barma 2002: 179).

By all accounts Rajbanshis' search for Kshatriyahood met with little success in as much as the upper castes had hardly had ever accorded recognition to their claim while many from their own community were insistent on re-invoking and retaining their tribal identity. The immigration of 'the upper caste gentry' guided as they were by the Brahmanical values – from outside North Bengal – brought about some sort of a tectonic shift in the society in a way that the Rajbanshis 'failed to get a respectable position in the status estimation of these immigrant caste groups' (Basu 2003: 62–3 ff). On the other hand, Debendranath Barma – an intellectual from the community – observes that Rajbanshis are 'in reality' not Kshatriyas but belong to the Indo-Mongoloid family of races. The followers of Manu (*Manuwadis*) have 'imposed Brahmanical culture on them' (Barma 2009: 21) and the Rajbanshis were 'inspired to intensively incorporate Brahmanical values and practices for a purified social image' (Sarkar 2006: 155). By 1947 the search for Kshatriyahood, according to Basu, 'lost its vigour and dynamism'.

A commentator argues that almost as a rebound effect of abortive Kshatriyaisation, there grew the realisation amongst the Rajbanshi intellectuals that increasing assimilation into the 'Bengali Hindu society' would lead them either to inevitable disappearance or to total subordination (Roy 2003: 11). It was from then onwards that the emphasis of the movement started shifting towards the assertion of the distinctiveness of their identity in the field of 'language, culture and literature' (Roy 2003: 12).

According to Barma, the language had to suffer first in the hands of 'the Muslims' and then in 1950 with the merger of Cooch Behar with West Bengal when parts of the erstwhile Kamata kingdom were split into Assam, West Bengal and East Pakistan/Bangladesh. The 'invasion' of Bengali language from the South dealt yet another blow insofar as Bengali became the official language of West Bengal thereby turning Kamatapuri into 'a dialect' ('upabhasha') of Bengali (1407 BS: 10).

Sanyal – one of the earliest historical anthropologists to write on the Rajbanshis and an upper caste himself – however argues that their language is only a *chalit bhasha* (dialect) of Bengali. More recently Nirmal Das concludes that although this 'language is different from colloquial Bengali, one (who knows Bengali) does not find it too difficult to understand it' (Das 1984: 18). In a derogatory reference to the advocates of Rajbanshi language as 'Rajbanshi-wallahs', he argues that they are bent on according 'the status of a full language' (*purna bhashar maryada*) while 'from the standpoint of Linguistics, the language of this area is nothing but a dialect of Bengali language' (Das 1984: 24).

Rajbanshis' search for identity turns out to be without an end; notwithstanding the fact that it has frequently changed its registers and trajectories. The persistent denials and exclusions make them what J. Prodhani calls a 'displaced' community – a community that is never a being but is caught in an endless process of becoming (Prodhani and Prodhani 2000: 5). The identity of the community is perpetually deferred. To reframe the question in a slightly different way, their quest for identity produces a *surplus* that refuses to be governmentalised into an identity. Inasmuch as they move perpetually, they refuse to be appropriated by any of the existing protocols of identification and government.

Insofar as the perpetually mobile nature of the Rajbanshis takes off from them their identity, they are reduced figuratively to their body – bare, pure and unmediated – unidentifiable by any of the known markers and protocols of caste or tribe.

The body that is too mobile to be invested with an identity is unhinged from both the caste society as well as the tribal society. It turns not only bare but pure freed from the obligation of any identification. Significantly Kancha Ilaiah argues that the body of a 'dalit bahujan' presents itself in its 'naturalness' (Ilaiah 2002: 34). Debesh Roy in his epic novel entitled *Teestaparer Brittanta*, (Chronicles by the Teesta Banks) describes Bagharu – the protagonist belonging to the

Rajbanshi community – as a naked figure wearing only a piece of loin cloth, naked not so much in the sense that he does not have any cloth to wear which is also otherwise true, but very much in the deeper sense that he has a body that no cloth can cover. It's a body that is emblematic of resolute refusal of the governmental grids of identity that society exhorts them to identify with. This body is neither the hapless *homo sacer*, nor one that renders itself available for being governed, but is a subject that is constituted 'as an entity that lasts, that is to say, that endures sustainable changes and transformation' (Braidotti 2006: 2).

Bagharu is therefore a naked figure – both figuratively and literally – a body without any trace of clothing, leave alone ornamentation. At one level, he stands as the unrepresented or may we say unrepresentable body – bare, pure and unmediated – so much so that he himself denies that he is a Rajbanshi or a Bhatiya, a member of the Uttarkhanda Party (the party that emerged as the spokesman of the Rajbanshi community) or even one of its flag-bearers. He wears no badge to represent anyone, for he does not have any piece of cloth on his body where the badge could be pinned. If he wants to enter a party meeting, he is asked to show his identity and is pushed out when he is sighted only with his *nengti* gloss around the waist. He stands as a lump of flesh – a mass of pure energy that cannot be directed towards any party, procession or meeting through which the Rajbanshi voice can be articulated. He is not only voiceless but his resolute voicelessness also constantly refuses to be represented through any other voice. Any form of identification is bound to elude this pure body – a body that does not belong to anyone.

A good deal of Rajbanshi politics, I argue, is not identity politics, but its opposite – a kind of body politics that refuses to desire and thus be governmentalised into any identity.

Killing Desire: The Gorkhas

While 'Gorkha nationalism' usually traces its genealogy to the King Prithvi Narayan Shah's (1723–1775) campaign of unifying various clans and tribes warring under the Malla Confederacy, at the root of the erstwhile Gorkhaland movement of the mid-1980s, however, there was the strong desire of reconstructing the tribal origins of the Gorkhas with consequences that only reintroduced the divisions within the community.

The idea of 'Gorkha' identity was to encompass a majority of the hill dwellers, and Nepali language had become an accepted medium of communication. All these contributed to the creation of a politically more articulate, more organised movement in Darjeeling. While the controversy around national integration and rights of the minorities were going on, the Gorkha League renewed its demand for special treatment for the district of Darjeeling. These demands found a more systematic expression when Gorkha League submitted its memorandum on 29 April 1952 to then prime minister of India in which it demanded some kind of autonomy for the hills and the recognition of Nepali as a major language. The language demand is believed to have brought various hill groups and tribes closer together, accelerated the pace of their integration and contributed to the development of Gorkha identity. Thus, to cite an instance, the comparative population figures of 1951 and 1961 censuses point to the phenomenal increase in the number of Nepali-speaking population presumably on this ground. Such hill tribes as the Gurungs, Magars, Tamangs and Rais, etc. who till then did not record Nepali or Gorkhali as their mother tongue, apparently did so with a vengeance in the 1961 Census.

Most of the early settlers of Darjeeling and Sikkim were members of tribal groups – now commonly described as the *janjatis* such as the Gurungs, Limbus, Magars, Rais, Tamangs or Thamis. Tanka Subba (1999) argues that in Darjeeling the political and cultural pressures of the 'numerically dominant and educationally superior Bengalis' forced various communities like the Gurungs, Tamangs, Rais, etc. to come under the umbrella of the Nepali/Gorkhali community. Beginning with the immediate aftermath of Independence (1947), the unifying struggle for recognition as Indian citizens of Nepali origin with full linguistic and cultural rights, the movement for Gorkha identity reached its peak in the 1980s with wanton violence accompanying the movement for a separate Gorkhaland state.

The process of unification has its own ramifications. Let us take the example of the Thamis of the Darjeeling Hills and Sikkim. Today their total population is estimated to be around 5,000 and 453 persons in the Darjeeling Hills and Sikkim respectively (Nepal and Thami 2011: 61). The Thamis of the Darjeeling Hills and Sikkim are reported to have faced extinction insofar as many of their members show 'a tendency of assimilation with the Nepali/Gorkhali culture around them' (Nepal and Thami 2011: 65). The younger generation, as a survey points out, has forgotten their mother tongue and a majority of them speak Nepali language (Nepal and Thami 2011: 66). This is also evident in their religious rituals and cultural practices. The pressure for assimilation took them away from animism (*Bonpo*) to Hinduism, although 80 per cent of the Thamis still claim themselves as *Bonpos*. Nepal and Thami conclude that they identify themselves as 'both caste and tribe' (Nepal and Thami 2011: 66).

In the immediate aftermath of the publication of the report of Mandal Commission, fearing that the mainstream political parties would not vouch for the Thami community, they formed the Thami Welfare Association in 1992 in their bid for being recognised as a Scheduled Tribe. The Thami Samaj submitted a representation to the leader of the opposition with a plea for recognition of their community as a tribe in December 1992. Whereas the Thamis continue to demand for recognition as a Scheduled Tribe; they were classified as an Other Backward Class (OBC) by the Government of West Bengal.

We know that in 1988, Darjeeling Gorkha Hill Council (DGHC) was set up, ending a fairly long agitation in the hills that more often than not turned violent. As Subash Ghising – its supremo – was facing criticism from various quarters, he tendered his resignation on 10 March 2008 and shifted gears by intensifying his demand for converting DGHC into an autonomous body under the Sixth Schedule. But for that to happen, an area will have to comprise at least 60 per cent tribal population going by the Constitutional provisions, whereas tribal population constitutes only 38 per cent of the total population in Darjeeling. While insisting on DGHC's rechristening under the Sixth Schedule, he started identifying the

Nepalis as 'tribals'. This brought about a new wedge between the erstwhile tribal groups and the Brahmins and Kshatriyas amongst the community who would not like to be described as tribals (Mukherjee 2011: 4). Ghising, as Mukhopadhyay points out, 'came out with his own theories of origin of various Nepali ethnic groups ... he also asked his community to return to animism and start observing their traditional customs and rituals' (Mukhopadhyay in Debnath 2007: 229). He also called a two-day bandh on 6–7 November 2007 demanding the Sixth Schedule status for the DGHC. If this could bring about bizarre results, it also reinforced the tribal-non-tribal rift amongst the Gorkhas.

Ghising, the caretaker administrator of the then DGHC, had issued a diktat on 17 September 2005 that only 'shilas' (stones) could be worshipped, not images of Durga during the Bengali Hindu festival of Durga puja. This was to 'prove' the tribal character of the people of Darjeeling. According to him, clay images could not be worshipped and only a stone should be placed in the pandals as the Darjeeling hills are 'tribal' in character. The largest Durga puja pandal in the hills, jointly organised by the DHHC and the Darjeeling Municipality at Chowrasta had no idol, but a chunk of 101-kilogram stone. In 2000, Ghising had introduced the worship of the 18-armed Durga instead of the conventional image of the goddess with 10 arms. This had also been an effort by Ghising to prove the 'distinctive character' of the Darjeeling hills. Though the worship of the 'shilas' at pandals reportedly dampened the enthusiasm of the celebration of the goddess' advent on earth, puja organisers, by and large, thought it imperative to carry out Ghising's 'orders' reportedly out of fear. In 2005, on Ghising's instruction a rally was held with people turning out in tribal clothing. This, according to him, 'proved' that the Darjeeling hills was inhabited by the tribes. Ghising had advised the hill people to wear traditional attire, drink only traditional brew and stop worship of idols. Accordingly, idols of Biswakarma, Durga and Saraswati were not worshipped in the hills in 2004. Ghising, who banned worship of idols in the Darjeeling hills in 2005 citing 'tribal traditions', evidently under pressure gave permission to four Durga Puja committees the next year to install clay images 'considering the sentiment and emotion of the people of non-Gorkha communities.' The overpowering desire of embracing tribal identity finally had to reconcile itself with the compulsions of the situation (Burman Roy 2005: 11–16ff).

Does a community exist before it expresses its desire of becoming a tribe? Or does the desire bring the community into existence. As we have seen, the modalities of desire make and unmake a community as much as they set forth the limits to its constitution into a tribe.

Acknowledgements

I thank Rajat S. Mukhopadhyay, Bijoy Sarkar and Swatasiddha Sarkar of North Bengal University for having made many of the materials actually used here, available to me – although I must admit, lapses – if any – are entirely mine. Unless otherwise indicated, all translations from original non-English sources are mine.

Notes

1. http://www.rgics.org/pdf1/wpn–55.pdf. Accessed on 23 April 2014.
2. http://www.ansi.gov.in/people_india.htm. Accessed on 23 April 2014.
3. '(M)ost scattered' of all castes in North India as Wise informs us (Wise 1883: 150).
4. Chains have the tradition of holding courts on issues critical to their existence as a community. Thus, *baishees* refer to courts held with the villagers of 22 villages while *chattishis* are held with those of 36 villages. The number can move up to 84 (*chourashi*) and the verdict given by them are supreme and final. Nowadays however the practice has been discarded.

References

Barma, Debendranath. 2009. '*Ouponibeshik Banglay Rajbanshi JanagoshthirJati Parichiti Prasanga – Kshatra Andolan: Ekti Sameekshan*' (in Bengali) [The Context of Ethnic Identification of the Community of Rajbanshis – KshatraMovement: A Review]. Kolkata: Bikas Publication.

Barma, Dharmanaryan. (2000) 'Nandiki' (in Kamatapuri). In *Kamatapuri Bhasha-Sahityer Ruprekha* (in Bengali), Edited by DharmanarayanBarma (ed.), [An Outline of the Language and Literature of Kamatapuri]. Tufanganj: Raidak Prakashan, 1407 BS.

Barma, Sukhobilas. 2002. 'Rajbanshi Samajer Atmaparichay' (in Bengali) [The Self-Identity of the Rajbangshi Society], pp. 156–181, in *Oitihye O ItihaseUttarbanga*. Edited by I. Sarkar [North Bengal in Heritage and History]. Dibrugarh: N.L. Publishers.

Basu, Swaraj. 2003. *Dynamics of a Caste Movement: The Rajbanshis of North Bengal 1910–1947*. New Delhi: Manohar.

Basu, Badal Kumar. 2008. 'Chain. in Shekhar Bandopadhyay, Tilak Bagchi and R.S. Bhattacharya, eds., *People of India: West Bengal*, Vol. XXXXIII, Part One, General Editor: K. Suresh Singh. Calcutta: Anthropological Survey of India/Seagull Books.

Beteille, Andre. 1992. *Society and Politics in India: Essays in Comparative Perspective*. Delhi: Oxford University Press.

Braidotti, Rosi. 2006. 'The Ethics of Becoming Imperceptible'. In *Deleuze and Philosophy*. Edited by Constantin Boundas. Edinburgh: Edinburgh University Press.

Burman Roy, Udaygobinda. 2005. 'Ghising's Dictat on Durga Puja', *Outlook*, 11 October.

Das, Nirmal. 1984. Uttarbanger Bhashaprasanga (in Bengali). Kolkata: Oriental Book Company.

Gupta, Pabitra Kumar. 2001. 'Foreword' to Sunil Chandra Mandal, *Paschimbanger Chain Samajer Bhasha-Sahitya O Sanskriti* (in Bengali) [Language, Literature and Culture of the Chain Society in Bengal]. Kolkata: Swadesh Charcha Kendra.

Harris, Errol E. 1993. *The Spirit of Hegel*. New Jersey: Humanities Press.

Ilaiah, Kancha. 2002. *Why I am not a Hindu: A Shudra Critique of Hindutva Philosophy, Culture and Political Economy*. Kolkata: Samya.

Laclau, Ernesto (ed). 1994. *The Making of Political Identities*. London: Verso.

Mandal, Amir Chand. 1982. 'Sanatan Dharma Varnashram Manav Dharma' (in Bengali) [Varna Hierarchy of Sanatan Dharma is the Religion of Man] in *Parichaya*, 3.

Mandal, Sunil Chandra. 2001. *Paschimbanger Chain Samajer Bhasha-Sahitya O Sanskriti* (in Bengali) [Language, Literature and Culture of the Chain Society in Bengal]. Kolkata: Swadesh Charcha Kendra.

Mandal, Tulsi Charan. 2010. 'Chain Samajer Andolaner Sankshipta Itihas' (in Bengali) [A Short History of Movement in the Chain Society] in *Chaturtha Duniya*, August: pp. 29–47.

Mandal, Tulsi Charan. 2012. 'Chain Samajer Diary', *Adol Badol*, July: pp. 44–46.

——. 2012 'Chain Samajer Diary', *Adol Badol*, November: pp. 40–41.

Mukherjee, Shyamaprasad. 2011. 'Ghisinger Tinti Tara Ebang Natun AshantirAshanka', *Uttarbanga Sambad*, 13 April.

Mukhopadhyay, Rajatsubhra. 2007. 'Tension and Anxiety over Proposed Sixth Schedule for Darjeeling Hills'. In *Social and Political Tensions in North Bengal (since 1947)*. Edited by Sailen Debnath. Siliguri: N.L. Publishers.

Nair, Bikarman. 1987. 'Chain Samajer Manushra Tapashilbhuktir janya Jhunkchhe Keno?' (in Bengali) [Why do the Chains settle for becoming being Scheduled?], *Ananda Bazaar Patrika*, 6 June.

Nepal, Padam and Ambika Thami. 2011. 'Democracy's Marginal Citizen: The Failed Demands for Recognition and Perpetual Marginalisation of the Thamis in Darjeeling Hills and Sikkim, India,'*Journal of Political Studies, An annual Journal of the Department of Political Science*, University of North Bengal, 5 March: pp. 61–73.

Prodhani, J., and Jyotirmay Prodhani. 2000. 'Secretary's Note' in Dwijendra Nath Bhagat (ed), *Rajbanshi Bhasha-Sahityar Parichay* (in Assamese) [Introduction to Rajbangshi Language and Literature]. Golakganj: Centre for Ethnic Studies and Research (CESR).

Roy, Debesh. 1990. *Teestaparer Brittanta* (in Bengali) [Chronicles by the Banks of the Teesta]. Kolkata: Dey's Publishing House.

Roy, Girindranarayan. 2003. 'Rajbanshi Jatir Parichay-Andolan Aar Itihaser Henyali' (in Bengali) [The Movement for Identity of the Rajbanshi Community and the Puzzle of History] in Nikhilesh Ray ed. *Degar1* (1): pp. 9–13.

Sarkar, I. 2006. 'The Kamatapur Movement: Towards a Separate State in North Bengal' in *Tribal Development in India: The Contemporary Debate*. Edited by Govinda Chandra Rath. New Delhi: Sage Publications.

Subba, Tanka B. 1992. *Ethnicity, State and Development: A Case Study of the Gorkhaland Movement in Darjeeling*. New Delhi: Har-Anand and Vikas Publishing House.

Weber, Max. 1978. *Economy and Society: An Outline of Interpretative Sociology*. Guenter Roth and Claus Wittich (editors/translators). Berkeley: University of California Press.

Wise, James. 1883. *Notes on the Race, Castes and Tribes of Eastern Bengal*. London: Harrison and Sons.

CHAPTER 4

Application and Distortion of Indigeneity as an Expression of Tribe

RAJAT KANTI DAS

I

Indigeneity as an expression of tribal identity has been receiving much attention these days. The two are almost inseparably connected. What does indigeneity actually mean? At present *'indigeneity'* is riddled with many meanings, which apply to 'indigenous peoples' in a loose sense and which does not find uniform representation among all of them. What matters is the legitimacy of claims made by 'indigenous peoples' themselves. The question is, do all of them carry the real indigenous tradition? Some of them have now been recognised as 'imagined communities' transformed into real communities. All in all, as an anthropological concept 'indigenous people' has become more problematic. Though historical context, regional specificity and national perspective are important considerations to anthropologists in their encounter with indigenous peoples, there is an apprehension that the question of indigeneity may not always be equated with ethnographic fact. Yet there was a time when ethnographic studies of indigenous peoples were pursued with much regularity. In the colonial situation there was a spurt in studies on indigenous peoples in Oceania, particularly in Melanesia, Papua New Guinea, Polynesia. These were carried out at the instance of the colonial governments with their emphasis on collecting information about the indigenous peoples and depicting their lifestyles in as much detail as possible. No serious attempt was made to concentrate particularly on political system. Social principles like reciprocal obligation, exchange, magical controls and chieftainship formed the governmental mechanism of these societies. On the other hand, African studies were not linked with tiny, bounded island populations, but with relatively large, extended and dispersed tribes and nations. The colonial rulers in Africa were more concerned with the methods by which such peoples could be most effectively administered and to the extent Lugord's principle of indirect rule could be adopted. For successful implementation of this principle some accommodation had to be given to traditional forms of government, as a result of which attention was particularly directed to political systems and social control.

In Africa, the encounter between traditional and modern societies had first of all taken place in the context of colonialism. In some form the encounter continues in the post-colonial period also. There have been attempts to conceptualise the various forms of encounters as reactions and responses, protests and movements, which include cults and millenary movements. In America, the encounter of the Europeans with the American Indians took an altogether different course. It was projected as the difference between the images of the 'self' and the 'other'. Now it has taken the form of a discourse between 'eurocentrism' and 'ethnocentrism'. In Australia, too, research on indigenous tribal populations was intense and well documented, though carried out not without purpose.

The Australian situation needs a little more elaboration. Before White settlement could take a firm root in the region, the native population was small, dispersed and homogeneous to an unusual degree. Variously described as tribes, bands and hordes, they had been in continuous occupation of the land. White settlement completely transformed the demographic composition of Australia so much, that there was a serious apprehension that the native populations might be eliminated from the mainland Australia. They had been marginalised to such an extent that they were not even recorded in the census. The encounter between the indigenous and White populations involved the contrasts in race, language, culture, and obviously, access to modern knowledge system. The White settlers were infinitely superior to the natives in terms of technological knowledge and displayed a sense of contempt, if not apathy, towards the natives, who were referred to as 'Aboriginals' or simply 'Abos' or 'Black fellows'. A sense of regret for not recognising the rights of the indigenous population came much later, prompted by a change in the political climate all over the world following the end of colonialism and rise of nationalism. In this respect the Australian situation bears close similarity with that of North America, but the populations involved there were bigger and differentiated too. Moreover, the native tribes in North America could be credited with putting up a stiff and prolonged resistance to White occupation of their land. Through their long encounter with the encroachers, native populations could not and did not remain rooted to their homelands. They were involved in long and continuous migrations, in course of which they were dispersed and fragmented into communities of various forms. This has been reflected in the ethnographic accounts at different periods of time. There are now 'councils' and 'camps' in Australia in line with 'grounds' or tribal enclaves and reserves in North America. But all is not well with those tribal concentration centres. Reuters from Alice Springs, Australia, reports on 5 July 2007:

> Aborigine Daryl Allen, 60, sits cross-legged in the dirt, dreaming of the good times when his outback people lived hunting kangaroo and working as cattlemen, instead of drinking themselves to death.
>
> Aborigine William Tilmouth, head of the Tengentyere Council that manages

> Alice Spring's 18 aboriginal camps, says the reasons his people are still struggling to improve their lives are because they feel powerless and continue to encounter racism.
> Australia's 4,60,000 Aborigenes make up 2 per cent of the 20 million population and have life expectancy 17 years less than White Australians. They have far higher rates of unemployment, imprisonment, alcohol and drug abuse, and domestic violence.

II

The tribal situation in India has of late started to reveal the degradation and deviance creeping into the tribal life. Some of those who can be naturally associated with indigenous society present a dismal picture. The Birhors may provide an example. It has been reported that the Birhors living around Amanguru, about 50 km from Ranchi towards south, present a picture of utter dejection and despondency. They have little control over resources, nor could they contribute in any way to generate resources, although they represent the original settlers of this village cluster. Half-starved and diseased, they have lost all zest towards life. A survey conducted sometime back revealed that more than 67 per cent of them were suffering from under-nutrition. Things are not much different even today. But the situation in India should not have been like this as the Indian tribes carry with them a different kind of history and tradition built around co-existence and mutual tolerance. In India,tribal and non-tribal populations have co-existed for centuries. There has practically been no instance of any encounter between the two in the way it had taken place in North America or Australia. Of course, there were confrontations, but these had not destroyed tribal populations in a manner suggestive of their total defeat and annihilation. It is difficult to place the 'tribal' and 'non-tribal' population in India in the same category as the indigenous and settler population of America, Australia, Africa or Oceania. No marked cleavage is discernible here between tribal and non-tribal populations at the physical or racial level as it does in Australia or Oceania. This does not mean that the tribals in India fail to satisfy the conditions of indigeneity.

They are indigenous in the sense that they have a long history of occupancy of 'jal, jangal and zameen' (water, forest and land). They are Adivasis, the term Adivasi being used to refer to autochthones. However, it is also true that some of the tribal groups arrived in India from outside in only recent centuries. For the confusion created because of the equation of tribes with indigeneity, the tribals themselves are not to be blamed. Our constitutional and legal experts, administrators as also some academicians and politicians have started using the terms 'indigenous' and 'tribe' almost at the same breath, probably with the intention that by strictly adhering to indigeneity it would be possible to bring tribal groups of all categories under one umbrella. No doubt, using the term 'indigenous' facilitates international communication and, as all of us know, 'indigenous rights' have now become an international issue. B.K. Burman (2006) observes that many tribal and non-tribal intellectuals and social activists use the term 'Adivasi' to people who are rooted in their immediate surroundings irrespective of the time-frame of their settlement in the current respective habitats. They are the people who live in close proximity with nature drawing sustenance from it, their culture and social organisation are considerably influenced by the natural surroundings; their ethos and attitudes towards life are also shaped by their close association with nature. Accordingly, tribal rights in respect of the endowments of nature are seen in the light of indigenous rights. They exemplify human – environment interaction pattern centering on interaction between the human social system and the rest of the ecosystem. The social system is a broad concept that takes in its stride all key determinates of a people's identity – their demographic composition, behavioural characteristics and social organisation that shape their behaviour. In human ecology, the social system occupies a special place and can be taken as a central concept because human activities having an impact on ecosystems are strongly influenced by the society in which people live, nurture values and acquire knowledge, all of which together form their worldview as individuals develop their capacity to sustain themselves within the fold of society. Yet the so-called 'ecosystem people' – hunter-gatherers, foragers and people engaged in forest-based activities including shifting-cultivation, are hardly in a position to sustain their livelihood today. Though they have a natural claim over the land and the natural resources therein, they could never exercise these rights because of government measures curbing their rights on the one hand and land grabbing by developers, business companies and private agencies on the other. A statement issued by the UN office for the High Commissioner of Human Rights in Cambodia to mark the International Day of the World's Indigenous Peoples on 9 August 2007 has underlined the need to take swift action by the government to halt land-grabbing in tribal areas. The statement noted:

> There are continuing concerns about the protection of indigenous land. Of particular concern is the growing number of economic land concessions and mining licenses granted over indigenous land, without community consultation.

Yash Ghai, the UN Secretary General's special representative for human rights in Cambodia, expressed deep concern over ethnic minority losing out land to business allies of the government. Following are some of the points raised by him in his report to the UN High Commissioner for Human Rights in June 2007:

> A wealthy and powerful social class has emerged on the back of the state through the exploitation of the people and the country's resources, relying on access to, and accumulation through, the apparatus of the state.
> ... The government tilts in favour of business companies whenever their interests clash with the interests of rural or urban people.

The above observations are no less true for India also. Acquisition of tribal land in Odisha, Jharkhand and even in West Bengal for setting up heavy industries has robbed the tribals of their rights over the ancestral land which signals an attack on their identity as an indigenous group. They have been facing the prospect of being marginalised with the loss of land, loss of cultural values, social structure and institutions, and above all, loss of recognition as an indigenous people together with lack of opportunities for them for effective participation in national, political and economic processes. For the indigenous people, equal access to both the factors and benefits of development remains a far cry. Their concern for social, cultural, environmental and community aspects of development are genuine because mainstream development leaves them with little chance to live with their heads high, keeping their rights to land, rights to forest and rights associated with the maintenance of culture intact. But with globalisation making rapid inroads into far-flung areas, not sparing even the remotest form of tribal life, their desire to protect their social, cultural and ethnic identity has received a severe jolt. It does not mean that they are against development. Actually they have no clue about how the development process, in which they have only the roles of part-time receivers, could be delinked from or equated with their basic identity. Their uncertainty, hesitancy and impoverishment prepare the ground for external political forces to lord over them. Some of them indulge in practising a type of 'national perpetuative nativism' (Frinberg 1993), which lays stress on cultural items or symbols to justify the existence of their society as a separate entity. It cannot be denied that ethnicity politics pose one of the toughest challenges to a government facing a plural situation and multiple voices. Indigeneity provides the necessary prop to such a course of action.

III

The international community is, however, more concerned about the protection of the rights of indigenous peoples and conventions and declarations of the international community provide a broad framework in this regard. The United Nations' Universal Declaration of Human Rights (1948) and International Convent on Civil and Political Rights (1966) hold much significance for the protection of indigenous people's rights. While the Declaration provides of common standard for the human rights of all peoples and all nations, the Convent highlights the civil and political rights and guiding principles based on the Universal Declaration. The first international instrument in specific support of indigenous peoples is provided by the 1957 International Labour Organisation (ILO) Convention No. 107, *Protection and Interaction of Indigenous and other Tribal and Semi-Tribal Populations in Independent Countries.* This was followed in 1989 by the ILO Convention No. *169, Convention Concerning Indigenous and Tribal Peoples in Independent Countries.* The Convention holds the view that indigenous and tribal peoples and their traditional organisations should be closely involved in the planning and implementation of development projects that affect them. But so far the Convention has only been partly ratified by a few countries, and none of the countries in Asia and the Pacific has taken any step in this direction. Significantly, Agenda 21 adopted by the United Nations Conference on Environment and Development (UNCED) in 1992 acknowledges the actual and potential contribution of indigenous and tribal peoples to sustainable development. It may be mentioned here that the United Nations 1993 *Draft Declaration on the Rights of Indigenous Peoples,* developed with the direct participation of indigenous peoples' representatives, address such issues as the right to participation, the right of indigenous peoples to direct their own development, the right of indigenous peoples to determine and develop priorities and strategies for the development or use of ancestral territories and resources, and the right to self-determination. Declaring 1993 as the International Year of the World's Indigenous People and the decade from December 1994 as the Indigenous Peoples' Decade were steps taken to arouse consciousness and genuine concern about indigenous peoples. The Government of India is rather slow in reacting to the growing concern for indigenous peoples' rights. The Scheduled Tribes and Other Traditional Forest Dwellers Act, 2006, passed by the Parliament after a lot of debate and discussion, is a belated attempt to rectify the 'Historical Injustice' done to the indigenous or/and tribal peoples in the consolidation of state forests during the colonial and post-colonial periods. The provisions are, however, yet to be strictly enforced. It may be noted here that although Schedule V of the Constitution provides for withholding laws considered to be detrimental to tribals, the state became the biggest violator of the spirit of the Constitution by 'vesting' huge areas of tribal lands in itself as 'state-forests'. Madhu Sarin (2005) observes, 'Sixty per cent of "state" forests today are concentrated in 187 tribal districts confined to only one-third of the country'. As has already been mentioned, some of the states have already given tribal lands for setting up big industries. In South Africa, indigenous African communities can now claim restitution of their lands forcibly appropriated during Apartheid. Compared to this, post-independent India has shown little concern for the proper implementation of indigenous peoples' rights. By taking resort to coercion, threat and other pressure tactics, it may be possible to bring some material benefits to some people, but what ultimately matters is to understand the spirit and conceptual validity of the indigenous society. Conceptual validity, however, involves restoration of well-defined rights, not just a step towards ensuring some material benefits mostly on an ad-hoc basis.

IV

Clearly the main problem with indigeneity today lies at the conceptual level. Equating tribes (both statutorily recognised and unrecognised) with indigenous societies, as has generally been followed in India, has created only more confusion. It gives scope for manipulation, twisting of facts, claims and counter-claims, and questioning the very ground of authenticity based on history and traditional continuity. Application of the latest bio-genetic methods may be able to determine age and composition of the populations, but how can it determine the authenticity of a community enjoying certain primordial rights? The African debate on indigenous society is between a live population whose rights, interests and education have been endangered and a society as projected by what Peter Pels (1999: quoted from Alan Barnard, 2006) calls 'salvage ethnography'. Salvage ethnography was not allowed to continue unchallenged by the 'revisionists' who had taken up a position of 'anti-Apartheid, anti-ethnic, class-based theories of society'. Now is the decade of activism as reflected in intensive action-oriented research by anthropologists working alongside indigenous peoples' organisations. This phase is indicative of the liberation of anthropology to pursue ethnicity as a topic in the context of South Africa. The installation of democracy coupled with successful land claims on the part of some indigenous groups in South Africa is in sharp contrast with the situation in Botswana, where the last remaining indigenous groups Glwi and Gllana have been evacuated from Botswana's Central Kalahari Game Reserve in the early 2000s. This is nothing but racism in another form. Incidentally, Botswana once earned the praise of all lovers of democracy and anti-racist groups because of its successful integration of minority and majority populations. But Africa holds an advantage in the sense that population-wise African states reveal less of diversity. Tribal state is the dominant feature of Africa, whereas in India tribals come under minority groups.

That 'indigeneity' like ethnicity has been reduced to a political concept is almost a known fact. It was a political concept during the colonial period and is still so as a nation-state politics. 'Indigeneity' is a popular notion now and as Alan Barnard (2006) contends, 'is grounded both in international law and in the practical politics of rights for oppressed minorities whose claims are fought under the guise, not simply of relations of oppression, but of presumed "indigeneity".' The fact is, 'indigeneity' is no longer an anthropological concept which may be attributed to the change in 'theoretical dispositions of the discipline' and active participation of 'indigenous' claimants themselves or their advocates in projecting their basic identity. Not that their claims or advocacy for indigenous status are more objective than the criteria followed by anthropologists as a scientific discipline, but that 'indigenous society' as historically part of larger social formations brings into focus 'the relation of dominance of one group over another, and especially the relation of different groups to the state, where the state is perceived (by the indigenous people) as protecting the values of non-indigenous over indigenous peoples' (Barnard 1998). Indigenous peoples are not generally the majority population of their states, and are therefore, victims of a system of domination and suppression perpetuated by the majority population in one form or the other. Even where they are in the majority, they are to follow the guidelines formulated by the mainstream. They seek to remain different, but with special rights or with their traditional rights recognised and reinstated. The point is, how far will it be possible for them to remain different? It partly depends on how non-indigenous people recognise them.

Sidsel Saugestad (2001) summarises the consensus in 'international discourse in politics, law and anthropology' in terms of relations between indigenous peoples and modern states with respect to four criteria: (1) First-come, i.e. 'indigenous people' are descended from people who were there before others; (2) non-dominance, i.e. they are under alien state structures; (3) cultural difference, i.e. they are different from majority population, assuming that 'indigenous people' are different from minority population, and assuming that 'indigenous people' are in the minority; and (4) self-ascription, that involves their own perception and a sense of belonging to the group of their origin. The critiques like Adam Kuper (2003) are of the view that definitions on the basis of such criteria would amount to creating imaginary constructs and resorting to false premises. Indeed, the four criteria of 'first-come, non-dominance, cultural difference, and self-ascription' as suggested by Sidsel Saugestad (2001) have their problems not only in Africa, but in all other parts of the world too. As a social construct, an indigenous society can no longer be seen as a self-maintaining unit. Obviously, the dynamics of inter-community relations demand closer scrutiny. The focus should be on larger composition of social formations of which indigenous peoples form only a part. The cultural integrity of indigenous peoples holds little meaning in the present situation unless it could improve their political economy. The continuation of indigenous aspects of culture is relevant only up to a degree, to ascertain their claim to 'indigeneity'. As is the case with 'refugee', which signifies concept of displaced people as defined by nation-states, by the UN and by other organisations (Good 2003), the relation with the state or states is crucial in case of 'indigenous peoples' also. 'Indigenous peoples', even if projected as 'imagined communities', carry with them a type of 'social reality' – a reality which is hard to dismiss outright. And here the anthropologist has a positive role to play not only to uncover that reality but to instill faith in our ethnographic vision and in 'our ability to think anthropologically that gives us insights that can solve problems for "indigenous peoples"' (Barnard 2006). But first of all, indigenous peoples need to be recognised within wider comparative contexts of anthropological depiction.

Though indigeneity may not be a typically anthropological concept today, but the need for anthropological validity of indigenous groups is far from over. It is an encouraging sign that the present-day anthropology has been putting in a lot of effort to generate and scrutinise its own discourse on the indigenous society and not simply freezes it in time and space. There may be indigeneity with or without tribe. In either case, no clear conclusion can be drawn about a tribe as a conceptual category of wider dimension, which has a validity established in its own terms.

References

Asian Development Bank. 1999. *Indigenous Peoples.* Manila: ADB.

Associated Press. 2007. 'Tribal Land in Powerful Hands', *The Statesman*, 9 August.

Barman, B.K. 2006. 'Indigenous and Adivasi Survival,' *New Age Weekly,* 24–30 September.

Barnard, Alan. 1998. 'The Foraging Spectrum: Diversity in Hunter-Gatheres Lifeways', *American Ethnologist,* 25(1): 36–37.

Barnard, Alan. 2006. 'Kalahari Revisionism, Vienna and the "Indigenous Peoples" Debate,' *Social Anthropology,* 14 (1): pp. 1–6.

Barnard, Alan and Justin Kenrick (eds.). 2004. *Africa's Indigenous Peoples: 'First Peoples' or 'Marginalised Minorities'.* Centre of African Studies, University of Edinburgh, Edinburgh.

Eriksen, Thomas Hylland. 1995. *Small Places Large Issues.* London: Pluto Press.

Frinberg, M. 1993. 'The Need for Unified Diplomacy in Identity Politics.' In *Yugoslavian War,* Edited by Tonei Kuzmaniac and Arno Truger. Austria: Ljubjena Peace Institute.

Good, A. 2003. 'Anthropologists as Experts: Asylum Appeals in British Courts', *Anthropology Today,* 19(5): 3–7.

Herzfeld, M. 1999. *Anthropology.* London: Blackwell.

Kuper, Adam. 1992. 'Post-modernism, Cambridge and the Great Kalahari Debate', *Social Anthropology,* 1: pp. 57–71.

Kuper, Adam. 2003. The Return of Native. *Current Anthropology.*44: pp. 389–402.

Lewis, I.M. 1985. *Social Anthropology in Perspective.* Cambridge: Cambridge University Press.

Pels, Peter. 1999. 'The Rise and Fall of Indian Aborigines'. In *Colonial Subjects, Essays in the Practical History of Anthropology.* Edited by Peter Pels and Oscar Salernink. Ann Arlior, Michigan: University of Michigan Press.

Sarin, Madhu. 2005. 'Scheduled Tribes Bill 2005: A Comment'. *Economic and Political Weekly,* 21 May.

Saugestad, Sidsel (ed.). 1998. *Indigenous Peoples in Modem Nation-States.* Occasional Papers Series A, No. 90, University of Tromso: Faculty of Social Science.

Saugestad, Sidsel. 2001. *The Inconvenient Indigenous: Remote Area Development in Botswana, Donor Assistance and the First People of the Kalahari.* Uppsala: The Nordic Africa Institute.

CHAPTER 5

On the Question of Inequality in Tribal Social Formation

RAJATSUBHRA MUKHOPADHYAY

I

The term 'tribe' had for a long time been used indiscriminately by missionaries, administrators, geographers and travellers to refer to a special category of people who were mystified and romanticised in a way that was far from reality. That trend continued till the time Lewis Henry Morgan himself undertook the scientific analysis of the primitive social organisation in the mid-nineteenth century and the time when Anthropology was becoming a scientific discipline. Taking into consideration the 'tribal' form of social organisation, L.H. Morgan preferred the nomenclature 'gentilitius society' instead of 'tribal society' as the former is run by a 'supreme government', where chiefs (in some cases a 'supreme chief') are elected by the *gentes* (blood relations) of the tribe (Godelier 1977). After about a century, Edmund Leach (1954) produced a strong case based on an empirical study of fact that the Kachins of Highland Burma represented a type of society that is simultaneously segmentary (in kinship terms) and class stratified. There were three classes among the Kachins: (1) the chiefs (*du*); (2) the free born (*darat*); and (3) the slaves (*mayam*). The people belong to the class of *mayam* (slaves) are owned by the village chief/headman. Such a chief, on the other hand is, or claims to be, the last born descendants of the last of the sons of the founding ancestor in the village. Above all, the chief's role as a central distributive agent accords him a special prestige by which he might extends his influence over others. The commoners were obliged to pay special respect to chief(s).

In Polynesian culture (Sahlins 1958) the distinction between producers and distributors corresponds precisely to that between non-chiefs and chiefs. The latter were responsible for the collection and distribution of goods and kept them divorced from production. There was also a preference among the chiefs for intra-status marriages, those which consolidate the economic, social and ceremonial prerogative of high rank. That led to institutionalisation of famous *mana tabu* complex in Polynesian society. The elaborateness of the *mana* (certain sacred power) as enjoyed/possessed mainly by the chiefs may be used as a measure of inequality and where the *tabus* (prohibitions) exist in the form of not touching these sacred persons. Moreover, the tribal societies like the Kachins in which the higher status members are divorced from production are taken to be more stratified or unequal in social terms than are those where such is not the case.

All the above facts locate the tribals in a particular form of social inequality mostly characterised by some kinds of ranked groups which are inbuilt or endemic in their social organisation that led to creation of a greater structural differentiation and inequality among the cultivating communities than that of the pastorals, hunters and gatherers. Even the tribal communities which are engaged in settled agriculture often vary in degree to which they are stratified.

Talcott Parsons (1966) viewed that there are inequalities in all societies. Hence some system of social stratification is intrinsic to the very concept of social system. Therefore, a sociological/anthropological understanding of inequality must take into account the insights gained from the study of tribal/primitive/simpler societies. Social inequality, like many other features of social life, is often ordered in these societies by some 'traditional' and 'non-traditional' considerations out of certain inherent requirements of the tribes themselves. From functional perspective, a few of such social differentiations and inequalities would have been institutionalised for meeting certain societal needs and to keep its social system rolling.

II

Let us quickly look into the inequality situation as is noticeable in tribal India. In this respect we get good insights from the writings of a few noted anthropologists. R.S. Mann's study (1984) reveals the inequality pattern as observed among some of the Western Indian tribes. In Rajasthan for instance, the Bhilale and Garasia, considered to be a mixture of Rajputs and Bhils, are treated by some, as sub-tribe of Bhil. Some treat them as independent tribes. Their surnames and clans resemble Rajputs (like Parmer, Solanki, Rathore, etc.). Considering themselves as socially superior to other Bhils, they at times differ even in dress and ceremonial representations. Intermarriages between them and other Bhils are normally avoided. They often give certain importance in making distinction between the descendants of sanctioned and unsanctioned unions. A study by Deliege (1985) shows that many families among the Bhils in Western India were rich and powerful, usually tribal chieftains claiming to be Rajas. They were able to get their women married into establish Rajput families, by which they could claim Rajput and Kshatriya status.

The Bhils are also socially ranked, high or low, considering the degree of their assimilation with the neighbouring Hindus. On this consideration some feelings of 'superiority' and 'inferiority' prevail among them and that influences their pattern of social interaction even within their own society. For instance, the 'Bhagat Bhils' who adopted various traits of higher caste Hindus now form a separate group and do not easily mix at the social level with the other Bhils. Similarly, the plain Bhils rank themselves higher than the Palvi (forest/hill) Bhils. The division of the Naikda tribe into *ooncha* (high) and *neecha* (low) is again attributed to the influence of Hinduism. In social scale, the former are ranked higher and are considered as Hindus, while the later are more affiliated to tribal base. These two groups of the Naikdas maintain a social distance and their relationships are tinged with inequality.

A kind of class-type inequality has been noticed among the Minas based on their attachment with particular occupation in the past. On this consideration a section is known as 'Zamindar' Mina and another as 'Chowkidar' Mina. The former were at times landlords and are presently engaged in cultivation. The latter included village watchmen and some of them are branded as born criminals and are alleged as dacoits. Any connubial relations between these two groups are hardly permitted. Also the Minas of Jaipur and Alwar consider themselves superior in social scale among the Minas. The social intercourses between the Jaipur/Alwar Minas and the common Minas are generally forbidden. Like the Minas, occupationally, the Bhils are also divided into two status groups: the *Kalia* and the *Palia/Ujla*. The Kalias are settled agriculturists whereas the Palias take out their living by fishing, collecting or rudimentary form of agriculture.

Some tribal people are ranked socially high and low on the basis of clan they belong to. For instance, the Garasias with Parmar, Thaiwar, Rathor, Chouhan and Solanki clans are considered socially higher or superior. Whereas the Garasia with non-Rajput clan names are ranked lower by their own tribesmen. Likewise, Bhil Garasia is considered socially inferior to Rajput/Baba Garasia. The latter include those who claim their descent from Rajput father and Brahmin or Lohar mother. In fact there is much to be learnt from studying such form of inequality in the Garasia society constituted on the basis of descent and clan.

Let us now take up the case of Gaddis, a semi nomadic tribe in Himachal Pradesh. Gaddi is a generic term and it includes two distinct status groups: *'savarna'* (the pure) such as the Brahmin, Rajput, Thakur, Rathi, and the non-'savarna' such as the Hali, Rihara, Sibi, Batual and Dagi. All these groups/sections are endogamous and hierarchically arranged. In this hierarchy the Brahmin and Rajput Gaddis belong to the higher status group, and the Sipi Hali, and Dagi to the lower ones. It is said that the Rajput, Thakur, and Khatri wear the sacred thread and regard themselves as 'true' Gaddis. They prefer to seek mates only from its own group. Another interesting fact is while the members of the savarna section call themselves as Gaddis whereas they address people of non-savarna section by their respective names (Pal 2008: 508). So, if we examine the social formation of the Gaddis vis-à-vis the anthropological notion of tribe, the identification and categorisation of this community as tribe becomes quite problematic and questionable.

Furer Haimendorf (1985) observes a rigid form of stratification/inequality among the Apatanis of Arunachal Pradesh. There are two classes in this tribal society who differ in social status: an upper class whose members own the large part of the land and wield political power in the clan and the village, and a lower class who used to consists of freemen to their own land as well as domestic slaves. The later have now been freed, but the endogamy of the classes persists. In another Nocte society, as also noted by Haimendorf (1962), the men of a chiefly clan seek their principal wives among the daughters of the chiefs of other villages. They can however select subsidiary wives from the commoners belong to other clans. But it is certain that a Nocte will never marry a Wanchu at any cost though they live in their close proximity. Similarly, in the case of Konyak Nagas, the *angs* (chiefs) establish marriage alliances only with the similar chiefly families from neighbouring areas. Like Apatanis, the Sherdukpen society is also divided into two unequal and endogamous status groups, viz. Thong and Tsao. The Thongs are supposed to be descendants from the legendry princely ancestors, whereas the inferior Tsaos are considered a stem from his attendants who came along with the prince at the same time.

N.K. Das's study (1989) offers valuable insights into the forms of inequality/stratification as noticed among the Nagas. He observes that in Naga polity certain special privileges have always been enjoyed by the members of higher order. For instance, among the Maring Nagas of Manipur the posts of priests and headmen are hereditary and confined to only two clans (*sibs*) namely, Dangsa and Charanga. In the social scale these two clans are considered superior to other clans. The Southern Angamis (Zounuo-Keythonuo), according to Das (ibid.: 147) on the other hand, are always conscious to attain the status of *pithimi* (a higher recipient of surplus in the 'exchange') and to accommodate more food and cattle to *out face* a rival in public esteem. This desire for surplus accumulation certainly refutes the notion of tribal economy as merely a subsistence oriented. The cases of Hmar and Southern Angami Nagas, as cited by Das, clearly reveal that elements of social inequality could be derived from within the social structures of respective tribes through the working of certain institutional forms.

In the case of Ahoms in Assam, Barua writes: 'the king was the supreme head of the State. But his selection was made only from one of the royal lineages that include Dihingiya, Chringiya, Tungkhungiya, Namrupiya, Samaguri, Tipamiya and Parvatiya' (cited in ibid.: 103). Among the Marings of Manipur, as noted by Rajat Kanti Das, 'their social structure is sustained by a principle of asymmetry, which goes hand in hand with the segmentary system. Segmentation is closely interlinked with unequal distribution of statuses and differential access to available resources' (2011: 3).

In fact, in many tribal societies of North-East India, as observed by K.S. Singh, 'there is a strong institution of chieftainship which exercises power in a manner that looks almost arbitrary and exercises control over resources which is more than unequal' (1994: 30). According to Pudaite, (1963: 39) the chief of the Hmar village in Assam was like a maharaja of a petty state. He was the sole owner of land, and his right can almost be compared with that of a zamindar in other parts of the country. The status of common villagers was like tenants at will. They were liable to pay *busungsadar* (a fixed quantity of grains and fore-legs of every game), and free/forced labour to the chief. The strata to which the Hmar chief belonged was something like the strata of despotic rulers. Ideally he was nothing but a simple custodian of common property and had the power to see to the proper allotment and use of land to each household for cultivation. But in reality, it offered altogether a contrasting picture and a frame of social inequality that adversely or negatively affected the land occupancy system in Hmar society. According to the estimation of some scholars the position of chiefs became more deep-rooted in the Hmar society following the adoption of settled agriculture in their economy. All these selected illustrations from the tribes of North-East India are clear reflections of the processes involved to institutionalise inequality in tribal social formation.

N.K. Bose's study (1972) reveals that the Saoras of Orissa can also be divided into an aristocracy consisting of the village chief's family (*gomong*), and the priest (*boya*) on the one hand, and the commoners on the other. The chief among the Saoras can take wife from among the 'lower' families, but would not give his daughter in marriage to any of them. That led to institute a kind of hypergamy in making marriage alliance between these two unequal status groups.

The Gonds of Madhya Pradesh are also divided into three classes: the aristocrats, the tenants and the labourers. The tenants include Patels, Malgujars, etc. By status, the Gonds are also broadly divided into two distinct categories. They are in particular the Raj Gonds and the Dust (Dhuriya) Gonds. The Raj Gonds are found jealous of their cultural identity, heritage and distinctiveness, and they seek to project it in various ways. They, including some others like Tanwar, Bhillala and Khaiwar used to feel happy on being called 'Thakur' and wore sacred thread. However, after Independence, they claimed a tribal identity to avail of the facilities given to the Scheduled Tribes in India (Ghosh 2008: 494).

Surajit Sinha (1957) noted that there is very little rigid stratification in the tribal society belonging to the category of hunters and gatherers. There is however, a tendency among the tribes especially among the settled agricultural groups towards stratification on the basis of following considerations: (1) relative political supremacy of the numerically dominant clan, compared to others; (2) superiority in landholding of the earlier settlers, relative to later settlers; (3) symbolic ritual superiority of one group over another, due to ritual degradations of others in traditional terms, and the tendency of the priest headman to form an endogamous class (priestly class). Such groups of statuses might be called 'social classes'. Examples of this kind of status group formation in the tribal society can be multiplied almost indefinitely.

Admittedly, a passage from hierarchy to stratification is also noticed in many tribal formations. This has been the result of the impact of development and other processes of modernisation on tribal society (Singh 1994: 33). Also, with reference to tribes in contemporary India, Sachchidananda asserts that, 'a significant impact of the politico-economic change in independent India is the accentuation of social inequality in tribal society' (1990: 297–98). In this respect, K.S. Singh, in another context, made an important observation that the emerging inequality and stratification in tribal society should engage our attention, particularly in the field of anthropological research (1989: 8). This may direct our attention, to the specific tribal situation and at the same time enable us to take a hard look at the stereotyped notion of tribe we have accepted uncritically for so long (Mukhopadhyay 2012).

III

The foregoing sections make it clear that it is difficult to idealise the notion of 'tribe' as a socially homogeneous, non-hierarchical/differentiated, un-stratified or egalitarian society. The tribes in India, both in their traditional and transitional settings have/had gradations and internal differentiations based on social honour/prestige, ritual statuses, resources/land position, engagement with certain occupations, position in lineage/kinship structures, places of origin and ethnic affinities, etc. Social inequality, like many other features of social life, is often ordered in Indian tribal societies on the basis of some of these considerations. It has a fundamental importance in addressing the question of inequality in tribal social formation.

Inequality in tribal society manifests itself in several forms. American ethnologist R.H. Lowie (1921) examined the nature of property rights in simpler societies. He found although rights in land were often held collectively by the clan or the lineage, movable property was commonly held by individuals. Even in the case of rules of inheritance, men and women are differentiated, and some special attention is paid to genealogical propinquity. In many tribal communities property is necessarily an important and possible criterion of inequality, which is articulated through the system of kinship. So there is much to be learnt from studying the interplay between the principles of equality and inequality within the domain of kinship in such societies (Beteille 1977: 159). Here one may take a note that 'kinship', which serves as a symbol of unity, is also divided, discriminating the members of a particular tribal community on the basis of their kin group alliance.

Kinship in tribal societies is an important basis for the formation of enduring groups including lineages. Two lineages originally founded by two siblings of unequal ranks have become unequally ranked in larger spheres in course of time. Their members might then enjoy unequal prestige and power without differing greatly in their material possession. In the case of tribal societies like Saoras of Orissa, the persons belonging to the *gomong's* (chief) lineage can take wives from among the commoners, but would not give away their daughters in marriage to any of them. So in this society the women-takers are distinguished from the women-givers and the two are unequally ranked. Here the women-takers rank superior to women-givers. It may be mentioned here that the core social structure of a number of North-East Indian tribal communities was built around the asymmetrical alliance system involving wife giving and wife-receiving lineages.

Both status and power are real issues among most of the Indian tribes, and even if inequalities are not visible on the surface, they still remain latent in the inner structure of the society. Therefore, the task of the anthropologists and sociologists is to deal with that reality instead of getting trapped or crippled by the 'ideal' notion of a tribe. They should not give an impression that they still continue to accept the simplistic, uncritical and conventional version of tribe at the conceptual level without even raising the question of its contemporary relevance.

References

Beteille, Andre. 1977. *Inequalities among Men*. New Delhi: Oxford University Press.

Bose, Nirmal Kumar. 1972. *Some Indian Tribes*. New Delhi: National Book Trust.

Das, N.K. 1989. *Ethnic Identity, Ethnicity and Social Stratification in North-East India*. Delhi: Inter-India Publications.

Das, Rajat Kanti. 2011. 'Social Structure as a Model of Studying North-East Indian Tribal Communities', *Journal of the Asiatic Society*, 53, No. 4: pp. 1–10.

Deliege, Robert. 1985. *The Bhils of Western India: Some Empirical and Theoretical Issues in Anthropology in India*. Delhi: National Publishing.

Fried, Morton H. 1975. *The Notion of Tribe*. California: Cummings Publishing Company.

Furer, Haimendorf Christoph Von. 1962. *The Apatanis and their Neighbours*. London: Routledge and Kegan Paul.

——. 1985. *Tribes of India Struggle for Survival*. New Delhi: Oxford University Press.

Ghosh, Abhik. 2008. 'Recreating the Tribe Ever a New', *The Eastern Anthropologist*, 61 No. 4: pp. 485–506.

Godelier, Maurice. 1977. *Perspectives in Marxist Anthropology*. Cambridge: Cambridge University Press.

Leach, E.R. 1954. *Political Systems of Highland Burma: A Study of Kachin Social Structure*. Cambridge, MA: Harvard University Press.

Lowie, R.H. 1921. *Primitive Society*. London: Routledge and Kegan Paul.

Mann, R.S. 1984. *Anthropological and Sociological Theory: Approaches and Applications*. Jaipur: Rawat Publications.

Mukhopadhyay, Rajatsubhra. 2012. 'Class Formation among of the Tribes in India: A Brief Review', *Man in India*, 92, No. 3–4: pp. 387–398.

Pal, Twinkle. 2008. 'On Concept of Tribe: The Case of Gaddis of Himachal Pradesh', *The Eastern Anthropologist*, 61, No. 4: pp. 507–514.

Parsons, Talcott. 1966. *Societies: Evolutionary and Comparative Perspectives*. Englewood Cliffs: Prentice Hall.

Pudaite, Rochunga. 1963. *The Education of the Hmar People*. Monipur, Sielmat: Indo-Burma Pioneering Mission.

Sachchidananda. 1990. 'Patterns of Politico-Economic Change among Tribals in Middle India'. In *Dominance and State Power in Modern India: Decline of a Social Order*. Vol. II. Edited by Francine R. Frankel and M.S.A. Rao. New Delhi: Oxford University Press.

Sahlins, M.D. 1958. *Social Stratification in Polynesia*. Washington: University of Washington Press.

Singh, K.S. 1989. 'Foreward', in N.K. Das *Ethnic Identity, Ethnicity and Social Stratification in North-East India*. New Delhi: Inter-India Publications.

Singh, K.S. 1994. 'Inequality in Tribal Society: A Brief Review', *IASSI Quarterly*, 13, No. 1 and 2: pp. 29–34.

Singh, K.S. 1994. 'People of India', Nagaland, Vol. XXXIV, Anthropological Survey of India, Culcutta.

Sinha, Surajit. 1957. 'Tribal Cultures of Peninsular India as a Dimension of Little Tradition in the Study of Indian Civilization: A Preliminary Statement,' *Man in India*, 37, No. 2: pp. 93–118.

PART II

Regional Focus on Identity Formation

CHAPTER 6

Politics of Identity and Growing Tribalism in the Darjeeling Hills

SWATASIDDHA SARKAR

It is rather non-problematic to argue that modern selves have multiple identities but the principal issue of concern for the students of sociology and anthropology is the question that when and how one particular base of identification (among many) becomes overpowering than others. What thus seem important are not merely the bases but their context – varying meanings, which are expressive of the concerns of individual/collective subjectivities as reflected in the dynamics of social, political and economic realities. Perhaps, that is why the identity theories of some genre grant agency in the articulation of identity. Whether it is agency driven or manufactured out of rational calculation, the questions of identity and identification become significant as and when they involve the discourse of power, in them. It is through the discursive practices of power, the horizontally arranged historical exigencies of everyday life processes give birth to hierarchically arranged sociations, i.e. the forms in individuals – realisable in different ways – grow together into a unity and within which their interests are realised. Identity is but one strategy of such various sociations organised through the productive punctuations of power relations. The notion of 'productive power' used in the essay – my indebtedness to Foucault is obvious – implies multiplicity of 'micro-practices' that actually organise the everyday life in modern society. This positive conception of power or for that matter the call for a 'politics of everyday life' situates power not as a property or a possession of a dominant class, state or sovereign but has a reference to 'complex strategical situations' implying 'multiplicity of force relations' operating in a 'situationally intentional' manner. By emphasising on ethnic revivalism, tribal identity and growing tribalism in Darjeeling hills the present paper seeks: (i) to explore the 'micro-practices' through which tribal identity issues come to the fore to dominate the everyday hill politics, and (ii) to hint at the possible outcomes of such processes for the hill society at large.

Conceptualising Politics of Identity

The idea of identity has been used here as a social construct and not just as a 'primordial given'. The articulation of any particular identity superimposing itself over others does not necessarily lead it to fixity. Nor even the overpowering presence of any identity in a given context and time does mean the inefficacy of the other bases. As argued earlier, the dominance of one identity over another is contingent upon the contexts of those underlying the power relations and the similar socio-cultural contingencies. Arguably, then the questions of identity and identification seem to be transitory, temporal and at best social constructs.

The trend of analysing identity as 'strategic' and 'positional', as Hall (1996) would suggest, attempts to interpret the issue of identification as an unending process of social construction. It does lead to the articulation, suturing and the overpowering presence of any one of the bases of identity (which may, however, arise out of the culturally given metaphors) at one point of time but not swallowing the other bases for ever. Once an identity is attained, it does not necessarily sterile the identification project forever. Hence the issues of identity and identification may appear as bounded serialities of modern mind but in reality these issues are never unified and are increasingly fragmented and fractured – never singular but multiple. They are constructed across different, often contradictory, channels of cultural practices and positions. Another significant analytical departure that took place through these processes of unbounded serialities, is that it has unpacked the entanglement that exists between the community and the 'modernist moment'. Increasingly, thus, we experience that communities in the East provocatively nurture the 'historical pasts' or 'cultural givens' of their own more as resources, as a sort of capital that actually helped them climb up in the process of 'becoming' rather than reviving their past heritages of 'being' to move back to the 'old golden days'.

Traditions are definitely getting invented but the foci of this 'invention' engage the tradition-modernity rupture and its bearing upon the notion of community and identity in a complex repertoire. Besides all these there exists a great deal of entanglement between questions of community identity and the political process that ran parallel at the local, regional, national and even at the international level. Scholars have already established tribes as post-primitives, the paradigmatic paraphrasing of the tribes in Indian context as 'colonial construct' has been on academic purchase for more than three decades now. The recurring need of the contemporary period is perhaps to project the tribe as a 'post-colonial construct' and the present paper is a preliminary attempt to meet such an analytical end. As such the present paper seeks to problematise the issues of tribal identity and growing tribalism in Darjeeling hills within the above-outlined conceptual framework.

Contextualising the Problem

The 'assimilationist' zeal as well as the 'melting-pot' theses of the so-called modernisation school has already been discarded both by the empirical experiences as well as by the intellectual probing. The same also seems to be true in case of Darjeeling hills. Of late, the so-called seemingly homogenous, Hindu

Nepali identity has been questioned as well as the claim that 'our identity crisis has been solved' (comment made by Ghishing soon after getting the Gazette Notification of 1988) is also at stake. Again it would be pertinent here to note that Subhas Ghishing, the chief architect of the violent Gorkhaland movement of the 1980s, once negated the offer of Sixth Schedule as a measure of settlement. He claimed that such a measure was meant for the tribes and that the Gorkhas are civilised modern people far better off than the typical tribes. Ghising since the beginning of the new millennium has been championing the 'tribal cause' for the hill Gorkhas. Even after being thrown out from the hill politics rather permanently, he continues trying his luck for regaining his lost power in the politics by playing out this tribal identity card for the hill Gorkhas leading towards the formation of Sixth Schedule for the hilly portion of the District of Darjeeling. Ghising failed to realise Gorkhaland but he succeeded in bringing Limbus and Tamangs (his own community) into the fold of Scheduled Tribes. Inspired by this success story and realising the near impossibility of Gorkhaland, Ghishing brought to the floor of hill politics the idea of Sixth Schedule for which he needed to establish that the majority of different castes/communities under the pan-Gorkha fold were 'tribes'. Dashain, Phulpati, Bhai Tika and many other supposedly Nepali Hindu caste rituals and festivities were abandoned and dictates were issued to replace idol worshipping by pieces of stone or anything else as totemic objects just to prove the Gorkhas as nature worshippers – one major qualification needed to attain Scheduled Tribe (ST) status. Instead of gaining any political mileage, the ST identity issue has made Ghising unpopular for his alleged *jati futaune* (nation destroying) activities emanated out of the politics of Sixth Schedule – the last trump card of Ghising. Speedy transformation took place in the hill politics and soon Ghising was replaced by one of his henchmen – Bimal Gurung – who founded a new platform called Gorkha Janmukti Morcha (GJM) in 2007 and revived the subdued agitation for a separate state. The politics of tribal identity received a back seat and Gorkha identity once again was revived but ultimately it yielded no prospect for the much-hyped Gorkhaland and left open the space for tribal identity politics once again. This time it emerged on the pretext of the entanglement that took place between the GJM leadership and the state. The demand of tribal identity raised by several communities in the Darjeeling hills and the ensuing political process that followed largely indicate that identities are constructed both within and outside the community life. It is for this reason the issue of tribal identity in Darjeeling hills needs to be framed within the intersections of community life and the state.

Why No Ethnicity within the Gorkha?

Besides its colonial moorings and the fames of tea and tourism, Darjeeling as a space has been well recognised as the citadel of Nepali national identity outside Nepal. Mostly as migrant labourers or as mercenary soldiers, the people from Nepal started inhabiting Darjeeling and contributed towards the increase of its moral density since the middle of nineteenth century. In addition to the Bhutias, Lepchas, Sherpas and Yolmos – the already designated tribes of Darjeeling District since India's independence – majority of the hill population are of Nepali ethnic stock. Nepali is a speech community that includes different Hindu castes and Mongoloid groups. Even in the earliest accounts of Darjeeling such as that of

Campbell's (the first superintendant of the 'British sanctuary' – Darjeeling) we find mention about Bahuns, Khas, Magars, Gurungs, Murmis, Limbus, Kirantis, Haioos, Sunwars, Chepangs (all of whom were instrumental in the production of a Nepali nation outside Nepal) besides Lepchas, Bhotias, Dhimals, Meches, Tharus, Rajbashis and others. Idiosyncrasies apart, the piece published in the pages of *Transactions of Ethnological Society of London* (1869) designed to facilitate colonial administration, contained some important observations. First, that all these communities, whom Campbell preferred to label as 'tribes', were the followers of mixed traditions – Hindu, Budhhist, and animist in particular. Second, that Darjeeling contained a polyglot population stock leading towards a situation, which Hodgson later narrated aptly as 'Babel of Tribes'. The heterogeneity of hill population was quite widespread and historically well known. The heterogeneity of population of the Darjeeling hills was also recorded even during the colonial period when first attempts of counting heads were made. The following table (Table 6.1) provides us a synoptic view of such a diversity that has been a persistent feature of hill demography:

Table 6.1

Caste/Community wise Population in Darjeeling District during Different Census Years

Caste/Community	*1872*	*1901*	*1911*	*1921*	*1931*	*1941*	*1951*
Bahun	904	6,470	6,195	8,174	8,791	8,999	11,317
Chetri	N.A.	11,597	12,599	N.A.	N.A.	25,941	30,463
Thakuri	56	N.A.	N.A.	N.A.	N.A.	N.A.	804
Kami	1,886	9,826	10,939	11,779	11,331	16,272	19,432
Damai	252	4,643	4,453	5,781	5,551	8,162	9,116
Sarki	328	1,823	1,992	2,036	2,432	2,778	2,932
Sanyasi	267	1,151	1,060	N.A.	N.A.	N.A.	1,085
Yogi	N.A.	N.A.	N.A.	N.A.	N.A.	454	474
Newar	1,117	5,770	6,927	8,751	10,235	12,242	14,827
Sunwar	1,194	4,428	3,820	3,691	4,055	4,822	4,803
Gurung	3,150	8,738	9,628	9,575	11,154	15,455	17,864
Magar	3,011	11,912	12,451	14,934	16,299	17,262	19,413
Rai	1,814	33,133	40,409	41,236	47,431	56,794	63,745
Yakhas	235	1,143	1,119	N.A.	850	824	N.A.
Bhujel	N.A.	N.A.	N.A.	N.A.	5,295	6,929	5,745
Gahtri	1,419	3,448	3,584	N.A.	2,053	496	998
Thami	13	N.A.	N.A.	N.A.	N.A.	N.A.	475
Tamang	6,567	24,465	27,226	30,450	33,481	43,114	49,890
Limbu	4,663	14,305	13,804	14,191	16,288	17,803	19,838
Sherpa	N.A.	3,450	N.A.	N.A.	5,295	6,929	8,998
Lepcha	3,952	9,972	9,706	9,669	12,101	12,470	13,394
Bhutia	N.A.	9,315	10,768	10,710	5,334	7,612	9,061

Source: Data collected from the respective census reports and official figures published in the Gazetteers

Being attuned with the civilisational mission of the British, these communities steadfastly followed modernity's attitudinal and ideological footprints. Caught in a liberal social order heavily loaded with the vestiges of colonial rule of law, these communities have developed a different social mapping where Divya Upadesh, Panchakhat, and above all, a Bahunbadi discourse of forging nationhood by annexation and conquest did never gain ground. People of Nepali origin more in a diasporic fashion felt the need of imagining a nation by following a differential route than that of Nepal. The liberal social space of Darjeeling hills and the laxity of traditional caste system have furthered the scope of this homogenisation. Inter-caste and inter-community marriages on the one hand and the similar proletarian life experiences on the other strengthened the bond amongst the different communities whose survival interestingly depended upon the Andersonian notion of 'print capitalism' (1991). The major role of nation building amidst the *mugalane* (staying away home) situation was thus played by Nepali language. In the words of late historian Kumar Pradhan *'Bhasa Eota Samajik Sambritti Ho. Darjeeling Ma Harek Jaat, Jati, Bhasagosthi Ko Afno Chuttei Kshetriyata Chaina Ra Palpalma Anyoharusang Samparkama Aonuparne Hunda Sajha Bhasako Rupma Nepali Bhasa Anibarya Bhandaicha'* (Pradhan 2004: 26) ('Language is like social capital. Castes and communities of Darjeeling having different dialects of their own were not territorial groups. This was precisely why they needed a common language to maintain their everyday social interaction and for which Nepali language was a must'). This linguistic homogenisation later on was successfully used in the political project of Gorkhaland.

Darjeeling has had community organisations since the colonial days (like Napali Tamang Buddhist Association 1922, *Sarva Kirat Chumlung* 1925). But the ideological commitment to linguistic homogenisation was so strong that the inter-Nepali/Gorkha identity did not gains ground till the 1990s. The notion that individual ethnic identities must be secondary to a united Nepali/Gorkha cause if Indian Nepalis were to gain any benefit from the state did hold the community together. Needless to mention that this feeling was at the core of Gorkha political aspiration that Ghising meaningfully utilised during the 1980s. It is also for this reason that whenever the clarion call for Gorkhaland was raised either by Ghising or later by Bimal Gurung inter-Gorkha, identity claims did remain a non-issue.

The 'Return of the Native' Phenomenon in the Darjeeling Hills

The notion that shifting from a Nepali national identity to group by group ethnic identity strategy would be a productive avenue for gaining resources from the state began to gain currency since 1990s. The decade of 1990 was marked by three significant experiences. First, the near failure of Gorkhaland movement that was increasingly becoming prominent; Second, the official declaration of the Mandal Commission Recommendations in the 1993 securing special benefits for SCs, STs, and OBCs; Third, the rise of Janjati movement and politics in Nepal since the 1990s. These three events played instrumental role in securing a process what may be termed by following Adam Kuper (2003) as the 'return of the native' in the Darjeeling hills.

Since the establishment of Darjeeling Gorkha Hill Council (DGHC) in 1988, the bemoaned masses of Darjeeling hills got disillusioned, leading towards a generation gap in assessing the neat outcome of the agitation in respect of the hardships meted out by them during the movement days. Case studies did reveal that younger generation Nepalis did perceive the Gorkhaland movement as a failure, particularly in matters of securing benefits from the government. Whereas the system of protective discrimination, particularly after post-Mandal period, has been assessed as a matter of double endowment that can possibly be achieved only when inter-ethnic differences are reworked. The measures of protective discrimination or for that matter the status of being a Scheduled Tribe are considered as double endowment. Firstly, because it has a ready assurance of entitlements and welfare benefits from the part of state. Secondly, by becoming a tribe one is not only accorded a 'privileged category' status but also a juridical and administrative recognition of being an Indian citizen, since protective discrimination measures are meant for the citizens alone. Hence, the rejoice for 'the return of native' quickly gained populism and became a fad indeed, that energised the Bahuns and Chhetris (the so-called *tagadharis* – men of sacred thread – the higher castes) even to join the race of 'enlistment movement'. 'The notion of tribe appeared as a doubly binding package whose achievement demanded group by group identification that can well run parallel with the so-called movement of Gorkhaland', as one of my respondents reasoned.

The Janajati Movement of Nepal and the Purport of the 'Outside'

The 1990s has been of tremendous significance for Nepal since during this decade the anti-Hindu stir in the name of Janajati politics was launched in Nepal. In Nepal the Janajati questions remained latent so long as the nature of political structure was authoritarian. However, with the installation of democracy, Janajati politics has gradually engulfed the state politics of Nepal. The long-standing domination of the Nepali society and politics by the so-called upper caste tagadharis – Bahuns and Chhetris – was at stake. The non-Hindu tribal communities, which did undergo fast mobilisation, have challenged the traditional power base of the Nepali society and polity, and they are demanding equitable redistribution of resources and goods (Upreti 2002: 8).

Much like Darjeeling, the emergence of community associations demanding tribal status was also a common phenomenon in Sikkim during this time. In fact, these community organisations like *Nepali Tamang Buddhist Association* (1922), *All Kirata Association* (1925) of the Limbus, and *All India Kirat (chumlung) Association* (1967) of the Rais have maintained trans-local and transnational organisational networks with their counterparts settled there in Sikkim and Nepal. They did share views as well as suggestions and financial support too for furthering the cause of community consciousness. Sara Shneidrman has made an in-depth analysis of how Thangmi activism took place in Darjeeling primarily depending upon this trans-national networks which she categorically analysed through the notion of 'feedback loop' (Shneiderman 2009). T.B. Subba likewise maintained that Limbu nationalism has always been trans-national (Subba 1990: 45). Some others do hold that these transnational networks particularly among the Kirata communities (Limbu, Rai, Yakha) are indicative of a *Kiratisation* process presently at work in Sikkim, Darjeeling and

Eastern Nepal (Sinha 2006: 1–22). These cases are suggestive of a sociologically relevant process, which Shneiderman (2009) has aptly narrated as a course in which ethnicity though emerges out of community-specific contingencies limited to the political boundaries of a country but continues to maintain its tapestry in a de-territorialised fashion regardless of where the communities live in.

Ethnographic State and the Classificatory Moment in Darjeeling

Dozens of communities constitute what we know as Gorkha. Some of them are already within arrangement of protective discrimination measures either as STs or as SCs or OBCs. The situation is more or less same in Sikkim but in other states they do acquire positions, mostly in the OBC category (Table 6.2). As noted earlier there has been a growing competition among the Nepali speaking communities in Darjeeling towards attaining ST status. The already designated tribes of Darjeeling since 1950 are the Lepchas, Bhutias and Sherpas/Yolmos. Recently Limbu and Tamang were also enlisted as STs in 2003 leading towards the rise of district total of 32 per cent of the STs (Middleton and Shneiderman 2008: 40). There are nearer to a dozen of communities who have submitted their case for enlistment while several other cases are pending decision.

Table 6.2

Status of Nepali/Gorkha Community in Different States within India

Caste/Community	*State*	*Status*	*Year*
Nepali (Thapa, Gurung, Lama, Gaine, Rai, Chhetri, Limbu, Magar, Lohar, Damai, Sarki)	Assam	OBC Central List	1993 1995
Nepali (Badi, Damai, Gainay, Kami, Sarki)	Manipur	OBC Central List	1995
Nepali (Limbu, Matwali, Rai)	Tripura	OBC Central List	1994
Gorkha	Himachal Pradesh	OBC Central List	1993
Gorkha	Punjab	OBC Central List	1993
Gorkha	Haryana	OBC Central List	1993
Gorkha (excluding Brahmin and Khastriya)	Uttarakhand	OBC Central List	2011
Bhujel, Gurung, Mangar, Rai, Sunuwar, Dewan, Thami, Jogi	Sikkim	Most Backward Classes (MBC)*	2003
Bahun, Chhetri, Newar, Sanyasi,	Sikkim	OBC	2003
Kami, Damai, Sarki, Majhi	Sikkim	SC	1978
Limbu, Tamang	Sikkim	ST	2001
Kami, Damai, Sarki	West Bengal	SC	1950
Limbu Tamang	West Bengal	SC	2003
Bhujel, Mangar, Newar, Thami Jogi	West Bengal	OBC	1995
Sunuwar	West Bengal	OBC	1999
Dewan, Rai (including Chamling)	West Bengal	OBC	2001
Limbu, Tamang	West Bengal	ST	2003

* Bifurcation of OBC into two categories Most Backward Classes (MBCs) and Other Backward Classes in Sikkim was made in 2003 (Notification No. 54/SWD/WD dated 17/9/2003).

Source: Required data were collected from the official website of National Commission for Backward Classes (NCBC) (Stable

URL: http://www.ncbc.nic.in/User_Panel/CentralListStateView.aspx accessed on 12.12.2013)

Gurungs and Rais who submitted their application in the late 1990s were accorded with a negative response from the side of the government. During this period Subhas Ghising had also submitted a memorandum to the government for the enlistment of all the Gorkhas as OBCs. Although Ghising's claim was scrapped, the Gorkhas were accorded the status of OBC in several other states. Notwithstanding this contradictory positioning of the state in regard to the question of classifying communities under reserved category, this very act of categorisation has enabled the post-colonial state to acquire the qualities of the colonial prototype of an 'ethnographic state' – to use Nicholas Dirks (2003) catchphrase – and to set in motion a 'classificatory moment' in which all the communities are dying hard to show off their 'tribality' and striving to live up to the requirements of an 'ethnographic state'.

Almost three decades back, André Beteille (1986) cautioned us that the problem in India is not about definition but about the identification of the tribe. Such requirements of classification and categorisation did never allow displacing the administrative and political contingencies for a scientific and theoretical discussion on the tribes. This is not to say that those engaged in drawing up lists of Indian tribes did not have their own conceptions of tribe, but those conceptions were neither clearly formulated nor were they systematically applied. The process of designating or 'scheduling' the tribes began during the

Figure 6.1

How to be a Tribe

Lokur Committee (1965)

- **(i) Identification of primitive traits**
- **(ii) Distinctive culture**
- **(iii) Geographical isolation**
- **(iv) Shyness of contact with the community at large**
- **(v) Backwardness**

CRI Survey Guideline

- (i) History of migration
- (ii) Genealogical table (father side)
- (iii) Traditional and present occupation
- (iv) Name of clan, sub-clan, totemic object
- (v) Rites and rituals (birth, marriage, death)
- (vi) Village festivals, festival calendar and community participation
- (vii) Educational status
- (viii) Availability of infrastructural facilities
- (ix) Food habits
- (x) Family size and present occupation
- (xi) Land and land records
- (xii) Traditional panchayat system
- (xiii) Magico-religious beliefs & practices, family deities, ancestral worship
- (xiv) Socio-religious ceremonies
- (xv) Rights of inheritance

Source: Adapted from Middleton 2011.

British rule and acquired a systematic character from the time of 1931 census. The criteria of scheduling some communities as tribes to the exclusion of others got further refinement in the reports of first Backward Class Commission 1955, the Advisory Committee on Revision of SC/ST lists (Lokur Commission) 1965, and the Joint Committee of the Parliament on the Scheduled Castes and Scheduled Tribes Order (Amendment) Bill 1967 (Chanda Committee 1969). Even though the question is still very nebulous as to how the tribes in India are to be identified, the Lokur Committee's five-fold recommendations are still considered as the official basis of determining a group as tribe. The typical classificatory arrangement as endorsed by five-fold criteria of Lokur Commission were further recast by the Cultural Research Institute (CRI), Kolkata, into fifteen more normative criteria constituting what is popularly known among the CRI officials as the 'ethnographic survey guideline' that they use while assessing, on behalf of the state government, the 'authenticity' and 'appropriateness' of the claim to be a tribe (Figure 6. 1).

Interestingly enough, the attempt to recast tribal identity following the codes of classificatory arrangement has led the aspiring communities go for practising tribalism as a peculiar process of social engineering leading towards the discovery of tribality almost as an 'invented tradition'. Such has been the case with the Gurungs, who after having denied tribal status by the government in 2011, started practising Buddhism notwithstanding the very fact they were heavily syncretised with Hinduism at the level of everyday religiosity. Almost in a similar vein the Akhil Bharatiya Mangar Sangh, Darjeeling, has taken pains to publicise the distinctiveness of Mangar culture. Since 2002 the Mangar Association has been consistently articulating elements of Mangar folk culture (viz., unique dress, musical instruments, folk songs, dances, scripts, etc.). The association has made a clarion call that all the Mangars of the Darjeeling hills should use *Mangrat* as religion for enlistment purposes of any sort and taken imitatives to produce trained *Bhusals* (Mangar religious specialists) as well. Likewise the repeated calls made by the Kirati Khambu Rai Associations that the *Dasain* (Dushera) has to be boycotted by the Rais are some such cases in point.

These claims of tribal identity raised by the majority of the hill communities and their associations have registered a marked tendency to politicse the everyday life by undoing the settled present for an unforeseen future. While at the level of everyday living, community identities in Darjeeling have been hybridised and syncretised for a common cause of Gorkha ethnicity, the claim of tribal status contradictorily is rooted in and routed through the ruptured distinctiveness of individual community identities (Middleton 2013: 18). Contemporary display of tribalism in Darjeeling appears to be more a result of such romanticised imaginations that tend to reify the cultural characteristics of communities as a part of institutionalised and idealised culture rather than as a matter of everyday practice. Tribal dress becomes a matter of staged demonstration; ancestral rituals become a matter of performance in front of the state-sponsored anthropologists.

With the near divination of Lokur Commission (1965) criteria or further refinement of those as made by the CRI, the idea of tribe has become politically poignant that tends to reformulate the idea of tribe much like what Jonathan G. Andelson has coined as 'an intentional community' (Andelson 1996). Following Morton Fried, it may thus be argued that in contemporary Darjeeling hills the idea of tribe has become a kind of 'secondary phenomena' (Fried 1975), which in the typical case acquires its form and identity from some external sources. The five-fold criteria of our ready reference situate the idea of tribe in the vestiges of colonial ethnology. Either none would be accorded tribal status or much of the already designated scheduled tribes are to be de-scheduled if the classification and categorisation of Scheduled Tribes are to be made by following the criteria presently in operation. The state-specified notion of tribe still hinges around 'tribal essentialism' while the need is actually to discredit such essentialisms and to bring into the fold of analysis the contemporary cultural dispensations of articulating indigeneity. Contemporary anthropology views culture as a dynamic concept, something that is continuously reconstituted. Unfortunately, tribal culture is still considered to be a static notion. It hardly moved an inch, while anthropology is prepared to traverse the globe.

Ethnicisation of Tribal Identity and the Concern of the State

The need is not just to critically assess the processes of growing tribalism but to point out that the over-dependence upon the discourse of authenticity so as to frame the claims of tribal identity has encouraged the claimants indulge in a self-defeating project of identity politics. Regrettably, though the present fashion of practising anthropology, either as a form of popular culture or as governmentality continues, in Darjeeling tends to shed light on the practising culture through the discursively framed disposition of 'authenticity', thereby enabling the articulation of a peculiar process of 'politics of recognition' in which communities go on producing a self-identity as something which they do not possess. The discourse of authenticity involved in the statist way of imagining a tribe anthropologically directs the politics of recognition move in the direction not only of misrecognition but perhaps of misidentification too (Middleton 2013: 20). This is how authenticity of tribal identity claims enters the arena of politics where the need is just to live up to its requirements of the state-endorsed discourse of authenticity no matter how contradictory it may be to the mundane practices of everyday community living. Contemporary tribal situation in Darjeeling largely approximates these forces and processes where both the content and context of tibalism get pejoratively framed in the arena of politics.

The seriousness of the problem under study becomes even more palpable when one takes into account the recent governmental decision to create separate development boards for the already designated tribes (viz., Lepchas and Tamangs) as a measure to better serve their interests. Luring the Lepchas and Tamangs through separate development boards and packages has added new incentives in the process of ethnicising the idea and concept of tribe, thereby leading it towards a theoretical dead end. The ethnicisation of tribal identity in the contemporary Darjeeling hills is certainly a new development, which also helped the state scale down the intensity and pace of the renewed call for Gorkhaland that took place in the recent past (July–October 2013), but the question that needs to be asked as to whether such a measure of 'engaging tribe'

– a strategy profitably used by the USA in case of pacifying anti-US and anti-imperial feelings of the Iraqis and Afghanistanis – will transform the concept of tribe merely as a 'political ploy' from being an 'ethnological category'?

Heading Towards a Conclusion?

What merits attention is the issue that through their acts of reviving the 'tribalist' cultural traditions the aspiring tribes of the Darjeeling hills are trying to depict their search to be known as 'something' and clarifies their relationships with the positions of power and privilege and thereby opening up the scope for inter-community conflicts based on differential political affiliations. This is how tribal identity issue has taken an 'ethnic detour' in contemporary Darjeeling hills, which is trying to get its justification realised within the circumstantial situation where the state itself is seen to encourage such activities (Sarkar 2014: 26). More in a fashion of outside contingencies of identity articulation, the situational waves, produced and reproduced through the discourse of power have provided the impetus for authentication and exclusivity. It is perhaps for this reason many communities in contemporary Darjeeling hills are dying hard to revive their erstwhile practices linked with ancestral worshipping coupled with animistic, shamanistic and/or Buddhist rituals, and so on. This is how the hill communities of Mongoloid origins are following the course of ethnicising tribal identity in contemporary Darjeeling hills. It would be too early to make a final statement as to whether Gorkha identity withstand the taste of time or it would be dismantled by the project of 'tribalisation' in the near future. Significantly, neither the GJM leadership nor even the aspiring tribal groups and communities of the hills do consider that the contemporary activism relating to the claim of ST status would jettison the spirit of Gorkha ethnicity. It is, however, not impossible to conceive of this act of balancing to be made by the Gorkhas or by the aspiring tribes who will have their one foot rested on the tribal identity claims and the other on the claim of a separate state for the ethnic Gorkhas. Such courses of action can be framed conceptually and, above all, when we know that the claims of tribe are made principally by the Matwali groups who constitute the core of Gorkha identity at the first place. However, it needs to be remembered that for those who are involved in such courses of action, activism for tribal status or the claim of a separate state are not intellectual questions to be solved by informed and rational understandings. Moreover, promises of increased inclusion or the addressing of grievances through 'confidence building measures' as was done by the state in case of the Tamangs and the Lepchas in the recent past has raised serious doubts as to how the act of balancing of tribal identity and Gorkha ethnicity can maintain the equilibrium necessary for a peaceful coexistence in the local society. The problem, at its core, is not in fact a lack of welfare benefits per se but of inter-community cooperation and communal solidarity, upon which Gorkha ethnicity rests. Keeping in view the recent associational public pronouncements made by the Lepcha and Tamang tribes, just on the eve of the 16th Parliamentary elections in May 2014, offering political support to the ruling party of the state that has attempted, time and again, to smash and grab or corner the Gorkha cause, are indicative of the very fact that tough times are ahead of the hill people as a whole.

References

Anderson, Benedict. 1991. Imagined Communities: Reflection on the Origin and Spread of Nationalism, New York: Verso.

Andelson, Jonathan G. 1996. 'Intentional Community'. In *Encyclopaedia of Cultural Anthropology*, Vol. 2. Edited by David Levinson and Melvin Ember New York: Henry Holt and Company.

Beteille, Andre. 1986. 'The Concept of Tribe with Special Reference to India', *European Journal of Sociology*, 27, No. 2: pp. 296–318.

Campbell, A. 1869. 'On the Tribes around Darjeeling', *Transactions of the Ethnological Society of London*, 7: pp. 144–159.

Dirks, Nicholas B. 2003. *Castes of Mind: Colonialism and the Making of Modern India.* New Delhi: Permanent Black.

Fried, Morton H. 1975. *The Notion of Tribe.* Philippines: Cummings Publishing Company.

Hall, Stuart, and Paul Der Gay (eds). 1996. *Questions of Cultural Identity.* London: Sage Publications.

Kuper, Adam. 2003. 'The Return of the Native', *Current Anthropology,* 44, No 3: pp. 389–402.

Middleton, Townsend. 2011. 'Across the interface of state ethnography: Rethinking ethnology and its Subjects in Multicultural India', *American Ethnologist,* 38, 2: pp. 249–266.

Middleton, Townsend. 2013. 'States of difference: Reconfiguring Ethnicity and its 'Crisis' at India's Borders', *Political Geography,* 25: pp. 14–24.

Middleton, Townsend and Sara Shneiderman. 2008. 'Reservations, Federalism and the Politics of Recognition in Nepal', *Economic and Political weekly,* XLIII, No. 19: pp. 10–16.

Pradhan, Kumar. 2004. 'Darjeelingma Nepali Jati Ra Janjatiya Chinarika Naya Udaanharu', (in Nepali) *Mahesh Chandra Regmi Lecture.* Laltipur, Nepal: Social Science Baha.

Sarkar, Swatahsiddha. 2014. 'Tribal Detour in the Darjeeling Hills', *Economic and Political Weekly,* XLIX, No. 32: pp. 25–26.

Shneiderman, Sara. 2009. 'Ethnic (P)reservations: Comparing Thangmi Ethnic Activism in Nepal and India'. In David N Gellner (ed) *Ethnic Activism in Nepal and India.* Delhi: Sage Publications.

Sinha, A.C. 2006. 'Search for Kirat Identity: Trends of De-Sanskritization among the Nepamul Sikkimese', *Peace and Democracy in South Asia,* 2, No. 1 and 2: pp. 1–22.

Subba, T.B. 1990. 'Limbu Ethnicity at Crossroads', *Himalayan Miscellany,* 4: pp. 40–45.

Upreti, B.C. 2002. 'Ethnicity and Politics in Nepal: Emerging Patterns of Socio-Political Mobilization and Alignments', *South Asian Studies,* 37, No. 1.

CHAPTER 7

The Teesta Warriors

A Study Focussing on the Cultural Dimensions of the Emerging Lepcha Identity in the Backdrop of the Anti-Dam Movement in Sikkim

JAYANTA MADHAB TAMULY

To the green fresh leaves I spoke,
To the pine and the oak,
To the flowers that strew the ground,
To the moss that gathers round.
To the far and to the nigh, to the blue and radiant sky.
To the insects sporting here,
To the water running there.
To the meadow, to the hill,
To the lively, to the still,
To one and all the things I love
On Mother Earth, in skies above.

(Translation of a Lepcha folk song)

Known by the exoethnonym, Lepchas are the autochthonous people of the Eastern Himalayas, spread over the hilly regions of Darjeeling, Sikkim, Eastern Nepal and Western Bhutan. Known for their deeper knowledge of botany and ecology, close relationship with nature and non-confrontational nature, Lepchas like to introduce themselves as Mutanchi Rongkup Runkup – the beloved son of the Mother Earth, the son of the snowy peak. Historically, Lepchas shared an intimate relation with all the animate and inanimate objects of Sikkim Himalayas, thus proving their demand to be the indigenous tribe of the region. Agriculture has been the chief occupation of the Lepchas. Lepcha agriculture is basically terrace-based hill agriculture that is concentrated on production of crops like paddy, maize, ginger, cardamom, millet, vegetables. The changing pattern of agricultural practices introduces newer crops like dal, soya bean, floriculture and different vegetables. The Lepchas have a low spatial mobility and they prefer to stick to their own place as long as they can. Unlike the Bhutias, they seem to be very reluctant to leave their home. In the social sphere, Lepchas follow patriarchal system with a flexible inheritance of property right for the female folk. Lepchas are known for their rich ethno-medicinal knowledge, riverine culture, hunting spirit and folk culture. The Lepchas are legally recognised as Indigenous people in India through the government's listing of their people as a 'Scheduled Tribe.' Earlier, they were also given 'primitive tribe' status.

Dzongu: The Lepcha Habitat of Sikkim

In Sikkim, Dzongu is the central habitat of the Lepchas. It is situated in the district of North Sikkim Dzongu and is a protected area. Dzongu is located at an elevation ranging from 800m and 6,000m above sea level and is about 70 kilometers away from the capital city of Gangtok. The Lepchas consist 38 per cent of the entire population of the district, thus forming the largest ethnic group of the district. In Sikkim, as a whole, Lepchas constitute 7.8 per cent of the state's population of 5,81,500 (Government of Sikkim 1961). Almost all the 7,000 inhabitants of Dzongu are Lepchas who practise Buddhism. Currently, Christianity has also had a great hold among the Lepchas. They also include shamanistic nature worshipping rituals in their worship, conducted by Lepcha *bongthings* and *muns* – male and female Lepcha priests. Owing to dense forest cover, the area experiences rain almost throughout the year. The Lepchas have their own indigenous script that dates back to the 18th century. They are one of the major communities of Sikkim along with the Bhutias and Nepalis. The Lepchas of Dzongu are protected by the Proclamation dated 30 August 1956 by His Highness Sir Tashi Namgyal, the Maharaja of Sikkim and the Notification No. 3069/O.S. dated 24 March 1958 and issued by the Home Department, Government of Sikkim. That was how Dzongu was 'earmarked' (Wangchuk and Zulca 2007) as a Lepcha reserve, the oldest, permanent settlement of the community.

Ethnic Identity

Ethnic identity is considered both as social and individual construct (Waters 1990). It is viewed as an individual's identification with 'a segment of a larger society whose members are thought, by themselves or others, to have a common origin and share segments of a common culture and who, in addition, participate in shared activities in which the common origin and seems most often to be a frame in which individuals identify consciously or unconsciously with those with whom they feel a common bond because of similar traditions, behaviours, values, and beliefs' (Ott 1989). These points of connection allow individuals to make sense of the world around them and to find pride in which they are. If, however, positive ethnic group messages and support are not apparent or available to counteract negative public messages, a particular individual is likely to feel alienated and detached from their own ethnic identity. Ethnic identity development consists of an individual's movement toward a highly conscious identification with their own cultural values, behaviours, beliefs and traditions. Ethnic and racial identity models provide a theoretical structure for understanding individuals' negotiation with their own and other cultures (Chavez and Guido: 1999).

The Anti-Dam Movement by the Lepchas of Sikkim

The movement against the hydro-power projects and dams over the river Teesta of Sikkim was led by the Lepchas of the state. Though reports vary, 26 dams have been proposed to be constructed over the river Tessta, the lifeline of Sikkim. Out of them seven were to be built in Dzongu. The Lepchas, since the beginning of the new millennium, have been continuing with their protest against the construction of these dams in Dzongu on the ground that the construction would disturb and reduce their cultural, environmental, economic and social integrity. The movement has been led by an organisation named Affected Citizens of Teesta (ACT), supported by other Lepcha organisations like Concerned Lepchas of Sikkim (CLOS), Sangha of Dzongu (SOD), Indigenous Lepcha Tribal Association (ILTA), Dzongu Holy Land Protection Committee (DHLPC), Save the Teesta campaign (SCT), Sikkim Association for Environment and numerous NGOs, environmental groups, human rights activists within and outside the country. The anti-dam movement has witnessed all types of protests including prolonged hunger strikes (63 and 96 days), rallies, sits-ins, protests in written forms (memoranda, letters, posters and banners, articles about the movement in magazines, newspapers, web portals, etc.). The movement has been able to attract critical attention both in the national and international level. It turns out to be one of the significant and persistent movements by an indigenous community for preserving their identity and rights. During this movement, cultural narratives have been used and revived to formulate an identity strategy. Simultaneously, the movement has helped in reviving the identity in the form of a cultural process.

The Anti-Dam Movement: A Movement for Lepcha Identity?

The official website of Affected Citizens of Teesta states that their prime objective is 'to resolve the true protected identity of Dzongu'. This one line statement is enough to demonstrate that the movement, which has started as a protest against the dams and the hydro-power projects in Dzongu, no longer remains an issue of protest against the threat posed by technological intrusions. It has now encompassed a cluster of issues involving protection of culture, livelihood, demography and identity of this simple, peaceful tribe in the foothills of the Himalayas. Lepchas' integral connection with the reserve of Dzongu and their embedded cultural bond with the Mother Nature make the anti-dam movement an issue of revolt against cultural threat against these eco-inhabitants, a popular term repeatedly used to refer to the Lepchas.

Dzongu and Teesta: The Symbols of Lepcha Identity

Irrespective of their religious practices, all Lepchas believe Dzongu and Teesta to be the symbol of their culture. Every myth, folktale, song, dance form, legend, food dish has references to Dzongu and Teesta. The cultural identity of this Himalayan ethnic tribe is inseparably related with them. They can be called the symbolic embodiment of Lepcha culture.

Lepchas believe Dzongu to be their holy land: the Mayel Lyang, the paradise. 'The very essence of being a Lepcha is derived from our physical and spiritual connection with Dzongu', – this is what the Lepchas believe. It is where the largest tree is never cut down or the strongest deer is never hunted. Historically, the dense forest of the reserve was the original habitat of the Lepchas and their livelihood was completely dependent on the forest. Each Lepcha clan has its own 'Chu', a Himalayan Peak, and 'Da', a lake. The clan members offer their prayers and supplications to their respective Chu. The 108 clans among the Lepchas are named after the 108 peaks of Mt Kanchenjunga. Identity of a Lepcha is inseparably connected with Dzongu. Innumerable references to Dzongu have been made in their stories relating to Creation, marriage and death; thus the entire lifecycle of a Lepcha is associated with Dzongu. Beliefs, rituals and customs of the Lepcha society have endless references of and relation with this sacred land. Lepchas believe that their ancestors, Fodong-Thing and Nazaong – Nyo, the first Lepcha Man and Woman were created from the virgin snows of Kanchenjunga of Dzongu. Lepchas believe that their souls go to Dzongu when they die. 'The soul will go to the confluence of Teesta and Rangyong rivers below Passingdang. The Mun will take the soul through Teesta River and when it arrives at the confluence of Teesta and Rangyong, it will follow Rangyong, the holiest river of the Lepchas that flows in the middle of Dzongu' (Tamsang, Lyangsong 2008). Such beliefs and associated customary practices provide the foundation of a community's identity. A song composed by a Kalimpong-based Lepcha lyricist Sukden Lepcha, which pays tribute to Dzongu, has assumed renewed meaning in the context of the movement. 'Rumlyang' was introduced to the anti-dam movement and it quickly became an anthem frequently chanted at rallies, protest meetings, festivals and any occasion where the Lepchas opposing the projects gathered.

Protection of Dzongu is the main objective of the anti-dam movement. Far from the humdrums of the modern life, Lepchas, for centuries, have been living in Dzongu. It offers their livelihood and shelter. Many of their holy places are also situated in Dzongu. Lingdong, Tung Kyong Doh, Kanchenbrung tung da, Sa Thong deh, Mayel Ney, Ta Ung deh are some sacred landscapes, lakes and groves where Lepchas go for worship as a mark of their holy life. Lepchas believe that they are protected by the hill God living in this place. During the years, Lepchas have identified themselves firmly rooted to this region. '... I could say that, despite minor variations due to long isolation and lack of outside influence here, much of our way of life that has been forgotten or coloured in other regions, I found to be still thriving here' (Foning 1997). The strategic choice for expressing the collective identity is always a crucial factor in formulating and leading a social movement. The place one lives in and the culture borne out of that place, make what the community is. 'A culture, we might say as a sighting shot, consists of the practices and forms of life which distinguish a social group from a group of animals: the styles, rules, values, and other elements distinguishable in various patterns of human life' (Wilson 1984), The dense, serene, isolated forest reserve symbolise the calm, peaceful and at times insular nature of the Lepchas where they enjoy 'free play of their own genius'. But the proposed Panan and Teesta IV projects bring major threats to these places. Influx of outsiders, impact of new cultures and technological advancement are feared to mess up the holiness and glory of these landscapes. Hence, ceaseless efforts to protect this land from any technology-induced cultural devastation turn synonymous with the protection of their identity.

The same is applicable to the river Teesta also. Lepcha legends, folktales, myths, beliefs and customs are intertwined with this river. In their marriage ceremonies, the tale of the river Rangeet and Rongnue (the other name of Teesta) is sung, which also find references in their dance forms. The bride and the bridegroom are always taken to symbolise the rivers Rongnue and Rangeet. The Lepchas wish the newly wedded couple a happy and prosperous life in future like the Rangeet and Rongnue. The newly wed Lepcha couple take a bath in the Teesta before starting a new life. Hence, while mobilising the mass against the prospective dangers of the hydro-projects or the dams, their impact upon Teesta has been discussed and analysed in greater details. In this process, Teesta has been imagined not merely a river, but also as the epitome of Lepcha culture. The cultural threat to the tribe has been enhanced by directly posing a threat to the river compounded by the environmental violations and exposed by the reports of different environmentalists, NGOs and environmental groups. Due to the loopholes in the Environmental Impact Assessment report of the Teesta V project, an ethnographic study was awarded to the Water and Power Consultancy Services (WAPCOS) and the biodiversity study was entrusted to Wildlife Institute of India, Dehradun. But, the project was cleared and granted environmental clearance before these studies could be completed. In effect, biodiversity and ethnographic concerns were not considered in the process of clearance of the project. There has been no information on downstream impact of the Teesta III, IV and V since 'these are run-of-the-river projects' (Mazumdar 2007). Scientists, civil society activists and local communities have cautioned against the construction of mega projects in a region that is geologically and ecologically fragile. Their concerns centre on the social and environmental impacts of 'run of the river' projects that re-route the river through tunnels bypassing long stretches of the natural river course. For example, the 'head race tunnel' of the Teesta V project bypasses a 23-kilometer stretch of the Teesta. While these projects are described as 'environmentally benign', as submergence areas and water regulation are lower than conventional storage dams, in practice, it has been argued that the diversion of water, extensive tunneling into the hillsides, and dumping of debris in surrounding areas threaten the river's ecology and livelihoods that depend on it (Asia Foundation Report 2013).

During the Public Hearing of Panan project held in Namprikdam, Lower Dzongu, the majority of those attending the Hearing said 'No' to the project. The environmental clearance to Panan was given on the basis of a flawed EIA and EMP. Affected Citizens of Teesta (ACT) had, on several occasions, written to the Expert Appraisal Committee (EAC) of the Ministry of Environment and Forests of Government of India (MoEF) citing serious flaws in the reports. Concern was voiced against the dumping of excavated soil, muck using explosive blasts for digging tunnels and the influx of workers in the Protected Lepcha Reserve. Brushing aside all concerns, the MoEF did accord environmental clearance to Panan. Subsequently, a condition was attached to the clearance which relates to the establishment of labour quarters and influx of workers appointed for the project. There was a clear directive from the MoEF that no labour quarter could be established within the Dzongu Reserve and that the workers would have to be transported in and out of Dzongu every day. This condition was violated by Himagiri (the patron agency) without attracting any action from the MoEF. The clearance conditions were never monitored by the MoEF (Lahiri 2012).

Cultural Dimension Turned Dimension of Existence

Social movement research states that culture representing collective consciousness is reflected in collective mobilisation. But at the same time it must be realised that it is not all emotion, but sound reason is working behind the action taken by the people. Reasoning and public consensus based on reasoning always open before us a shared hope for a flexible multi-layered organisational structure 'that could create arenas for confrontation among different associations and subjectivities, by which they would not just act in common but also transform each other reciprocally, building new identities, values and communities' (Porta 2001).

The issues of protection of Dzongu and Teesta thus transcend its cultural or sentimental boundary as numerous charges of violation, miscommunication, deprivation, manipulation and discrimination have been revealed by different parties. Significantly, all these violations and discrimination show how Lepchas have been tactfully deprived of their age-old rights and cultural integrity. Though the ancient nature-worshipping of the Lepchas have been replaced by formal religions of Buddhism and Christianity, Lepchas still consider some particular places, lakes or caves sacred and representative of their cultural ethos. But due to the dams and the migration of outsiders, many of such places have lost its significance. The Armed Forces and Border Roads Organisation is found to change the original names of the surrounding names of lakes, ridges, villages, which the Lepchas consider a direct attack on their culture. For instance, the holy Guru Dongmar Lake was renamed as the Guru Nanak Jeel. Further, the holy stone (*Leydo*) complex at Chungthang was encroached upon and the name of Chungthang was changed into Changithang. All the history connected with Sikkim's Patron Saint Guru Padmasambhava has been changed and attributed to Guru Nanak, thus erasing the factual history of the place. The National Hydroelectic Power Corporation (NHPC) not only defaced the slopes of Kewzing but also changed the name of the place to Rangit Nagar. During the time when these processes were on, they neither tried to look into the cultural attachment of the community to these names nor did they discuss the matter with the community members. These dictatorial steps deepened the fear of the loss of their identity among the community. Fear of cultural loss or defacement having a direct impact on their identity made the Lepchas rethink about their existence. A group of Lepcha research scholars from Sikkim University and North Bengal University, during an interview, expressed how this cultural oppression compelled them to rethink about their duty. 'We never thought that the changing of a name of a place can be such a serious matter. But when we read our folklores and beliefs associated with these places, we felt that it was a serious oppression. If one's name is the basic identity for him/her, why not with the places?' 'They are playing with our emotion', said Rebeka Lepcha, a research scholar in the Department of Sociology, Sikkim University. Akit Lepcha, an MBBS student of Sikkim Manipal College of Medical Sciences, expressed concern over the loss and extinction of the medicinal plants of Dzongu due to the dam projects. Lepchas have a great knowledge of traditional medicine that they practice with the available plants in Dzongu. The hydro projects and the dams, by occupying a large area of Dzongu land, may lead to the extinction of such traditional herbs.

Such activities are nothing but a form of cultural violence, instigated to erase the cultural history of the region. Lepchas gradually realise that these are not accidental steps, rather intended strategically. The word 'intent' is central in the interpretation of any form of violence. Physical or psychological harm that occurs by accident, in the absence of intent, is not violence. Johan Galtung emphasised on the element of 'intent' in studying about violence. Galtung (1990) opines that it is necessary to check whether violence is intended or unintended to measure the element of guilt, since the concept of guilt has been tied more to intention. Violence committed with conscious intention is destructive. It is destructive not in the sense that it causes immediate loss, but it determines the development of the seeds of hatred and enmity for future conflict of a bigger dimension. Even our legal system recognises the critical role that 'intent' plays. 'If you deliberately plot to kill someone, and succeed, you will be charged with murder; conviction can imprison you for life or even sentence you to execution. On the other hand, if you kill someone by accident, you would typically be charged with manslaughter, a less serious offence that, in some cases, does not even warrant imprisonment' (Englander 1997). Attack over the cultural ethos, 'the historical reservoir' leads to reshaping the collective identity. This threat helps the Lepchas come out collectively to raise voice to protect their identity.

Other Developments

Identity politics and new social movements suggest a special form of agency – a self-conscious 'collective agency.' Identities emerge and movements ensue because collectives consciously coordinate action; group members consciously develop offences and defences, consciously insulate, differentiate, and mark, cooperate and compete, persuade and coerce. In such a context, agency encompasses more than the control and transformation of one's social environment. Charles Taylor suggests that in a collective agency there is a conscious attempt of group as an agent. In case of the Lepchas, culture acts as the agency at the internal level, while the different organisations that lead the anti-dam movement act in the external sphere.

In this process, we have witnessed other significant cultural developments that considerably contribute to the process of formation of a collective identity among the Lepchas. For instance, publication of separate collection of Lepcha folklores and folktales, composing and recording of songs in Lepcha language, publication of literary text in Lepcha language, promotion of the Lepcha culture and language through internet in the form of websites, blogs, Facebook profiles, have been in rapid progress. Lepcha *Aachualy* magazine (aachualy.blogspot.in), owned by Azuk Lepcha, is an honest effort to inform and share everything about Lepcha tradition: from language, grammar, font to folksongs, stories or academic write ups. *Ani Sikkim runcha* (weepingsikkim.blogspot. com) contains – detailed account of the ACT-led movement, their concerns, methodologies, objectives supported by PDF files of letters, memorandums, articles, media responses of the movement, etc. *Zorborthing.blogspot.in* is another blog which provides recent updates related with the Lepchas. Most of these internet-based sources also provide good photographs of Lepcha tradition, culture, places and the movement. This visual sharing helps people to know and learn more about this isolated community. The responses of the followers and users are tremendous and inspiring. Separate pages for the Lepchas on Facebook offer all political updates related with the community. Seminars, conferences, traditional fashion fests have been organised exclusively for the Lepchas. The colleges of the state of Sikkim have witnessed a new trend of organising 'Lepcha Freshers' Welcome' meant to welcome exclusively the Lepcha students. In such functions, traditional dresses are worn, traditional songs and dances are performed and traditional foods are served. Though seemed trivial, these small developments help uniting the community successfully and bringing their ethnic identity to the fore.

The participants attending these occasions come in their traditional outfit-the *gada, dumdyem* (female outfit) and *dumpra* (male outfit). Though the new generation is very much familiar with modern clothing styles, they too attend such occasions only in the traditional attire. Renewed interest in this traditional outfit is closely related with the display of their collective identity borne out of the anti-dam movement. The very famous Satyagraha by the ACT members, and the holy pilgrimage to Dzongu from Kalimpong witnessed the long, large crowd of Lepchas in their beautiful traditional outfit fighting for their land, their river, their culture, in short, their identity. Clothes display, express and shape identity, imbuing it with a directly material reality. They offer a useful lens through which the older identities get expressed in conformity with the new demands, new commitments. The traditional clothes stand for a symbol, a code whereby the Lepchas send a message in favour of their ethnic identity. During the process of revitalising their identity, the Lepchas, are found to explore their rich heritage of traditional forms of material culture. Like other elements, clothes are cultural artefacts, embedded in current and historical sets of meanings, shaped by social and economic forces, reflecting current social and cultural concerns (Twigg 2009). This seemingly ordinary phenomenon has been found to be an effective channel in the invigorating process of the commuminty's identity. While explaining the objective behind the Himalayan Ethnic Lepcha Fashion Event – the event that showcased Lepcha designers and Lepcha models, the organisers clearly said that it was more than a mere fashion show as it was an effort to 'keep our tradition recognised by every individual world'. A community, under the threat of a technology with destabilising effects and a ruthless government, try its best to keep its identity alive by such fashion shows and display of indigenous art forms.

Identity Through Culture

Culture stands for the symbols and signs, whose meanings have a generalised status, provide categories for understanding, relate and sort elements of social life in hierarchical orders, as well as mediate between and blend with structure and action. The meanings attached to signs and symbols are subject to contention and reinterpretation. The bounded sets of differences between the meanings of signs and symbols that stand for things and relations in social life constitute cultures (plural). Thus, cultures in this sense allow us to identify and pin down specific meanings a given society or social group attributes to things and social relations and analyse how they favour or impede social movements and their practices at different points of its life-course.

Scholarly research on the identification process explores different mechanisms by which collectivities create distinctions, establish hierarchies and renegotiate rules of inclusion. James M. Rubenstein in his research proves that cultural objects, particularly clothing, has been commonly used as an object or medium to articulate and project identities. Demand for a separate cultural identity is always accompanied by the group's efforts for preservation of their heritage and symbols, which they have considered and projected as symbolic of their identity (1998). This eagerness for preservation of culture and its heritage can be attributed to the feeling of losing one's own identity as the groups' associate identity with symbols that are thought to represent their unique characteristics. The process of identification is interrelated with economic, political and historical contexts. Multi-tiered investigations view identification at critical junctures in a group's history, including periods of identity formation, its institutionalisation, and periods of identity interpretation. The negligence of the government and the structured ignorance of those in power compel the collectives to look for a new identity, and in this process, they generally opt for cultural elements to legitimise their demand. An objective condition of socio-economic inequality leads the group to pick up a visible, immediate and effective cultural element to announce their new demands and aspirations. Identity politics creates 'new social movements,' collective initiatives that are self-reflexive and sharply focused on the expressive actions of collective members (Melucci 1995).

Intellectual concerns with agency and self-direction have re-energised the study of identification processes. At the level of collective endeavour, scholars are examining the mechanics by which distinctions are created, maintained and changed. Collective identity is a concept grounded in classic sociological constructs. So rooted, the notion addresses the 'weness' of a group, stressing the similarities or shared attributes around which group members coalesce. Early literature approached these attributes as 'natural' or 'essential' characteristics-qualities emerging from physiological traits, psychological predispositions, regional features or the properties of structural locations. A collective's members were believed to internalise these qualities, suggesting a unified, singular social experience, a single canvas against which social actors constructed a sense of self. Richard Alba (1990) argues that ethnic identity is no longer anchored in strong ethnic social structures. Rather, he presents ethnicity as a symbolic entity 'concerned with the symbols of ethnic cultures rather than with the cultures themselves'. Identity politics and study on new social movements suggest a special form of agency – a self-conscious 'collective agency.' Identities emerge and movements ensue because collectives consciously coordinate action; group members consciously develop offences and defences, consciously insulate, differentiate, and mark, cooperate and compete, persuade and coerce. In such a context, agency encompasses more than the control and transformation of one's social environment. In this critical juncture, cultural elements appear to be the most effective medium to express the 'weness'.

Conclusion

The anti-dam movement of the Lepchas is still going on. The issue has led to newer developments in the field of politics, economics, academics in general and policy-makers. The emergence of a strong pro-dam Lepcha lobby, bolstered by the recent declaration of the West Bengal Chief Minister Mamta Banerjee, strengthening the native status of West Bengal Lepchas, and the debate over the issue of participation of the West Bengal Lepchas in the anti-dam movement are some crucial developments that have given new twists and turns in the identity-formation process of the tribe. The state has also experienced misuse of power by a group of the so called 'movement leaders' who have been using their power and status to fulfil their mean political needs. But, if examined closely, it seems that culture has been deployed as an effective element or tool in mobilising the masses as well as making them aware of their ethnicity. Unlike the other states of North-East India, identity issue of Lepchas is not grounded on the demand of autonomy or a separate statehood. The need of the reconstruction of the Lepcha identity was founded on the threats caused by the hydro-power projects and the fear of extinction of their land and identity. For the Lepchas, identity is an issue entangled with nature and geography. So, to raise their voice, they did not opt for an extreme option. They rather choose culture to be their main weapon. In this process, the clever use of day-to-day cultural activities and dissemination of knowledge derived through technology-oriented services help in keeping the issue alive.

References

Alba, R. 1990. *Ethnic Identity: The Transformation of White America,* New Haven, CT: Yale University Press.

Bernstein, Mary. 2005. 'Identity Politics', *Annual Review of Sociology*, 31: pp. 47–74.

Carrying Capacity study of Teesta Basin in Sikkim. 2006. Socio-cultural environment, Volume X: Centre for Interdisciplinary study Mountain and Hill environment, University of Delhi.

Chavez, Alicia, Fedelina and F. Guido. 1999. 'Racial and Ethnic Identity and Development', *New Directions for Adult and Continuing Education,* No. 84 (Winter): pp. 39–47.

During, Simon. 1993. *The Cultural Studies Reader*, New York: Routledge.

Englander, Elizabeth Kandel. 2007. *Understanding Violence.* New Jersey: Lawrence Erlbaum Associates.

Foning, A.R. 1987. *Lepcha: My Vanishing Tribe.* Kalimpong, WB: Chyu-Pandi Farm.

Galtung, Johan. 1990. 'Cultural Violence', *Journal of Peace Research*, Vol. 27, No. 3, (): 291–305.

Gorer, G. (1938) 1987. *Himalayan Village: An Account of the Lepchas of Sikkim.* Reprint, Delhi: Gian Publishing House.

John, Wilson. 1984. 'Art, Culture and Identity', *Journal of Aesthetic Education*, Vol. 18, No. 2. Special Issue: 'Defining Cultural and Educational Relations – An International Perspective'. University of Illinois Press.

Lahiri, Souparna. 2012. 'Hydro Power Projects in Sikkim: A Story of Violation, Coercion and Suppression'. In *Independent People's Tribunal on Dams, Environment and Displacement.* Edited by Doma Bhutia. Delhi: Human Rights Law Network, India.

Lepcha, Dawa. 2012. 'Affected Citizens of Teesta Fighting the Goliath'. In *Independent People's Tribunal on Dams, Environment and Displacement.* Edited by Doma Bhutia. Delhi: Human Rights Law Network, India.

Little, Kerry. 2008. 'Lepcha Narratives of their Threatened Sacred Landscape', *Transforming Cultures* e Journal, Vol. 3 No. 1. February.

Little, Kerry. 2010. 'From the Villages to the Cities: The Battlegrounds for Lepcha Protests', *Transforming Cultures* e Journal, Vol. 5, No. 1. June.

Melucci, Alberto. 1995. 'The Process of Collective Identity'. In *Social Movements and Culture.* Edited by Hank Johnston and Bert Klandermans. Minneapolis: University of Minnesota Press.

Menon, Manju and Niraj, Vagholikar. 2004. *Environmental and Social Impacts of Teesta V Hydroelectric Project, Sikkim: An Investigation Report.* Kalpavriksh. Pune.

Oommen, T.K. 2010. *Social Movements I, Issues of Identity*, New Delhi: Oxford University Press.

Political Economy analysis of the Teesta River Basin. 2013. New Delhi: The Asia Foundation.

Polletta, Francesca and J.M. Jasper. 2001. 'Collective Identity and Social Movements studies', *Annual Review of Sociology*, Vol. 27: pp. 283–305.

Press Releases – Affected Citizen of Teesta, 23 June 2007, 22 July 2007, 13 October 2010.

Press Release. 'Joint Action Committee for Protection of Holy land Dzongu', 17 October 2007.

Rubenstein, J.M. 1998. Cultural Landscapes: An Introduction to Human Geography. Prentice Hall Inc. London.

Twigg, Julia. 2009. 'Clothing, Identity and the Embodiment of the Age'. In *Aging and Identity: A Postmodern Dialogue.* Edited by J. Powell and T. Gilbert. New York: Nova Science publishers.

Vagholikar, Niraj and Partha J. Das. 2010. *Damning North East India.* Mumbai/Pune/Guwahati: Kalpavriksh, Aaranyak and Action Aid India.

Wangchuk, Pema, Dorjee. 2007. 'Lepchas and their Hydel Protest', *Bulletin of Tibetology,* Vol. 43, No. 1–2, pp. 33–57.

Waters, M.C. 1990. *Ethnic Options: Choosing Identities in America.* Berkeley: University of California Press.

Web Sources: www.actsikkim.com., (the official website of ACT), weepingsikkim.blogspot.in, himalmag.com, aachualy.blogspot.in. Last accessed on 25 May 2014.

Zulca. 2007. 'Protest in the Hills', *Talk Himalaya*, Vol. 1, No. 1, July – August, 2007.

PART III

Mainstream Development and Tribals

CHAPTER 8

The Need for Promoting Indigenous Indicators to Tribal Development

A Case Study of the Paniyan Tribe from Kerala

ARUN D. PAUL

One may start with the following statements about Kerala development scenario:

> The fact that the Indian (federal) State of Kerala has achieved impressively high life expectancy, low fertility, and high literacy and so on despite its low income level per head is certainly an achievement worth celebrating and learning from. And yet the question remains as to why Kerala has not been able to consolidate on its successes in human development to raise its income level as well, which would have made its success more complete. As it is, it can scarcely serve as a 'model' as some have tried to claim (Sen 1999).

'Kerala Model', actually refers to the 'average' situation. Only the central tendency of the distribution of the indicators is used to establish the point.

However as in all distributions, the 'Kerala Model' also has its 'outliers' represented by communities that seem to have been left out of the domain of public action for what Jean Dreze and Amartya Sen have referred to as 'capability building' (Kurien 1995). Two points of consideration would emerge from the above arguments. The first is to recognise Kerala's development experience as a success story of development practised and public policy-making, which have resulted in its high Human Development Index (HDI). The second one is the realisation that even such a development experience can't be called as a model and can end up focusing on central tendencies, leading to the exclusion of peripheral communities. An attempt is made here to explore the process of exclusion inside an 'inclusive' development experience. The paper explores the case of remote community in Kerala by closely studying Paniyan tribe in Wyanad district of Kerala whose abysmal existence is a paradox to Kerala's development experience.

To analyse the dynamics of exclusion process, the paper looks at the nature of the tribal development in Wyanad, which is a residue of complex power relations and interactions of tribal with outsider communities for more than four centuries. Thus, a historical analysis has been undertaken by looking at outsider communities as actors entering into the space of tribals propagating new modes of production, production relations and knowledge systems related to technology and livelihood practice.

Tribes and Human Development Indicators in Kerala

Kerala has the highest HDI (UNDP 2011) among all Indian States, which is even comparable to developed nations. Kerala has achieved almost cent per cent literacy rate, high life expectancy, better universal health coverage, better public food distribution systems, participatory planning and governance, without major economic growth but by 'expansion of basic education, healthcare and equitable land distribution' (Sen 1999), thus supposedly ensuring equity with development. But all these aspects attain sharp inequity when seen against the prevailing tribal situation in Kerala in general.

To understand the level of inequity among tribal in comparison to all other populations in Kerala, one indicator of human development, namely education is taken into consideration. Education is taken into focus for this analysis because Kerala has been credited with the status of a leading state in mass education programmes with it's near cent per cent literacy rate. Following aspects would delineate the invisible inequities in such a claim, when the focus is on tribal communities:

- *Literacy Inequity:* When the overall literacy rate in Kerala is 94 per cent, the tribal communities in Kerala lag behind with 65 per cent (Census of India 2011). This gap of almost 30 per cent forms the highest inequality in literacy rate between any tribal and all other communities in any state of India.
- *Low Access:* Among all tribal communities in India, children of tribal communities in Kerala have the least access to school (DISE 2011–12).
- *Gender Inequity:* Kerala is among the three states in India with least percentage increase in tribal girl child enrollment in schools (DISE 2011–12).
- *Economic Impairment to Schooling:* Tribal communities in Kerala are among the six most impoverished tribal communities of all Indian states with a poverty rate of 44 per cent, which is close to the national average of 47 per cent (Planning Commission of India 2007).
- *Non-inclusive Pedagogy:* Kerala is among the three states in India to have least percentage increase of tribal teachers, which is an important for tribal education (DISE 2011–12).

Similar to education, one could find the presence of inequalities, in its access, availability and quality, in other areas essential for human development too. Regarding tribal communities in Kerala three crucial aspects are important: their heterogeneity, large socio-economic inequity in between tribes and small size of population. Tribals in Kerala are a heterogeneous group of thirty five notified communities, diverse with respect to livelihood (hunter gatherers, shifting cultivators and settled agriculturists), range of socialisation and exposure (urbanised to particularly vulnerable tribal groups) and geographic allocation spreading around the hilly tracts of northern Kerala (majorly in the districts of Wyanad, Palakkad and Kasargod) and southern Kerala (districts of Idukki and Trivandrum). To take a note of the socio-economic disparity, it can be found that when tribal communities in Kerala like Malai Arayan have the high literacy rate of 94.50, communities like Maha Malsarare languishing with literacy rate of 20.83 per cent (Narayana 2010). Another crucial feature of the tribals in Kerala is their low population. Kerala has the lowest population of tribals in India constituting only 1.45 per cent (Census of India 2011) of its total population.

The Paniyans are the largest (almost one fifth of total tribal population) as well as the most deprived tribal communities in Kerala (CSDS 2007). Further, Wyanad district has the highest concentration (36%) of tribes in Kerala, especially Paniyan with almost three fourth of Paniyan population. Other major tribal communities in Wyanad include Adiyan, Kattunayakan Kuruman/ Mullukuruman, Kurichiyan, Vetta (or Urali) Kuruman, ThachenadanMoopan, Wayanad Kadar, Mala Arayan, Karimpalan and Ulladan. As in the case of Kerala, in Wyanad also one could find the features of heterogeneity and large inequity among tribes, but unlike the general trend in Kerala, with 18.53 per cent they form a significant population here (Census of India, 2011). The factors of heterogeneity and inequity in between tribes of Waynad district can be observed from Table 8.1 (KILA, 2011):

Table 8.1

Descriptive Information on the Major Tribes of Wayanad District, Kerala

Tribe	*Percentage Break up of ST Population*	*Literacy Rate*	*Percentage Breakup of Drop Outs among STs*	*Livelihood*
MulluKurman/ Kuruman	13.70	86.94	7.02	Land Owning, Tertiary jobs
Kuruchian	16.49	84.76	15.72	Land Owning, Tertiary jobs
Adiyan	7.31	66.18	8.51	Landless Agricultural Labour
Paniyan	45.12	64.72	51.59	Landless Agricultural Labour
Kattunayakan	11.13	60.15	11.35	Landless, Food Gatherer

Of all tribal communities, the socio-economic deprivation of Paniyan who forms the largest tribal community in the district is more than apparent. Their deprivation is added by the widely reported cases of land alienation, sexual exploitation, exploitation in the field, cases of unwed mothers, death of agricultural labourers following their migration and exploitation at Coorg in Karnataka, farmer suicides, larger number of under-trail prisoners, etc.[1] Further, during this study it could be identified that in Wyanad there was stratification among tribes, which in some cases reached the extremes level of practising untouchability. Paniyan and Adiyan occupy the lower position in such stratification whereas Kurichiyan and Kurmar occupy a higher position. This is later reflected in terms of their educational status, employment, claiming of ST reservation benefits. Thus, one could see that for the marginalisation of the Paniyans, outsider communities as well by other tribal communities are no less responsible. The whole question needs to be seen with respect to the impact of outsider communities on the Paniyans.

For a thorough social investigation, one will have to look at the particular social milieu which exists in the multiplicity of interaction of different actors in its space; the formation and sustenance of inequities in these interactions over time; formation and responses in the public domains of action. Such an approach raises a fundamental question as the indicators conceal the inequality and reality and focus only on aggregates, which become a knowledge source for the purpose of governance to monitor, control and confirm through subjectivity (Merry 2011). What is fundamental is to look at the process of systematic marginalisation of subalterns (here, Paniyans) in Kerala (Kunhman 2002 as quoted by Tharakan 2006)

Phases of Alienation and Dispossession

'Paniyan' in Malayalam means 'labourer': clearly the etymology of their name is rooted in their occupation. Here two aspects have to be noted. Firstly, for their occupation as agricultural labourers, they are highly dependent on other communities. Secondly, the word Paniyan is used in a derogatory sense by other communities. One could find such a trend in the naming of different occupation based castes in other parts of India such as *Chamar/Mochi* (tanners and cobblers), *Bhangi/Balmiki* (Scavengers) and the usage is essentially a reference of caste identity and oppression. The impact of such a language among tribes can be profound as James Frazer notes in the 'Golden Bough' (1890),

> ... the North American Indian regards his name, not as a mere label, but as a distinct part of his personality, just as much as are his eyes or his teeth, and believes that injury will result as surely from the malicious handling of his name as from a wound inflicted on any part of his physical organism.

In the onomastic of 'Paniyan' itself, one could find the presence of two cardinal positions and two actors. The first is the conscious or unconscious understanding of the relevance of name in Paniyan's identity and the usage of this identity marker for oppression. As the Paniyan started interacting with different outsider communities, they became familiar with a language of oppression and internalised it. The emerging of phases of historical progression are important in this context when the language of oppression (which is identified here as the new mode of knowledge production or livelihood practice) developed by an outsider community is deconstructed. Such a historical approach also aligns with particular case of tribes in India because of their transitory nature and as their process of transformation is a historical process (Beteille 1970).

Kulirani (1996) has described different historical phases of Paniyan based on history of Wayanad and corresponding livelihood strategies taken by Paniyans, which are as follows: (1) an early phase of food gathering, (2) a period of bonded labour where major part of the payment only in kind supplemented with food gathering, (3) introduction of daily wage earner-payments in cash, and 4) dependence on welfare measures of the state after being sidelined in the competitive labour market and with a sense desperation setting in. Unlike such a demarcation, in this study different historical phases are demarcated on the basis of arrival of an outsider community or emergence of a new political authority because the earlier demarcation makes the outsider communities conspicuously absent and tends to look at Paniyan as subjects who are adapting to a situation that is quite unknown to them. Further, such a repositioning of history here is essential for a change in the local popular culture which demeans Paniyans and subsequent change in the state policy towards them. Thus six historical phases through which Paniyan went through are identified in this paper: (1) The early phase of hunting and food gathering; (2) Arrival of Goundar and Chetty communities; (3) Invasion by the Kottayam dynastic rulers; (4) Invasion by the colonial British; (5) Arrival of marginal farmers from outside; and (6) Formation of the Indian states and civil societies. A brief account of all these phases is given below:

Early Phase of Hunter – Gatherers

The myth of Paniyan genesis is prevalent in their oral tradition. According to these genesis narratives collected during the field work and recorded in different studies on Paniyan, the first parents of Paniyan are believed to be Ippimala Uttappan and Ippimala Uttama, a brother and sister who came out of an egg. Nair (1976) adds that Ippimala refers to a mountain and Paniyans identify them as Ippimalamakkal, the children of Ippimountain. Another narrative mentions Paniyans as those who have been freely roaming around in jungles as hunter and food gatherers.

As Kulirani (1996) highlights, three aspects have to be noted in this phase. First is the heterogeneity of tribes in Wyanad in terms of their livelihood and their language (possibly hinting at their non-indigenous origin). At this phase there was the presence of other food-gathering groups like Kattunayakan, Adiyan, shifting cultivators like Urali Kuruman who spoke dialects of Kannada; and the presence of Malayalam-speaking tribes like the hunting tribe Kurichiyan and the agricultural tribe Mullu Kuruman from the southern plains. Secondly, the autonomous existence of tribes with the presence of Kurumbi/Kurumba-Veda rulers (of Mullukuruman and Vetta Kuruman tribes) at this period is important. Finally, comes the out-migration of Paniyans to other districts of Kerala like Kozhikode, Kannur and Malappuram. As Vinod CP (2000) notes, this phase can be summarised as follows:

> ... it is widely believed that the whole region was an abode of 'jungle tribes' like Paniyan and Adiyan till the 5th century A.D. and since then the movements of people from the plains started to penetrate into Wayanad region.

Arrival of Jain and Chetty Communities

From 8th century onwards, immigration of Jain population from Karnataka has been assumed to have strengthened as evidenced by a number of Jain temples in different parts of Wyanad. This community introduced settled agricultural practice in Wyanad where land was plentily available and the existing tribes like

Kurichiyan and Mullu Kuruman practised only *punamkrishi*, i.e. shifting cultivation. Introduction of settled agriculture forced these tribes to change from shifting cultivation to settled agriculture (Johni 2010). Similarly, Hindu agricultural communities – Wyanadan Chetty (Malyalam speaking), Idanadan Chetty (Tamil speaking) and Mandatan Chetty (Kanada speaking), who practised settled wet land cultivation are presumed to have come at different points of time from the plains of Kerala, Tamil Nadu and Karnataka (Vinod 2009).

The most important contribution of both these immigrant communities was in the form of introduction of settled agriculture in Wayanad. When Kurichiyan and Mullu Kuruman changed to settled agriculture Paniyans and Adiyans became bonded labourers and agrestic slaves (Johni 2010: 66). The Paniyan genesis myth narratives indicate that because of their physique they were considered suitable for hard agricultural labour. It is said that Mullu Kuruman captured Paniyans from the forest for serving a group of Jain cultivators at Goundar. The myth also refers that the captured Paniyans were a brother and a sister who were asked to treat themselves as husband and wife. Thus Paniyans were 'domesticated' for agricultural labour and they became bonded labours. Chetty communities' also organised the Paniya labour through *Chemmi/Moopan* who were religious heads or local leaders of the Paniyan Community (Vinod 2009).

Two aspects have to be noted in this phase. Firstly, Paniyans entered into the first phase of exploitation by becoming bonded agricultural labourers. But, they still had free access to natural resources. At this phase, their name Ippimakkal has been supposedly changed into Paniyan, meaning labour. Similarly Ravulvar came to be known as Adiyan (Slave) tribe (Kulirani 1996). Secondly, land in Wyanad started gaining importance among different outsider communities as a property worth owing because of its unique geographical location, wet climate and high soil fertility. As a result, more and more outsider communities were attracted to come to Wyanad.

Invasion by Kottayam Dynasty

The land relations of different tribes acquired a crucial change with the arrival of Kottayam/Cotiote dynasty by the late 13th century. A narrative (Johni 2010) mentions that once the Kumbla ruler (from Kumbazha in present Kasaragod district of Kerala) who came to Thirunelli temple in Wyanad (famous from that period for its Hindu religious sanctity) saw the Wyanad's unique land. Later he brought his army to conquer the land but was defeated and captured by the Vedar ruler and imprisoned at Velikumbam fort (present Veliyambam near Pulpally in Wyanad). Upon knowing about this Kottayam and Kurumbranad rulers (from the present Kannur and Kozhikode districts) came to his rescue. But after seeing the mighty Vedar army, they reached an agreement of marriage between Kumbla ruler and Vedar princess. But during the wedding, the Kottayam-Kurumbranad ruler attacked the Vedar and later took control of Wayand. Though another narrative of colonial British account (Nair 1911) has a different version of it, the common point of the story is the invasion of Wyanad by Kottayam and Kurumbranad rulers and later taking over the whole Wyanad by the Kottayam dynastic rulers.

Under Kottayam dynasty one could see the strengthening of feudal system in Wyanad. The country was divided into ten *Nads* (divisions) and *Nair* Chieftains were assigned the post of administrators called as *Janmi* (feudal landlords). All the agricultural communities like Chetty, Goundar, Kurichiyan, Mullu Kuruman became tenants under the Nair Janmi, whereas Paniyan and Adiyan got into a structured bonded labour system called *Kundalpani or Vallipani* (Nair 1911; Kulirani 1996).

Paniyan families were attached to *Edoms* (houses or places) or *Devaswams* (property of temple deity) under Nair landlords. Devan (2006) gives a detailed account of the Kundalpani. Under the system, Paniyans were recruited as bonded labour during the 'slave market' associated with the annual festival at Valiyurkav Bhagavathy temple by advancing an amount called *Nippupanm*or *Valiyurkavpanm*. After that the Paniyan recruit was to stand in front of *Sreekovil*, the most sacred place of the temple and pledge to serve the employer until the next temple, festival by reciting a song called Kakkapattu.

The slaves were divided into three ownership categories: *Janmam, Kanam* and *Pattam.* In the case of Janmam slaves, ownership was unconditional and absolute and they had the highest price of 250 to 300 *panms* (1 Rupee = 3.5 panm). *Kanam* slaves were mortgaged to the master (for two-thirds of the slave's value and annual payment of paddy) and *Pattam* slaves were *Janmams* slaves rented out for a certain period (man for 8 panms and woman for 4 panms). The slaves were paid *Valli* (daily payment; thus the name *Vallipani*) of 2.5 sers (1 ser = 1 litre) of paddy for man and 2 ser for woman.

Three features marked this phase. Initially, the emergence of feudal system had marginalised the non-cultivating tribes without any knowledge of land titles into slaves. Second and the most important feature was the beginning of the process of Sankritisation among tribes in Wyanad. Chattopadhyaya (2004) finds the Sankritisation of forest space as a part of Brahmanical perception of state in early Indian history. In the case of Wyanad one could see the rise of a bonded labour system structured in a Brahmanical social order. For example, though the Valiyurkav temple was constructed by the Kottayam dynasty and managed by Nairs, the deity of Valiyurkav has a permanent place in the psyche of tribes. The festival associated with the deity is still faithfully observed by the tribes in Wyanad (Johni 2010). Thus, the bond between master and slave made here has become a sacred agreement. Devan (2006) records one of the *Kakkapattu,*

> Vallookav Bhagavathikku
> Janmamayitullapadathilu
> Moovayiram Vithuvithakkannudu
> Udaneparayannu Chinnuanneram
> Enneonnumcheyyaruthuvalluracha
> Ivideadimayayinikkumnjanu
> Vallooruadimayayininnu Chinnu

> [Chinnu, a Paniyan, is taken as a captive and is produced before the deity by the non-tribal employer, then, he says that he has to sow in the paddy field of Valliyoorkav deity. He pleads to the revered deity to leave him unhurt and in turn he promises to work for his master (Santhosh 2008)]

One could also see that with the growing importance of land, the cultivating tribes positioned themselves as elites over non-cultivating tribes, which signalled the formation of tribal hierarchy in Wyanad. Practice of purity and pollution was also evolved during this phase. As Ayyapan notes,

> Feudal land relations based on slavery of the 'untouchables' developed in the subsequent periods. Many characteristics of the Hindu caste system penetrated into the local social life and value system. Internal stratification on the basis of purity and pollution, a universal feature of the pan Indian caste system, made its marks even among the tribal people in the area.

During the fieldwork, it could be observed that cultivating tribes like Kuruman and Kurichiyan still identify themselves as tribal elites and consider Paniyans as 'dark-skinned' who stay in unhygienic dwellings, have pleasure seeking behaviour and are lazy. This is a classic example of Sankritisation (Srinivas 1956) of tribes in Wyanad.

The third aspect to be noted in this phase is the introduction of *Valli,* daily payments in paddy as part of *Kundalpanni* system. Such a process increased the dependence of non-cultivating communities on landlords who saved them from the risks of being engaged in cultivation for food and kept them away from the idea of surplus for future, a feature of hunter gatherers.

Invasion of Colonial British

The invasions of Mysore dynasty from Karnataka to Kerala through Wyanad by the end of 17th century are significant as it led to conflicts with the British East India Company and their subsequent arrival in Wyanad. Against the backdrop of the domination of Malabar, including the present districts of northern Kerala with its sea ports that were of importance to Mysore, but were equally crucial to the British, the possession of Wyanad became strategically important for both the powers. The Kottayam dynasty under Pazhassi Raja defended the Mysore's invasion with the aid of British. Following the treaty of Coorg in 1786, Wyanad came again under the Kottayam dynasty, but it led to conflicts with the British.

Pazhassi Raja along with Nair chiefs organised Kurichiyan and Mullukurman tribes into guerrilla model armed collectivities to defend against the British. Thus, this phase led to the initiation of the tribal communities into politically organised groups to defend their land. Their struggle was curbed by the assassination of Pazhassi Raja in 1805 leading to the total British entry to Wyanad. But in 1812 Kurichiyan and Mullukuruman organised a revolt against the British using traditional weaponry of bow and arrow. Though the motive behind such an armed conflict could be their dissent with the British policies of imposition of high tax and banning of shifting cultivation, it could be presumed that this was the first tribal resistance against a colonial power in South India (Johni 2010).

Three major features of the British rule have also to be noted. At the first instance, the British retained *Janmi-kudiyan* system in Wyanad, which was already prevalent in Malabar (*Jaysree*). In fact, Malabar had the largest population of slaves in India covering about 15 per cent of its population (Slavery in *Encyclopedia Britannica*) Further administrative reforms brought by the British like massive land surveys led to appropriation of land under them. The land was divided into: tilled land, private forest, revenue forest and reserve forest. Obviously, the government had high stakes on all categories of land and it was too preoccupied with it. In this task, it was asserted by the members of the Nair community and by doing so they rose to prominence in the government structure. The agricultural communities could act their property rights but only at the cost of high tax payments. Other communities like Brahmins, Moplah (Muslim tradesman), Goundar maintained their landlord – tradesman role in the social structure. The revenue system based on the capitalist concept of property rights was alien to Paniyans and they remained as bonded labourers or slaves. Further marginalisation of Paniyan happened as the access to their forest-based livelihood has been curtailed by different colonial administrative reforms like declaration of Wayanad Reserve (leading to excessive tree felling and teak plantation) and Indian Forest Act of 1927.

Secondly, the strengthening of tribal hierarchy and practice of sankritisation went on unabated as can be observed from the note prepared by Goplan Nair (1911), a civil officer under the British. He classified tribes like Kurichiyan, Karimpalan, Mullu Kuruman, Vetta Kuruman, Thachandan Moopan as hill tribes and Paniyan, Adiyan as 'predial' slaves. Kurichiyan tribe enjoyed the highest status among them and purified their worship places by holy water from a Brahmin, Karimpalan tribe wore *kuduma*, hair tufts like Brahmins, Kadar tribe referred to their house as *Ilams*, like Namboodri Brahmins in Malabar and Kattunayakan were responsible for 'lowering their status' by eating monkey's flesh.

Thirdly, considering the high-altitude climate, the British introduced plantation economy based on coffee (1820), black pepper (1875), tea (1892), rubber (1904) and cardamom in Wayand, which ultimately found their place in international exports (Nair 1911). Following the demand for labour force and reports of different Christian missionary commissions (See Jaysree) the slavery system in British Colonies was legally abolished by the British in 1843, though it continued *de facto* due to the influence of slave owners and the ritual compulsions. A colonial, upper caste perception of Paniyan at this phase can be observed from Nair's account (1911):

> The Paniyars are a necessity to Wynad cultivation; they alone are able to control the wild cattle of this country and in the soft and clayey soil, which sinks to the touch, they alone can handle the plough. Their habits are migratory and unless the employer is kind, they suddenly give him the slip and are not easily caught. In moral turpitude they stand high. They are professional burglars, waylay and rob travellers and do not hesitate to commit the gravest crimes and yet they are excellent-field labourers. They are fond of music, sing during work in the fields, spend whole nights singing and dancing to the accompaniment of a peculiarly shaped drum and a reed-flute.

Arrival of Marginal Farmers

By 1940, farmers from the erstwhile Cochin and Travancore princely states in southern Kerala started migrating to Wyanad. It was of such high influx that the population growth rate of Wyanad between 1951 and 1971 was as high as 55 per cent, when it was only 25 per cent in all Kerala as a whole. Largely of Christian and marginal farming backgrounds, these communities were affected by food scarcity during the World War II and 'grow more food' campaign. Further, they had 'exposure to European planters and plantation systems and could internalise the logic of agricultural practices that was required for a commercially viable agricultural production' (Vinod 2009). These immigrants acquired large tracts of land from Nair landlords on lease and in some cases they even illegally acquired forests and wastelands. The settlers obtained tribal land through counterfeit land titles by bribing the government officials, giving alcohol to tribals for land at cheap rates, by taking their land on lease and illegally obtaining ownership rights (Aufschnaiter 2007)

The immigration of marginal farmers further increased the demand of labour, which resulted in larger integration and monetisation of indigenous labour economy with domestic market leading to the gradual end of tribal slavery system, Kundalpanni and the beginning of Kulipanni, a cash-based wage system. It furthered marginalisation of tribes caused by large-scale alienation from their lands and increase in the number of landless tribal agricultural labourers. The proportion of tribal agricultural labourers in Wyanad increased from 43 per cent in 1961 to 72 per cent in 1976 (Bijoy and Raman 2003). Once again, it is to be noted that as land in Wyanad attracted more and more agricultural communities from different geographical regions to Wyanad, the tribal land alienation in Wyanad increased and non-agricultural tribes like Paniyans became increasingly dependent on the outsider communities.

Regime of State and Civil Society: Policy, Legislation and Rights

With the formation of Indian Union in 1947 and the federal state of Kerala in 1956, a large number of affirmative polices were taken for tribal development. While analysing these, we would be looking at how these affected the land relations that were against the interest of tribes.

In the post-independence period, land reforms in Kerala were initiated by the communist-led government with the passing of Kerala Agrarian Relations Bill in 1957. It included ceiling on holdings, permanent occupancy rights to tenants, etc. Such radical reforms aroused protests from the landed gentry leading to 'liberation struggle' against the government and its absolution, and imposition of the President's Rule in 1959. The following Congress-led government passed a watered down version of the previous bill, Kerala Land Reforms Act, 1963. But such legislation was ineffective because of the instability of, government and Kerala coming under President's Rule again (Radhakrishnan 1981).

Tribal issues in Wayanad came for serious consideration of the state machinery following the tribal and marginal farmer uprising, initiated by the Naxalites against local landlords in 1960s. But the movement soon got diluted, for which two reasons may be advanced. One, the marginal farmers who played crucial role in the movement, were conferred ownership rights on the lands leased in by them under the Kerala Land Reforms (Amendment) Act of 1969 by the Communist Government. Further, the movement was curbed by the strong police action infamous for the fake encounter death of the movement's prominent leader, 'Naxal Varghese' in 1970. But such movements later prompted the government to pass legislation in favour the tribal land issue.

The Kerala Private Forest (Vesting and Assignment) Act entitling around 23,000 hectares of land to landless tribals was passed in 1972, and in 1975, following 1950 Debhar Commission guidelines, the interests of Kerala Scheduled Tribes were safeguarded (restriction on transfer of lands and restoration of alienated land) through the legislation of the Tribal Land Act with effect from the 26th January 1960 (Bijoy and Raman 2003). The Act received mandatory assent from the President of Indian and was included under the Ninth Schedule of the Constitution so that it would not be challenged in any court of law. Following the weakening of land struggles and the rise to prominence of the lobby of landed class and encroachers in Wyanad, one could see the government legislation during post-1975 contravening its previous legislation.

The Kerala Forest Produce Act 1978 restricted access of tribals to forest produces, the Forest Conservation Act 1980 led to large tribal evictions and though after 11 years, the rules of Tribal Land Act 1975 were formulated in 1986 diluting the previous act. The time period for restoring alienated land was changed from 26 January 1960 to 1st January 1986. Tribal beneficiaries were asked to return the sum they collected during the land transaction to non-tribals along with a charge on the improvements made on the land and the compensation was decided by the revenue divisional officers. Though government provided a loan for compensation with 20 years of time period, none took the loan. Even claims to land were not properly filed as they lacked proof of ownership due to hefty compensation (Bhuria et al., 2004)

Following the non-implementation of the act, in 1988, a writ petition was filed at Kerala High Court by a non-tribal, Dr Nalla Thampi Thera. In 1993, the High Court issued a writ of mandamus for implementation of the same within 6 months with a series of remarks against the callousness of government in its non-implementation of legislation for oppressed classes in support of the settlers' lobby. At the same time, the state government appealed for extending the deadline, mentioning that tribal were not taking loans and even brought an ordinance for amending the 1975 act. Following the governor's rejection of the ordinances brought by both Congress- and Left led-governments, the Kerala Scheduled Tribes (Restriction on Transfer of Lands and Restoration of Alienated Lands) Amendment Act, 1996 was passed, which was rejected by the President of India as it fell under the Ninth Schedule of the Constitution. Thus, a second amendment bill, the Kerala Restriction on Transfer by and Restoration of Lands of Scheduled Tribes Bill was passed in 1999, replacing the term 'tribal land' with 'agricultural land'. The Kerala High Court rejected the validity of both 1996 and 1999 amendment bills in 2000. But the Kerala government could file a writ petition and obtain stay order from the Supreme Court against the High Court verdicts in 2001.

Muthanga Adivasi Land Struggle: Before and After

As the state government legislation reduced the claim of tribes on their land, ironically the same political organisations that were in power mobilised the tribals for land struggle. Organisations ranging from CPI(M) forming Adivasi Kshema Samithi and Adavasi Dalit Samra Samathi, rightist factions forming Wayanad Adivasi Sangam were significant in forming an Adivasi identity based on land against the settler encroachments (see Kjosavik and Shanmugaratnam 2004). The formation of this identity led to a series of sporadic events that culminated in what came to be known as 'Muthanga Adivasi Land Struggle'.

In 1993, 220 landless tribal families under Adivasi Vikasana Pravathaka Samathy constructed houses in 67.5 acres of 128 acres of vested forest in Ambukuthy in Wyanad. The following combined action of police and forest officials led to the arrest of 317 tribals, and a case was filed on 1993. In 1995, 229 families under Adivasi Aikya Samathy and South Zone Adivasi Forum forcefully settled in 100 acres of Chengeri Tribal Rehabilitation Project, which was followed by the detention of 120 activists and arrest of 244 people. In the same year, 106 tribal occupants were arrested at Panvally. In 2001, 32 starvation deaths of tribals were reported from Wyanad, Palakkad and Kannur districts of Kerala. In the same year, a group of tribal supported by radical left groups looted food items from vehicles of government civil supplies department in Wyanad and the same were distributed among the tribals.

The critical phase started when Adivasi Dalit Samara Samiti started a camped protest in front of Kerala chief minister's residence on 30 August 2001 and in 48 days the protest led to an agreement with the state government. The major points of the agreement included the constitution of Tribal Resettlement and Development Mission to provide five acres of land to tribals having less than one acre before 31 December 2002, inclusion of tribal lands in the Fifth Schedule.

Two significant crucial aspects have to be noted at this phase of the struggle. One, the formation of Adivasi Maha Gothra Sabha, (AGMS), a grand assembly of 31 tribal communities. Two, when the previously agricultural tribal communities like Kuruman and Kurichiyan took part in the struggle for their land alienated by settlers according to 1975 Act, for the first time in the history non-cultivator landless communities like Paniyan and Kattunayakan also asserted for vested forest lands which were to be distributed to them under 1972 Act (See Kjovasik and Shanmugaratnan 2004).

Following the failure of the government agreement of 2001, AGMS convened a tribal court and decided to continue the protest. In January 2003, around 4,000 tribals forcefully entered and settled in deforested portions of Eucalyptus plantation area of Muthanga in Wyanad. Following a forest fire, which was claimed to be set by tribals, a heavy police assault was made on the occupants leading to the death of two, burning of several huts and arrest of more than 300 tribals. Though the movement failed, this phase influenced the crystallisation of tribal identity as D.J. Kjosavik and N. Shanmugaratnam quote a tribal:

> The 44 days in samara bhoomi were like a dream. My husband did not drink alcohol. We had no fights at home. My children were happy and read their school books. We hoped that the government would let us stay there.' The hopes and dreams of the adivasis are reflected in these statements. Evidently, adivasi lives were changing through the experience at Muthanga. Each one

reminds the other, this is our self-rule area. So we must set an example with our exemplary behaviour (2004).

Muthanga incident points to the political mobilisation and how the memories of it were suppressed by the state. It is to be noted that the cylce of events that predated Muthanga continued uninterrupted, which include passing of the Forest Right Acts (2006), Supreme Court verdict (in 2009) on 1999 act in favour of tribals, tribals occupying forest land in Pulpally in 2012, death of 58 tribal infants due to malnutrition in 2013, etc.

Means of Production and Patterns of Knowledge Production

In the first section, we have closely looked at the paradoxes inside Kerala's development experience and in the second section we have tried to explore the historicity of the process of exclusion involved in it. Now, through a pattern analysis of the historical phases of alienation and dispossession, we have discussed so far, a fresh attempt has been made to look at the tribal identity, especially that of Paniyans evolving in relation to patterns of knowledge production in that period. It is fundamental to look at this identity transformation in the wider context of Kerala's development experience, which has supposedly empowered the marginalised communities through public action for basic access and rights, resulting in high social sector spending. Jean Dréze and Amartya Sen point out that the success of Kerala in spite of such a low level of income is the result of the public action aimed at promoting people's basic entitlements and capabilities (as quoted in Tharkan 2006). Each outsider community came into the space of tribal with superior livelihood/knowledge practice. Later, the tribal identity evolved in response to this practice but in a submissive form.

Table 8.2

Genesis of Tribal Identity and the Role of Outsider Communities/Agents

Outsider Community/Agent	*Knowledge Production*	*Distorted Tribal Identity*
Jain-Chetty	Agriculture practice	Bonded Labours
Kottayam Dynasty	Caste-based landlordism; Sanksritisation of the tribes	Organised into slaves, Formation of tribal elites, Paniyan 'untouchables'
British Colonial Rule	Land revenue system, Plantation Economy	Deprived of access to forest
Immigrant Farmers	Cash crop-based small agriculture, linkage with labour market	Land alienated, increasing role as agricultural labour
State	Legislations and development Policies, HDI-Decentralisation based approach	Land alienation, Starvation deaths, Dependency on welfare measures
Political Parties and NGOs	Land rights, Political mobilisation and organisation	Developing Adivasi Identity based on land, Stigmatised by memories of struggles

Here, one may observe that the tribal identity has always remained as a subject of transformation and exploitation in their relationship with nature and social systems. This is in sharp contrast to the experience of social mobilisation in Kerala. As Patrick Heller (1996) notes:

> Since the last decade of the nineteenth century, Kerala has been the site of a nearly continuous succession of social movements: a social-religious reform movement in the early part of the century; nationalist, agrarian and prodemocracy movements on the 1930S and 1940s; a series of rural and industrial labour movements (from 1930 to 1975); and most recently various new social movements including state wide campaign for decentralisation orchesatred by state reformers and non-governmental organisations (NGOs). These high levels of social mobilisation have been directly tied to what is widely known in development circles as the 'Kerala Model', namely levels of social development unparalleled in low-income societies.

But such a model conceptualised tribes as a 'frozen working class', who were property-less and denied of mobility for generations, unlike workers in a modern capitalist social structure. So it followed the broad development programmes planned by the national government. Further, the class reductionism approach sidelined the customary land tenure systems of Adivasis causing failure of allocating space for forest commons in exemplary land reforms established in Kerala (Kjosavik and Shanmugaratnam 2004)

When the government followed the frozen working class approach, at the micro level one could identify a different dynamics. The ideological platform developed by the present agrarian social structure to tap the labour supply by the Paniyans is crucial here. In Paniyan myth of their genesis, mentions about the story of the Paniyan who freely roamed around the forest before being captured and tamed by Ippimalachetti and Kaunda – Upper caste landlords for agricultural labour after seeing their strong physique. During the fieldwork, similar narratives of branding Paniyans as intellectually weak but physically strong could be collected. Other narratives also stated that when settled farmers moved to Kodagu in Karnataka for ginger cultivation, they could not find any labourer among the local population as good as Paniyan. So they took Paniyans along with them for working in the fields. In 2008 it was reported that this migration led to death of more than 200 tribals in two years due to their maltreatment in fields (Tehelka 2009). During interviews even school teachers were very particular about mentioning Paniyan students being weak in Mathematics but good in sports. In some cases, Paniyan students were asked to sit separately at the back seats of classrooms.

Another aspect is the cultural hegemony set out by Malayalam over Paniyan language, which is a scriptless language formed out of mixture of Malayalam and Kannada. John Zerzan (1998) in his essay on 'primitive communism' quoted Levi-Strauss: 'the primary function of written communication was to facilitate exploitation and subjugation'. Such a domination of Malayalam over Paniyan language was observed in different narratives obtained such as ostracising Paniyan students from schools, lack of educational materials to support Paniyan children in primary schools, etc.

Another feature attributed to Paniyans is their laziness and recalcitrance to industriousness. The Planning Commission Report on Western Ghats

Development Programme (1982) identifies the failure of Sugandhagiri cardamom project for tribal rehabilitation with 40 per cent absenteeism of tribal workers. Different studies on high rate of dropouts among tribal children identify the lack of motivation among parents and students as single largest cause for school dropouts. Here, it would be important to note Tanaka's (1980) observation that hunter gatherer communities spend 'strikingly less time labouring and much time at rest and leisure'. The Paniyans have been exploited by outsider communities as they were frequently involved in exchanging liquor for land transactions and labour leading to unjust payments and increasing the frequency of addicts.

Few dimensions of complex Paniyan identity have emerged in the course of the above discussion. The imagery of Paniyan being physically strong, gullible and unclean is rooted in the popular culture of Wyanad, supporting hegemony over Paniyan culture and passing the way for further exploitation.

Further, the Paniyan's livelihood development has also been curbed due to their entrapment in the agrarian economy of Wyanad. In an economy with 57 per cent (Wayanad Initiative 2006) of land under-cultivation, the Paniyan community became the labour reserve for labour intensive paddy cultivation, followed by plantation and cash-crop cultivations. This was furthered by different control mechanisms manipulated from outside like slavery, bonded labour system, etc. Further, this labour reserve formed an informal economy that could absorb the fluctuations during agrarian distresses in Wyanadas in 2004 (George and Krishnaprasad 2006).

Relooking at the Development Paradigm

Clearly the HDI-based approach to tribal development is problematic because it masquerades social realities by looking only at certain indicators and eulogising positive experiences. Such an approach is situated in an ideological framework that looks at creating a universe against multiversals by following a linear approach. It is in sharp contrast to the capability approach developed by Amartya Sen, from where it ironically has taken its philosophical framework: when capabilities mean improving capabilities and developing agencies so that they may lead a life they have reason to value. The values, he considers as product of larger 'public discussions and democratic understanding and acceptance' by the community (Sen 2000). By focusing only on the 'evaluative aspect' of the approach, pinpointing only income, literacy and life expectancy and disregarding of 'the agency aspect', one is led to a situation where the approach gets 'trapped in its own measure' (Fukuda-Parr 2003).

With regard to literacy, Felix Padel (2011) rightly quotes a Native American leader, Russell Means, in 'Sacrificing People':

> I detest writing. The process itself epitomizes the European concept of 'legitimate' thinking. What is written is given an importance that is denied the spoken. My culture, the Lakota, has an oral tradition, so ordinarily I reject writing. It is one of the white world's ways of destroying the cultures of non-European peoples, the imposing of an abstraction over the spoken relationship of a people.

By citing the particular case of Orissa, he observes that most of non-tribal people there apart from Brahmins rarely used writing, which epitomises knowledge as something obtainable only from books, not through experience of living with nature, in the midst of other people. Further such an approach camouflaged two aspects of tribals in Kerala: abysmal status of tribals in Kerala left out in policy circle and one of the longest ever historical exploitation of tribals in India as is exemplified by Wyanad. The indicator-based approach not only focused upon central tendencies, it also failed to see the subtle sociological realities that inhibit the development. Thus the values that are so dear to the Paniyans and their worldviews are not included in policy framework, denying them a life they have reason to value. Moreover, the approach has become an apparatus to continue the exploitation mechanism at micro level aided by legislations, which can ensure its continuance.

What can probably replace the indicator-based approach? As we look back on positions developed in the paper, it should begin by looking at the formation of tribal identity, else any such attempt would end up merely as another exercise in gaining knowledge and about production of exploitation. The following argument of C.R. Bijoy is worth considering:

> Unlike others, adivasis have a special relationship and dependence on land which gives them the notion of territoriality. Their existence as communities is possible only if their inalienable right to their territories is acknowledged.

The fact that 96 per cent of tribal households in Kerala have less than one hectare of land indicates that they form one of the largest landless (NSSO 2006) and the largest small and landless agricultural labourers in India. How effective would be a development indicator if it fails to show this aspect? Further, the same logic can be applied to the denial of access of tribals to forest and water resources, outright rejection of ethnic organisations and self-governance. One can argue about the rights and legislative framework developed by the state to ensure them. But the case study of Paniyans in Kerala highlights that just legislative framework or welfare state policies cannot solve all the issues around development. Probably development indicators need to be indigenously developed and linked to the consolidation of tribal identity.

HDI-based development approach in fact contradicts the tribal development. Such an approach misses the cultural and historicity factor and increases its vulnerability in the context of its full range application. As Amartya Sen (2000) notes:

> The right approach would have to be sensitive to the circumstance involved – both the nature of public services to be offered and the characteristics of the society to which they are to be offered. The latter must include the behavorial values of different kinds, which influence individual choices and incentives.

The present study may be defended on the premise that it is important to analyse the inclusive nature of HDI-based development approach, when applied to small but compact tribal communities, which may qualify to be called as indigenous communities.

Acknowledgements

I am grateful to MS Swaminathan Research Foundation, Kerala, Institute of Development Studies, Kolkata, and Indian Institute of Public Administration, Delhi, for their assistance during the study and paper preparation. I would like to thank Professor Felix Padel, Dr D Narayana of CDS Trivandrum, Dr Bidan Kanti Das of IDSK, Varun Sharma and Namami Sharma of Delhi School of Social Work for their valuable comments, kind guidance and support.

Note

1. These issues have been brought together in 'Paniya Sadas', an International seminar organised by Centre for Development Studies, Trivandrum held on 13–15 March 2010 at Shreyas, Sulthan Bathery, Wayanad, Kerala.

References

Aiyappan, A. 1992. *The Paniyan: An Ex-slave Tribe of South India*. Kolkata: Institute of Social Research.

Beteille, Andre. 1977. 'The Definition of Tribe'. In *Tribe, Caste and Religion*. Edited by R. Thapar. Delhi: Macmillan India.

Bijoy, R., and K. Ravi Raman. 2003. 'Muthanga: The Real Story of Adivasi: Movement to Recover Land', *Economic and Political Weekly*, 38(20): pp. 1975–1982

Bourdieu, P. 1986. 'The Forms of Capital'. In *Handbook of Theory and Research for the Sociology of Education*. Edited by J. Richardson. NewYork: Greenwood.

Chattopadhyaya, B.D. 2004. 'State's Perception and the "Forest" and the "Forest" as State'. In *Tribes, Forests and Social Formation in Indian History*. Edited by BB Chaudhuri and A Bandhopadyay. New Delhi: Manohar.

Devan, P.K. 2006. 'September Kundalpani: Bitter Days of Bygone Adivasian slavery. Kerala Calling. pp. 30–31. Retrieved from http://www.old.kerala.gov.in/kercalsptmbr06/pg30-31.pdf. Last accessed on 25.11.2013.

Frazer, John. 1890. *The Golden Bough: A Study in Magic and Religion*. London: Temple of Earth Publishing. Retrieved from http://www. templeofearth.com/books/goldenbough.pdf. Last accessed on 12.10.2013.

Fukuda-Parr, Sakiko. 2003. 'The Human Development Paradigm: Operationalizing Sen's Ideas on Capabilities,' *Feminist Economics* 9(2 – 3): pp. 301–317.

George, Jose and P Krishnaprasad. 2006. 'Agrarian Distress and Farmers' Suicides in the Tribal District of Wayanad', *Social Scientist*, Vol. 34: pp. 70–85.

Heller, Patrick. 1999. *The Labor of Development: The Workers and Transformation of Capitalism in Kerala, India*. New York: Cornell University Press.

Jayasree, C.H. Patterns of Institutionalized Servility: The Case of 19th Century Malabar. Retrieved from http://www.fihrm.org/documents/DrCHJayasreepaper.pdf accessed on 15.10.2013.

Johni, O.K. 2010. *Wayanad Rekhakal* (in Malayalam). Kozhikode: Mathrubhumi Books.

KILA. 2011. Scheduled Tribe Communities Basic Information – 2011 (Waynad District), Thrissur, Kerala.

Kjosavik, Darley Jose and N. Shanmugaratnam. 2004. 'Integration or Exclusion? Locating Indigenous Peoples in the Development Process of Kerala, South India'. *Forum for Development Studies*, 31, No 2: pp. 232–273.

Kurien, John. 1995 'The Kerala Model: Its Central Tendency and the Outlier'. *Social Scientist* 23(70).

Kulirani, B. Francis. 1996. The Shrinking Livelihood Strategies of the Paniyar. Retrived from http://www.sasnet.lu.se/conferences/livelihood-strategies-among-forest-related-tribal-groups-south-india. Last accessed on 5.11.2013.

Merry, Sally Engle. 2011. 'Measuring the World: Indicators, Human Rights, and Global Governance'. *Current Anthropology*, 52: S83-S95.

Nair, C. Gopalan. 1911. *Wayanad: Its Peoples and Traditions.* Madras (Chennai): Higginbotham and Co.

Nair, P.S. 1976 Paniyar. (Malayalam). Kottayam: National Book Stall/London: Routledge and Kegan Paul.

Narayana, D. 2010. 'Educational Deprivation of Scheduled Tribes in Kerala'. Keynote Address at Panya Sadas, Waynad, Kerala.

NSSO. 2006. National Sample Survey Organization, Government of India Report No. 516, Employment and Unemployment Situation among Social Groups in India, 61st Round.

NUEPA, Elementary Education in India: Towards Universal Elementary Education, DISE 2011–12.

Padel, Felix. 2011. *Sacrificing People.* New Delhi: Orient Blackswan.

Planning Commission of India. 2008. *Eleventh Five Year Plan 2007–2012*, Volume 1, Govt. of India.

Radhakrishnan, P. 1981. 'Land Reforms in Theory and Practice: The Kerala Experience'. *Economic and Political Weekly*, 16(52): pp. A129–A137.

Santhosh, Rachel. 2008. 'Mapping of an Ethnohistory of the Paniyan: Some Preliminary Reflections', *Indian Anthropologist*, 38(1): pp. 61–76.

Sen, Amartya. 1999. *Development as Freedom.* New York: Alfred A. Knopf.

Srinivas, M.N. 1956. 'A Note on Sanskritization and Westernization', *The Far Eastern Quarterly*, 15: pp. 481–496.

Tanaka, Jiro. 1980. *The San Hunter Gatherers of the Kalahari: A Study in Ecological Anthropology.* Tokyo: The University of Tokyo Press.

Tharakan, P.K.M. 2006. 'Kerala Model Revisited: New Problems and Challenges'. Working Paper No. 15. Centre for Socio-Economic and Environmental Studies, Kochi, Kerala, India.

UNDP. 2011. Inequality – adjusted Human Development Index for India's States. http://www.undp.org/content/dam/india/docs/inequality_adjusted_human_development_index_for_indias_state1.pdf Last accessed on 10.11.2013.

Vinod, C.P. 'Ethnicity and livelihood practices at the confluence of the local and the global: a study of Paniyas in Wayanad, Kannur University', 2009. Accessed from http://shodhganga.inflibnet.ac.in/handle/10603/4533. Last accessed on 07.12.2013

Wayanad Initiative. 2006. 'A Situational Study and Feasibility Report for the Comprehensive Development of Adivasi Communities in Wyanad', KIRTADS-CREST-IIMK. Last accessed on 14.12.2013.

Zerzan, John. 1998. 'A Post Historic Primitivism'. In *Limited Wants, Unlimited Means: A Reader on Hunter-Gatherer Economics and the Environment.* Edited by John Gowdy. Washington, DC: Island Press.

CHAPTER 9

Towards Demarginalisation of the Lodhas in West Bengal

A Study in the Assessment of the Impact of Development Efforts by the State

SANTANU PANDA AND ABHIJIT GUHA

Demarginalisation is used mainly in the social science literature to refer to the process of bringing back specific social groups in the mainstream of the society. Gender related and racial issues are dealt under the concept in which the efforts of the state and other non-state agencies towards the liberation of women and the non-white sections of the population in Western societies are often viewed to 'demarginalise' themselves. In the Indian context, the process of demarginalisation can be looked as a much broader process involving the protests of not only women but also groups of people (e.g. Dalits) who have been subjected to discrimination and marginalisation by the state and the economically and politically powerful and dominant sections of the society (Narayan 2008: 163–184).

The attempts by the state to uplift the conditions of these marginalised groups and communities can also be approached from the angle of demarginalisation in which the role of the state, various non-governmental actors and the members of the marginalised communities may be studied from historical as well as synchronic perspectives.

The Lodhas of West Bengal is one such community that has a long history of marginalisation and oppression by the state and the dominant communities, and they also have a history of demarginalisation that had started in the post-colonial period by the efforts of the state and non-state actors as well as the members of the community themselves.

In this article an attempt has been made to look into the twin processes of marginalisation vis-à-vis demarginalisation of the Lodha tribe in some specific geographic and administrative locations in a historical context. The first part of the article, which has several sub-sections, deals with the story of marginalisation of the tribe in a historical frame of reference, while in the second part a synchronic narrative of the process of demarginalisation of the community is constructed based on anthropological fieldwork and observations.

The Story of Marginalisation of the Lodhas in a Historical Context

Criminal Tribes in Colonial India

The Criminal Tribes Act dates back to various successive pieces of legislation enforced in India during British rule. The legislation was first enacted in 1871 as the Criminal Tribes Act, 1871, which applied mostly in North India. The Act was extended to Bengal Presidency and other areas in 1876, and, finally, with the Criminal Tribes Act, 1911, it was extended to Madras Presidency as well. The act went through several amendments in the next decade and, finally, the Criminal Tribes Act, 1924, was enacted incorporating all the aforementioned provinces. (http://en.wikipedia.org/wiki/Criminal_Tribes_Act). Interestingly, in an article entitled 'The Criminal Tribes of India' published in the *Journal of the Royal Society of Arts* in 1923, a retired British administrative officer Frederick de L. Booth Tucker wrote:

> Crime in most countries is committed by individuals, in India usually by tribes, communities and gangs, who are highly organised and trained in it from childhood as a profession. The entire family and the relatives of an Indian criminal, including the women and children, are usually associated with him in the commission of crime. It is looked upon by these tribes very much as we regard the military profession, and is considered to be both honourable and lucrative (Tucker 1923: 158–168).

According to Tucker, there were 18 settlements of criminal tribes and in the then Bengal Presidency there was only one such settlement and the community that was recorded by him as criminal was not the Lodhas but 'Karwal Nats'. Moreover, he stated in the same article that most of the families in those settlements were found to practise agriculture combined with petty commodity production and the rest were engaged in industrial occupations. (ibid.). Tucker's description does not fit to the traditional occupation of the Lodhas practising hunting gathering as was reported by the anthropologists much later. The question is how were the Lodhas included under the Criminal Tribe category and brought under the purview of the Criminal Tribes Act, 1911?

In the same volume of the journal published after five months, another British official of the police in his correspondence in connection with a remark made by Sir Edward Henry in the discussion on Commissioner Booth Tucker's paper dealing with Criminal Tribes Act observed:

> The chief motive of the Act is to save criminal tribes from themselves; to reform and to reclaim them, so far as is humanly possible. The Act, as it stands, supplies to the criminal classes a method by which they may be able to improve themselves and to lead decent lives. To the general public it affords a scheme of protection while it places at the disposal of the police a lawful means for keeping potential criminals under proper supervision (Faulkner 1923: 449).

Faulkner in the conclusion of his correspondence mentioned about how the Lodhas of the then Bengal Presidency might have been designated as a criminal tribe by the local administration who were empowered by the law to declare a whole tribe as criminal if a certain section of the community was found to commit certain non-bailable offences. We should quote Faulkner verbatim:

> If only a part of the tribe is addicted to the systematic commission of non-bailable offences, then only that part of the tribe may be declared a criminal tribe for the purposes of the Act. This was, to my knowledge, done in the case of certain gangs of the tribe of Lodhas in the district of Midnapur (ibid.).

The above exchange between the two experienced British officials revealed the truth that the Lodhas as a community were not initially included under the designation of a criminal tribe, at least like the other communities of India, but some members of the community were definitely declared as 'criminal' as early as the first half of 20th century and then by the immense scope of the law and the discretion of the British officials the whole community was classified as a Criminal tribe. Be that as it may, one thing was clear in the basic premise of the Criminal Tribe Act. The premise was clearly explicated in the first quote from Booth Tucker's article wherein he opined that crime in India was committed by *'tribes, communities and gangs'* who were *'trained in it from childhood as a profession'* and they regarded crimes *'to be both honourable and lucrative'* profession like the westerners who viewed military profession as admirable (emphases by us).

From Criminal to Denotified: The Post-Colonial Story

After Independence, a number of communities in India who were designated as 'criminal tribes' by the British colonial administration were redesignated as denotified tribes and later some of them have been classified as primitive tribal groups (PTG) (Verma 1990). The Lodhas of West Bengal are one of them, who suffered from continued poverty and marginalisation (Devi 1983). In 1952, the Criminal Tribes Act was repealed by the Government of India, and all the communities who were designated as criminal tribes were reclassified as denotified communities. Once again, in the name of 'positive discrimination' they were reclassified into another governmental category without being given equal status with the mainstream communities of the nation. Furthermore, the denotification process also carried the colonial hangover of looking at those 'criminal tribes' as born criminals. G.N. Devi, a noted scholar-activist and the editor of *Budhan, the Newsletter of the Denotified Nomadic Tribes Rights Action Groups (DNT-RAG)* narrated the passage from the Criminal Tribes Act of the colonial period to the post-colonial Denotified Tribes Act in a succinct manner:

> Soon after Independence, the communities notified as criminal tribals were denotified by the Government. This notification was followed by substitution of a series of Acts, generally entitled 'Habitual Offenders Act! The HOAs preserved most of the provisions of the former CT Acts, except the premise implicit in it that an entire community can be 'born' criminal. Apparently, the denotification and the passing of the HOAs should have ended the misery of the

communities penalised under the CT Act. But that has not happened. The police forces as well as the people in general were taught to look upon the 'Criminal Tribes' as born criminals during the colonial times. That attitude continues to persist even today (Devi 1998).

In the post-Independence period the 'ex-criminal' and 'denotified' Lodhas also suffered extreme humiliation and human rights violation not only from the higher Hindu castes but also from the Santals, the dominant tribe of the region. The anthropologist, Probodh Bhowmick, in an article narrated how the Lodhas in the bank of river Subarnarekha in erstwhile Midnapore district were chased and thirty-nine of them were brutally beheaded and the rest were taken to the custody of the killers in September 1979 (Bhowmick 1981: 6). In the same article Bhowmick reported that in an earlier incident in 1968 the houses of eighteen Lodha villages were burned by the Santals (ibid., 1981: 6). The famous litterateur and social activist Mahasweta Devi reported in her 1983 article published in *Economic and Political Weekly*, 'Lodha killing is a regular feature in West Bengal', and she enumerated the killing of thirty four Lodhas in West Bengal from 1979–1982. (Devi 1983: 947). Budhan, a member of the 'Denotified Tribe' Kheria Sabar (also known as Lodhas) was arrested by the police and brutally tortured within the police lock-up for seven days and he died in custody. The police however reported that he committed suicide by hanging himself in the lock-up. Later, Paschim Bangya Kheria Sabar Kalyan Samiti, a civil rights organisation under the leadership of Jnanpeeth-Magsaysay award winner Mahasweta Devi took this case to the Calcutta High Court and alleged that Budhan was beaten to death and filed a writ petition in Calcutta High Court against the police (Writ Petition No. 3715 dated 1998). It was revealed that Budhan was killed by police torture (Amnesty International Report 2001: 24). Justice Rama Pal of the Calcutta High Court rejected the police story in the judgment delivered and ordered the state government to pay compensations of Rs 80,000 to his wife and Rs 5,000 to his parents. The judgment also directed the state to punish the jail superintendent of Purulia and the office in-charge of Burrabazar police station.

Under this post-colonial scenario, various welfare measures have been undertaken by the central government to improve the living conditions of the Lodhas. After the Independence many plans and projects of specific nature have been initiated by the government to resettle the forest dependent and semi-nomadic Lodha minority community in an agriculture-dependent sedentary life. Meanwhile, a good number of rehabilitation schemes have been formulated and implemented on the Lodhas. Most of these schemes failed and no lasting impact of them could be made (Bhowmick 1985: 17). In the post-Independence period the main aim of the government was to put off the stigma of criminal tribe designation of the Lodhas. At the same time, the government also wanted to uplift the socio-economic condition of this tribe who mainly depended on forest produce and daily labour. After the sixties, the Lodhas were included under the denotified and nomadic tribes along with 19 communities of West Bengal (https://www.indianfolklore.org/journals/index.php/Mukt/.../134 2012).

The central government had taken special initiatives for improving their living condition and rehabilitation, by providing facilities for housing, agriculture; cottage industries and education through ashram hostel from the primary level (Bhowmick 1985: 15). But the traditional life of the Lodhas has not changed much. Still they are dependent on forest produce collection and hunting animals for livelihood (Bhowmick 1963: 26).

Still later, since 1971, the Lodhas were redesignated as one of the 'primitive tribal groups' (PTGs) of India, another governmental category (Verma 1990: 277). Special funds have been sanctioned by the government to organise a development cell under the project officer and backward class welfare officer (PO and BCW) of the state government (Bhowmick 1985: 14).

Through the cell (PO and BCW) of government has delivered various types of development inputs for strengthening of the socio-economic condition of this marginalised community. Another important component of the governmental perspective centring round the development of the Lodhas was to settle this tribe as an agriculturist population.

The traditional and intimate knowledge of the Lodhas about the forests and the animals on which the community sustained its livelihood were rarely studied and used by the governmental and non-governmental development agencies. Even the anthropologists, who have studied the Lodhas, did not study the relationship of the Lodhas with the forests in detail. One striking fact in this regard is the virtual neglect of the Lodhas by the forest department of the government. For example, in the joint forest management movement the participation of the Lodhas is still very much negligible. Most of the benefits gained through the activities of the forest protection committees are enjoyed by the members of the economically and socially dominant castes and tribes. This truncated approach towards the development of the Lodhas operated in such a manner that the socio-economic condition of the Lodhas did not improve appreciably in the long, post-Independence period. As a result of the failure of the government to improve the condition of the Lodhas and other tribes under similar conditions, the Government of India coined a new designation for such tribes in the year 1971 for their development, which was 'primitive tribal group' or PTG. The Lodhas of West Bengal were put under this new category. The overall approach towards the development of the Lodhas, however, did not change much after the introduction of this new designation, except for the fact that more funds for the development of the Lodhas were allocated. In a later period, another new idea for the development of the 'backward districts' came into existence. This scheme was launched by the Planning Commission of India and it is known as the Rastriya Sama Vikas Yojna (RSVY). The RSVY scheme is a recent initiative undertaken by the central government. The scheme was launched during the period 2004–2005. The scheme aimed at focused development programmes for backward areas, which would help reduce imbalances and speed up development. Under the RSVY scheme, the central government aimed to cover 100 backward districts in India.

Government launched another programme, i.e. Indira Awas Yojana (IAY). It is a Government of India social welfare programme: to provide housing for the rural poor in India. It is one of the major flagship programmes of the Rural Development Ministry, Government of India to construct houses for BPL population in the villages. This scheme started operation since 1985. Under the scheme, financial assistance worth Rs 45,000 in plain areas and Rs 48,500 in difficult areas (high land area) is provided for construction of houses. The houses are allotted in the name of the woman or jointly between husband and wife. The construction of the houses is the sole responsibility of the beneficiary and engagement of contractors is strictly prohibited. (en.wikipedia.org/wiki/Indira_Awaas_Yojana. Accessed on 9 November 2012).

The government also builds up some houses under the backward class welfare section through Lodha Development Cells. These houses have been implemented by Lodha Savar Kalyan Samiti of Paschim Medinipur district. Under this background an attempt has been made in this article to record the comparative findings on the implementation of development programmes under the various developmental schemes. The comparative study consists of three administrative blocks of Paschim (west) Medinipur district of West Bengal, which was earmarked as a 'backward district' by the Government of India.

Lodhas as Viewed by the Anthropologists and Activists: The Second Part of the Post-Colonial Story

The Lodhas are now treated as one of the denotified communities by the central government. In West Bengal, Lodhas are mainly concentrated in the districts of Paschim (West) Medinipur and Purba (East) Medinipur. As mentioned earlier, in the pre-Independence period they were treated as a criminal tribe till the revocation by the Criminal Tribes Act in 1952. In the first Census of India after Independence, the Lodhas were recorded as a Scheduled Caste and their total population was returned to be 8,346 only in West Bengal (Mitra 1953: 89). According to the Census of 1951 the Lodhas were found to be distributed in the districts of Burdwan, Birbhum, Bankura, Midnapore, Hooghly, Howrah, 24 Parganas, Calcutta, Murshidabad and Jalpaiguri. In 1951, they were not found in the North Bengal districts like Nadia, Maldah, West Dinajpur, Darjeeling and Cooch Behar. In the same census the total number of Lodhas in erstwhile Midnapore was 7040, that is, 84.35 per cent of the then total population of Lodhas in West Bengal (ibid.: 89–90).

The Census of 1981 shows that the total population of the Lodhas including the Kharias and the Kherias of West Bengal is 53,718. The Lodhas are concentrated in Midnapore district and their total number according to the Census of 1981 was 16,534. Besides West Bengal, they are also found in the Mayurbhanj and Baleswar districts of Odisha. Originally, they inhabited hilly rugged terrains covered with jungle. Their mother tongue is Lodha, which is close to Savara, an Austro-Asiatic language. They are fluent in Bengali. Traditionally they were forest dwellers but now they have started cultivation either as owner or as agricultural labourer and are also engaged in hunting and fishing. More than 80 per cent of them follow Hinduism with traditional belief in spirits and nature (Mandal, et al., 2002: 32).

At present the Lodhas do not live exclusively in the forest-covered areas, but have spread out in other deforested regions and are found to work there as agricultural and non-agricultural labourers. But their main economy is still based on collection of minor forest products, such as leaves for preparing leaf-plates for sale. According to Bhowmick, the Lodhas were found to collect edible roots and fruits for household consumption and sell the surplus in the local markets. They are also found to be engaged in the collection of tussore cocoons and sell them in the market for cash. Lodhas also catch snakes and lizards and sell their hides and consume the flesh of these animals. They also catch fish and tortoises from the water bodies for domestic consumption as well as for sale (Bhowmick 1981: 6).

Bhowmick also reported that various types of developmental initiatives had been undertaken by the government and some non-governmental organisations to settle the Lodhas for leading a sedentary agricultural life. In 1950s a rehabilitation project was taken up on an experimental basis for the Lodha families at Daharpur of Narayangarh block in erstwhile Medinipur district. This project included development inputs like house building, land purchase, land recovery, supply of domestic and agricultural training to be imparted to the Lodhas for their resettlement. But these could not be implemented in the aforesaid area owing to some serious difference of opinion among the organisers and social scientists associated with that project (Bhowmick 1981: 7).

According to Ajit Danda, the Lodhas belong to Mundari speaking population who are mostly found in the forest covered areas of Singhbhum District of Jharkhand, Mayurbhanj District of Odisha and Midnapore District of West Bengal, which is also known as Jungle Mahal since the colonial period. They speak a dialect composed of distorted Bengali, Oriya and words of Mundari origin (Danda 2002: 103).

The Government of Independent India repealed the Criminal Tribes Act in 1952. Even after denotification as criminal tribes, the Lodhas continue to suffer from the social stigma and the non-tribal neighbours still behave unsympathetically towards them. Over the decades, the Lodhas gradually changed their occupation from hunting gathering to agriculture as an alternative means of livelihood owing to deforestation (Danda 2002: 110–111).

An important observer of the marginalised condition of the Lodhas in West Bengal is Mahasveta Devi who is a famous Bengali litterateur and a human rights activist. Mahasveta Devi not only wrote on the abject poverty and exploitation of the Lodhas, she also worked for decades to fulfil the various demands of the community as regards their socio-economic condition. Although, not an anthropologist, Mahasveta Devi has first-hand experiences of the failures of governmental schemes and shortcomings of the government policies directed towards the development of the Lodhas in erstwhile Midnapore, and the adjoining districts of West Bengal. Unlike academic anthropologists, she practised activism through the publication of a literary magazine in which many literate tribal persons including Lodhas wrote about their living conditions, violence committed to them by the state and higher classes of the society and the demands of the different tribal communities. Mahasveta Devi herself wrote a number of articles in Bengali and English in which she depicted the ground realities regarding the problems of the implementation of development inputs and schemes among the Lodhas. In one article published in the *Economic and Political Weekly* in 1983, she cited examples of some Lodha villages in the present Paschim Medinipur district in which government schemes have failed to reach the beneficiaries, although they were badly in need of the development programmes. In the article Mahasveta Devi categorically pointed out:

> Usually the schemes are made by people not knowing or caring to know what the tribal really need. The plan is then, after the usual procedures, left to the contractor .... I have seen contractor – made construction works meant for the Lodhas. It is better to make specious earthen huts. With a structure of cement, brick and sand, the inevitable contractor is bound to enter the scene. To whose benefit? Not the Lodhas'. Over three decades, huge sums have been spent in the name of the Lodhas and the community has gone much below the poverty lines (Devi 1983: 948)'.

Mahasveta Devi' s long experience of working actively for the cause of the Lodhas led her to recommend certain concrete solutions, which she thought should have been adopted by the policy-makers and government functionaries for the development of this small and marginalised community of Bengal. According to her, plans with big budgets may not work for the real development of the Lodhas and secondly, development inputs for the community should be executed and managed by the Lodhas themselves. In another article published in the *Economic and Political Weekly*, Mahasveta Devi narrated her experience of observing the enthusiasm created among the Lodhas when in 1982–83, they revived their own community organisation (Lodha-Sabar Kalayan Samiti). We quote from the author:

> The Lodhas had revived the Samiti in sheer desperation for physical survival. The awakening of the Lodhas surprised the state government. The sluggish serpent eternally in winter hibernation covering the Lodha name seemed to stir a little. Six Lodhas were appointed as Lodha cell social workers, including Chuni Kotal. And three boys were appointed as village welfare supervisors in Chakua, Chandabila and Pranabpalli, on contingency basis, at ten rupees a day. All were employed in September 1983 .... This encouraged the Lodhas, through their devotion and dedication Lodha and some non-Lodha children came to the community centre for studying. These workers could persuade the Lodhas to give up drinking, to save from their wages, to live hygienically. They felt that the state government was coming forward with schemes for development and the Lodhas should be prepared to reap the full benefit of such schemes (Devi 1985: 1467).

Demarginalisation: The Synchronic Narrative

The Locations

Our study area was located in the two subdivision, viz. Jhargram and Khargapur of Paschim (West) Medinipur district. Under the two sub-divisions we have studied three blocks, viz. Binpur II, Nayagram and Narayangarh. Binpur II and Nayagram are rural administrative blocks in Jhargram sub-division of Paschim Medinipur district. These two blocks are covered by terrains with dense forest. Total populations of both blocks were about one and half lakh (2001 census). The tribal populations of both blocks were about fifty thousand. Most of the Scheduled Tribe populations depended on forest produce collection. According to *District Human Development Report: Paschim Medinipur*, the Human Development index (HDI) of Binpur II and Naygarm blocks were very low and the rank is 27 and 29 out of 29 blocks of paschim (west) medinipur district. (DHDR 2011: 17). Narayangarh block consisted of 16 gram panchayats and there was no urban area under this block. this block contained the agricultural area and most of the tribal populations depended on cultivation. According to 2001 census, the total population was 2,66,675 and the Schedule Tribe population 57,527.

The primary data for the research have been collected from three hundred thirty two (332) Lodha households and the total population is 1,382. The blockwise populations are as the followings.

Binpur II ⇨ Surveyed population is 319
Nayagram ⇨ Surveyed population is 720
Narayangarh ⇨ Surveyed population is 343

The villages in which we conducted fieldwork were in a very poor condition as regards the communication. Most of the villages were surrounded by dense forest with hilly terrain. There were no regular public transport systems in these villages, so people had to walk long distance to reach the market, hospital or other public facilities. The villagers belonging to various communities including the Lodhas mainly depended on daily labour and forest produce collection. Most of the villagers had no agricultural land. Electric facilities, drinking water and health centres were not available to the villagers within a radius of 25 km.

Development Scenario in the Lodha Villages

The Lodhas are regarded as a marginalised and economically backward tribe by the government and both the central and the state governments have allocated funds under various development schemes to improve the socio-economic condition of the tribes since Independence. The anthropologists, social activists and the media had been emphasising the traditional socio-cultural life, food habit, pattern of living conditions of the Lodhas and it was also reported by the anthropologists and in the media how the community was deprived and oppressed by state and the dominant higher castes and tribes. The government has given various types of development inputs to the Lodha beneficiaries for their upliftment. The administration also attempted to bring them to the mainstream from their traditional forest-depended life and settled them as agriculturists. Apart from these, the government has given various types of development inputs under the Rastriya Sama Vikas Yojana (RSVY), Indira Awas Yojana (IAY), Mahatma Gandhi National Rural Employment Guarantee Act (MNREGA) and Lodha Development Cell through Backward Class Welfare office, etc. Special attention has been given to the Lodha children through the Lodha Development Cells'. In 2012, the administration built up buildings for crèche centres in the Lodha settlements for the outside-home-rearing of the Lodha children in the day time in the absence of their parents in all the three blocks although not a single crèches have yet been started.

The anthropologists, however, have not yet made any empirical attempt to assess the impact of the development inputs given to this marginalised community. In this study we have made an attempt to assess the utilisation of the various developmental inputs given by external agencies towards the demarginalisation of the Lodhas. The following table was constructed on the basis of our prolonged enquiries conducted in the government departments and the target villages of the three administrative blocks. This gives an overview of the development scenario of the Lodhas.

Table 9.1

Utilisation of Development Inputs among the Lodhas of Three Administrative Blocks

S. No	*Name of Development Inputs*	*Number of Beneficiary who Received the Inputs*	*Utilised the Development Inputs*	*Could not Utilise the Development Inputs*
1.	Patta Land given by Government	(3.26)45[7.95]	(1.95)27	(1.30)18
2.	Land given by NGO	(0.72)10[1.77]	(0.51)07	(0.22)03
3.	House	(12.66)175[30.92]	(7.38)102	(5.28)73
4.	Job card	(8.32)115[20.32]	(6.22)86	(2.10)29
5.	Pond	(0.29)04[0.71]	(0.29)04	00
6.	Money for domestic animal	(1.01)14[2.47]	(1.01)14	00
7.	Training for skill development	(0.43)06[1.06]		(0.43)06
8.	Husking Machine and Spray Machine	(0.79)11[1.94]	(0.79)11	00
9.	Loan (MT and Babui Cultivation)	(2.46)34[6.01]	(1.09)15	(1.37)19
10.	Old age Pension	(1.16)16[2.83]	(1.16)16	00
11.	Solar	(7.60)105[18.55]	(4.63)64	(2.97)41
12.	Cattle	(1.95)27[4.77]	(1.23)17	(0.73)10
13.	Blanket	(0.29)04[0.71]	(0.29)04	00
	Total	(40.95)566[100.00]	(26.56)373[64.84]	(14.40)199[35.16]

() Represents percentages out of total population.

[] Represents percentages out of the total number of beneficiaries.

The above table revealed the pattern of distribution of various types of developmental inputs given to the beneficiaries in the surveyed population. We have found thirteen type of development inputs: (i) patta, (ii) house, (iii) solar cell, (iv) job card (v) pond (vi) cattle (cow, goat and bullock) and only eight poultry bird, (vii) skill development training and (viii) loan (MT, Babui cultivation and agriculture), etc. in the study area. Our findings revealed that at the time of our survey, about 41 per cent beneficiary families out of 1,382 have received various types of developmental inputs in different combination. The distribution of agricultural land has not been used in the appropriate method. So, the beneficiaries could not use the patta land but they have patta record. Through our observation and interviews with the beneficiaries, we have found that most of the houses were built in a hurried manner and seemed to be weak in structure. The beneficiaries also expressed their dissatisfaction with the newly built houses. We have also found that the majority of the beneficiaries who received solar cells either sold them against cash to well-to-do neighbours belonging to other communities or could not use them properly (Panda and Guha 2009: 69–75).

As regards skill development through training, we have found that only six persons were given training and that too was done in the Narayangarh block. Training was given to middle-aged men in mushroom cultivation and micro-credit. Mushroom seeds were given to persons but no arrangement was made in their houses so that they could grow the seeds under proper condition. The persons trained in mushroom cultivation finally consumed the seeds and the training could not be utilised in future. The distribution of cattle and poultry birds among the Lodhas of our survey population also revealed that the beneficiaries could not manage their cattle and birds owing to lack of basic knowledge in rearing those animals. As a result, we have found that many cattle, particularly goats have died within a short period of time after those were given to the beneficiaries. The overall scenario of the utilisation of the various development inputs showed that the majority of the beneficiaries utilised the development inputs, although there is large amount of variation among the different inputs in terms of their consumption.

A Comparative Account of Development Inputs among the Lodhas in the Three Blocks

In this section, we have made an attempt to compare the utilisation pattern of the three major (patta land, house and solar cell) development inputs given to the Lodhas in the study area. The justification behind the comparison is twofold. Firstly, through this comparison we have presented the overall scenario of the utilisation vis-à-vis non-utilisation of the development keys by the study population at a glance.

Secondly, the comparison also reveals the variation among the households in the three blocks in the utilisation of the development keys.

Table 9.2

Profiles of Patta Records and Cultivation on Patta Land among the Lodha/Sabar Households in Binpur II, Nayagram and Narayangarh blocks of Paschim Medinipur

Surveyed Households			*No. of Households who Received Patta Record*				*No. of Households Found to be Actually Cultivating Patta Land*			
Binpur II	*Naya-gram*	*Narayan-garh*	*Binpur II*	*Naya-gram*	*Narayan-garh*	*Total*	*Binpur II*	*Naya-gram*	*Narayan-garh*	*Total*
87	182	63	10 [11.94] (3.01)	28 [15.38] (8.43)	17 [26.98] (5.12)	45 [13.55] (13.55)	01 [10.00] (0.30)	11 [39.28] (3.31)	15 [88.28] (4.51)	27 [60.00] (8.13)

() Figures in parentheses represent percentages out of the total number of households.

[ ] Figures in parentheses represent percentages out of the block wise Patta holder.

The above table shows the scenario of patta land distribution by the government and its utilisation by the Lodha families in the three blocks of the study area. It is found that the condition of the Binpur II block is worst both in terms of patta distribution and its utilisation by the beneficiary families. About twelve per cent of the total number of surveyed households received patta land from the government and only one family was found to use it whereas, in Narayangarh, twenty seven per cent of the total number of families received patta land and as high as eighty eight per cent of the families were found to cultivate their land. In Nayagram the percentage of recipients was about fifteen, while the users turned out to be thirty nine per cent (Case study 2).

Table 9.3

Profiles of Housing Scheme Distribution and Utilisation among the Lodha/Sabar Households in Binpur II, Nayagram and Narayangarh blocks of Paschim Medinipur

Surveyed Households			*No. of Households who Received Financial Assistance Under The Scheme*				*No. of Households who Actually Utilised the Benefits of the Scheme*			
Binpur II	*Naya-gram*	*Narayan-garh*	*Binpur II*	*Naya-gram*	*Narayan-garh*	*Total*	*Binpur II*	*Naya-gram*	*Narayan-garh*	*Total*
87	182	63	36 [41.37] (10.84)	124 [68.13] (37.35)	15 [23.81] (4.52)	175 (52.71)	12 [33.33] (3.61)	75 [60.48] (22.59)	15 [100.00] (4.52)	102 [58.29] (30.72)

() Figures in parentheses represent percentages out of the total number of households.

[ ] Figures in parentheses represent percentages out of the block wise patta holder.

From the above table it is found that the highest percentage of families of the Nayagram block received financial assistance from the government to build their houses and the lowest percentage was found among the Lodhas of Narayangarh. But the financial assistance towards house-building was best utilised by the Lodhas of Narayangarh, indicating higher level of consciousness of the beneficiaries. In Nayagram also the scenario of uitilisation was found to be fairly good, whereas the utilisation percentage at Binpur II was found to be very poor (Case study 2).

Case Study 1

Name of informant: Madhu Sabar Age: 43 Sex: Male
Village: Chirakuti JL. No: 91 Block: Binpur II

According to Madhu Sabar (name changed) there are four members in his family. The family did not possess any agricultural land and no patta was given to this family by the government. They are totally dependent on minor forest produce collection for survival. Madhu told that he is not a member of the Forest Protection Committee under the joint forest management programme of the forest department. He received a solar cell in 2004 from the government under the RSVY scheme although he had to deposit Rs 500 to the panchayat pradhan for receiving the solar cell. No money receipt was given to him. Madhu did not think it was illegal. He frankly admitted, 'Once I received the solar cell, I decided to sell it. After a few days, two men came to me from Ghatshila of the neighbouring Jharkhand state and wanted to buy the cell. I agreed to sell it at a price of Rs 1,000. Then there was a bargain and finally I sold it at a price of Rs 700 since I was badly in need of some money. Already I deposited Rs 500 to Panchayat Pradhan'.

Madhu further added 'I sold this gadget because it had no use for a poor man like me. My net gain was Rs 200 and still I was happy because I decided to purchase some utensils which was more useful for the family and I was looking for the money since long.' However, when I pointed out that the actual price of the solar cell was between Rs 8,000 to Rs 10,000, Madhu was really surprised. In fact, he had no idea about its price, since nobody told him about the market price of the gadget and the government officials did not give him any training for using the gadget.

Table 9.4

Profiles of Solar Cell Distribution and Utilisation among the Lodha/Sabar Households in Binpur II, Nayagram and Narayangarh Blocks of Paschim Medinipur

Surveyed Households			*No. of Households who Received Solar Plate*				*No. of Households Found to be Actually Use the Solar Plate*			
Binpur II	*Naya-gram*	*Narayan-garh*	*Binpur II*	*Naya-gram*	*Narayan-garh*	*Total*	*Binpur II*	*Naya-gram*	*Narayan-garh*	*Total*
87	182	63	23 [26.64] (6.92)	82 [45.05 (24.69)	Nil	105 (32.63)	04 [17.39] (1.20)	60 [73.17] (18.07)	Nil	64 [60.95] (19.28)

() Figures in parentheses represent percentages out of the total number of households.
[ ] Figures in parentheses represent percentages out of the block wise patta holder.

The distribution of solar cells by the government was done in Binpur II and Nayagram. The Lodha families of Narayangarh block were not covered under this scheme. Our respondents of Narayangarh reported that according to government officials, the families of this block were considered to be in a better economic condition so they were not provided with solar cells. The percentage of families who received solar cells was much higher in Nayagram and we have also found better utilisation of this gadget in this block. In Binpur II only four families out of twenty three were found to use solar cells. Most of the families in

Case Study 2

Name of informant: Sambhu Sabar Age: 42 Sex: Male

Village: Amlasole JL. No: 25 Block: Binpur II

According to Sambhu (name changed) they are dependent on forest product collection and daily labour for their survival. The informant received (i) *patta* land from the Block Land and Land Reforms (BLLRO) Department, (ii) financial assistance for house building under IAY scheme from the government and (iii) domestic animal from panchayat department in 2005. He said, 'I have received the papers on patta land in 6 December 2005. The plot nos. 206 and 203 in the Amlasole mouza were allotted to me and the total amount of the land was 0.60 acre only, but till now I could not cultivate the land.' He again narrated: 'the patta was issued in favour of my father late Samba Sabar. But I could not cultivate these lands because a man belonging to the Mahata community was cultivating the land and he did not want to forgo his rights. I complained the matter to the BLLRO but the government officials told me that the patta land should have been transferred under my name after the death of my father and only after that I may be able to cultivate in the land.' Sambhu reported about the financial assistance given to him for building his house. According to him: 'The newly built house was not suitable for living and I am still living in my old ancestral house and use the new house for keeping the minor forest products and the domestic animals'. This is due to the poor planning of the house by the contractor appointed by the panchayats who did not care to consult us.' He further added: 'I also received six goats in 2005 but after thirteen days all the goats died because the goats were not vaccinated and the goats were also very weak. Moreover, I have not been provided with any training regarding the rearing and proper upkeep of the domestic animals.'

Binpur II were found to have sold out the solar cells at very low price to outsiders in order to meet their domestic needs (Case study 1).

In Binpur II block, 79 beneficiary families have received three major development inputs. In Nayagram Block, 236 beneficiary families have received three major development keys. But In Narayangarh block, they received two major development keys, their beneficiary families are 32.

The comparative scenario of the utilisation of the three major development inputs in the three blocks among the Lodhas showed a marked overall variation. Details of these variations are highlighted below.

- The development inputs given to the Lodhas have been utilised by them most successfully in the Narayangarh block and, interestingly, solar plates have not been distributed in this block.
- The most horrible scenario is found in the Binpur II block in which non-utilisation of all the development inputs predominated the scene. Nayagram lies in the middle position in terms of the utilisation of the development keys.
- The utilisation of financial assistance for house construction given as a development input showed that even the overall worst performers (Lodhas of Binpur II) have made a substantial utilisation of house construction as a development key.

- Regarding patta land, we do not find full utilisation in any of the blocks studied but in case of house we find full utilisation in Narayangarh Block.
- The development assistance given in the form of high technology solar cells revealed a grim scenario both at Binpur II and Nayagram blocks while the Solar cell has not been given to the Lodha families of Narayangarh block. But the beneficiaries of Narayangarh block showed the overall best performance towards the utilisation of other development keys was found to be fairly well.

A Few Final Words

Going by the specifics, we have found differences in terms of the utilisation of the developmental inputs by the Lodha families of the three administrative blocks of Paschim Medinipur district. In case of patta land, 90 per cent beneficiaries have not used because the Lodhas have received the patta record in paper but they have not seen the plot. About 61 per cent beneficiaries of Nayagram block have not used the patta land owing to lack of agricultural implements and proper irrigation. But we have found in Narayangarh block there were about 90 per cent beneficiaries utilising the patta land.

Another development input, i.e. housing, showed a grim scenario. Under the governmental scheme, about 67 per cent of the houses remained unutilised in Binpur II and 40 per cent of the houses were found to be incomplete in Nayagram. The major reason behind the non-utilisation of constructed houses lay in poor and non-participatory nature of planning towards the construction of the houses by the concerned department of the government. But in Narayangarh block they were fully utilised the inputs. The 83 per cent Lodha beneficiaries have not used the solar cells in Binpur II, whereas about 27 per cent beneficiaries have not used the gadget in Nayagram but in Narayangarh the solar cell has not been given.

In Binpur II block, the beneficiaries suffered from terrible lack of communication and transport system, and lack of access to the panchayat members of the area although the local panchayat leader belonged to their own community. Both the central and state governments have not yet been able to organise any skill development training programmes for the Lodhas towards the implementation of the development schemes funded by the government.

In Nayagram block, the Lodhas were found to be in better condition than they were in Binpur II, in terms of communication and access to local panchayat leadership. Here the government had also taken up some training programmes as part of awareness programme through an NGO. It was also found in this block that an NGO played a good role towards monitoring of the implementation of the development schemes.

In Natrayangarh block, the Lodhas also seemed to be more aware about the development inputs than their counterparts in the other blocks. They also owned cultivable land and got training in agriculture and other skill development training programmes organised jointly by an NGO and the state government. In this block, the Institute of Social Research and Applied Anthropology (ISRAA), founded by the anthropologist Probodh Kumar Bhowmick, played a catalytic role in raising the consciousness of the Lodha community towards the development efforts undertaken by the government.

In Lieu of a Conclusion

The narrative of demarginalisation of the once 'criminal' made 'denotified' and then categorised as a 'primitive tribal group' is a gloomy story of the failure of a welfare state and its citizenry in dealing with this subjugated mass of people. It appears that most of the funds pumped into the development of the Lodhas were either misplaced or remained unutilised. The governmental approach to sedentarise this community who loved and lived with the forest seemed to be rather misplaced and even when some of the community members showed willingness to lead an agricultural way of life, the right of the Lodhas to the basic resource of agriculture, i.e. land, was usurped. The state machinery remained just an onlooker. This basically points to the colonial hangover of looking at the tribe from an alien angle, which attempted reforms towards the community without knowing their real needs and aspirations, and when development inputs failed to reach the goals, the Lodhas were blamed again as suffering from drunkenness, nomadism, laziness and criminal habits. They are, therefore, still regarded as 'primitive' if not 'criminal' under the modern jargon, and the anthropologists have also agreed with the governmental categorisation without going through the history and the present empirical realities of the development story.

Acknowledgements

We are very much grateful to the coordinator of the national level conference organised by the Institute of Development Studies Kolkata (IDSK) in collaboration with the Anthropological Survey of India to present a preliminary version of the paper in the conference. We owe our debts to the members of the Lodha community of the selected blocks for their help and cooperation during my fieldwork and we also express gratitude to the government officials of Paschim Medinipur district. We also express our gratefulness to the Indian Council for Social Science Research (ICSSR) for providing financial support to attend the conference and the fieldwork. Last but not the least, we express our deep sense of gratitude to Dr Bidhan Kanti Das for providing untiring support to write the final version of the paper for publication.

Note

1. The criteria of inclusion of a tribal community under Primitive Tribal Group (PTG) are: (i) pre-agricultural level of technology, (ii) very low level of literacy, (iii) declining or stagnant population and (iv) a subsistence level of economy. (Meena 2009: 13)

References

Amnesty International Report. 2001. pp. 1–51.

Bhowmick, P.K. 1985. 'Tribal Situation West Bengal', *The Anthropologist*, Vol. 15, No. 1: pp. 1–19.

——. 1981. 'Rehabilitaion of a "Denotified Community": The Ex-Criminal Lodhas of West Bengal', *Royal Anthropological Institute Newsletter*, 44: pp. 6–8.

——. 1966. Some Aspects Tribal Transformation in India', *'Proceedings of the Summer School in Anthropology'*, edited by N.C. Choudhury. Darjeeling: Anthropological Survey of India.

——. 1963. *The Lodhas of West Bengal.* Kolkata: Institute of Social Research and Applied Anthropology.

Chanda, A. 2005. 'Tribal Women'. In *The Changing Status of Women in West Bengal, 1970–2000: Tthe Challenge Ahead.* Edited by J. Bagchi. Delhi: Sage Publications.

Danda, A.K. 2002. 'Predicaments of a Marginalised Community: The Lodha' *Journal of Anthropological Survey of India.* 51: pp. 103–111.

Devi, Mahasveta. 1983. 'Lodhas of West Bengal–1', *Economic and Political Weekly*, Vol. 18, No. 22: pp. 947–949.

——. 1992. The story of Chuni Kotal. *Economic and Political Weekly*, Vol. XVII, N0. 35, 1992: pp. 1836–1837.

Devy, G. 2000. 'For a Nomad Called Thief', *India International Centre Quarterly*, Vol. 27, No. 2, Marginalised: pp. 51–60.

Devy, G.N. 1998. 'The Branded Tribes of India', *Peoples' Union of Civil Liberties Bulletin,* September.

Faulkner, L.P. 1923. 'Settlements of Criminal Tribes of India', *Journal of the Royal Society of Arts*, Vol. 71, No. 3677: p. 449.

Mandal, H. et al. 2002. 'West Bengal'. In *India: An Illustrated Atlas of Tribal World.* Kolkata: Anthropolgical Survey of India.

Mitra, A. 1953. *The Tribes and Castes of West Bengal: Census 1951.* Calcutta (Kolkata): Land and Land Revenue Department, Govt. of West Bengal.

Narayan, B. 2008. 'Demarginalisation and History: Dalit Re-Invention of the Past', *South Asia Research*, Vol. 28, No. 2, (July): pp. 169–184. doi: 10.1177/026272800802800203.

Panda, S., and Guha, A. 2009. 'Development Inputs among the Lodhas in a District of West Bengal: Problems of Implementation and Recommendations', *Journal of the Indian Anthropological Society*, 44: pp. 69–75.

Radhakrishna, M. 2009. 'Starvation among Primitive Tribal Groups'. *Economic and Political Weekly,* Vol. 40, No. 18: pp. 13–16.

Singh, Suresh Kumar. 1994. *People of India: The Scheduled Tribes.* Delhi: Oxford University Press/Anthropological Survey of India.

Tribal Health Bulletin (Special Issue), 2014. pp. 1–126.

Tucker, B. 1923. 'The Criminal Tribe of India', *Journal of the Royal Society of Arts*. Vol. 71, No. 3661: pp. 158–166.

Verma, R.C. 1990. *Indian Tribes through the Ages.* Delhi: Ministry of Information and Broadcasting, Government of India.

Web references

*https://www.indianfolklore.org/journals/index.php/Mukt/.../134. Accessed on 12.12.2012.

*http://en.wikipedia.org/wiki/Criminal_Tribes_Act. Accessed on 11.07.2014.

*http://en.wikipedia.org/wiki/Indira_Awaas_Yojana. Accessed on 09.11.2012.

* http://en.wikipedia.org/wiki/Criminal_Tribes_Act. Accessed on 11.07.2014.

*http://www.pucl.org/from-archives/Dalit-tribal/branded-tribes.htm. Accessed on 03.08.2014.

PART IV

Forest and Tribals

CHAPTER 10

Forest Policies and Tribal Livelihood

An Organisational Perspective

PRADEEP KUMAR MISHRA

Forest Policies in India have invariably influenced tribal livelihood pattern. The commercial forestry focus during colonial era not only excluded concerns of tribal people but also deprived them of their rights over the forests. After Independence the same policies continued in meeting the industrial interests. In 1980s, however, the situation started changing when the conservation focus was brought in; but here also the tribal livelihood aspects were not recognised. Only after the National Forest Policy of 1988 the importance of tribal livelihood was recognised, which received a further boost after the Scheduled Tribes and other Traditional Forest Dwellers (Recognition of Forest Rights) Act, 2006, popularly known as Forest Rights Act (FRA) was passed in 2006.

Besides, several programmes have also been designed and implemented on forestry, initially those areas related to teak plantations, pine plantations, bamboo plantations and in the recent decades, programmes on social forestry, farm forestry, joint forest management (JFM), etc. Teak plantations required huge number of labourers for a long time and hence labourers had to be settled inside the forest and such settlements later became permanently branded as forest villages. People settled in such villages did not have entitlements to land and were considered as encroachers until the passage of FRA. Similarly, tropical pine plantations in Bastar created resentment among tribal people (Mishra 2008).

In formulating of these policies and implementation of forest-related programmes, several organisational stakeholders were involved. The direct stakeholders obviously are the politicians (policy-makers), industries that influence the forests and people living there, and the tribal people whom these policies and programmes influence. The role of such stakeholders and the impact of the forest policies have been the focus of many academic discussions in the past.

But there is another category of stakeholders who are engaged directly in policy formulation and implementation. They are agencies such as Ministry of

Environment and Forest (MoEF), Forest Department (FD), civil society organisations, research institutes, funding agencies and implementing agencies who convert the policy statements to deliverable actions. Their role becomes important in the quality and magnitude of outcomes realised. The organisational influences are different from the political influences and interest groups, who lobby like an industry because the latter tries to affect the policies per se, while the organisational stakeholders, though working work well within the framework of the policy statements, yet influence the ultimate outcomes in no uncertain terms.

The influence of such organisational actors on policy and programme implementation, which in turn affect the tribal livelihoods (as an outcome of the programmes implemented), has not been given due attention. Here an attempt has been made to look into the forest policies and their linkage with tribal livelihoods from the perspective of associated organisations. The focus is particularly on the implementation processes that affect the policy and programme outcomes.

Literature Review and the Research Problem

The evolution of forest policies and various programmes have been well analysed from political economy perspectives wherein the interests of industry has been emphasised at the cost of tribal rights and their natural assets (Gadgil and Guha 1992). A few scholars have looked into the issue of forest policies from a cultural point of view wherein they have argued against the narrow economic focus. Tribals have their distinct cultural identity and practices. If the cultural elements are not considered, economic policies vis-à-vis forest utilisation and conservation would not stand a chance of success (Sharma 1989). There is also an ecological point of view that has received high priority in the policy statements of conservation programme.

Earlier organisational role in policy implementation was sometimes seen from a Weberian point of view, according to which the bureaucracy plays a neutral role. The rational perspective of policy processes matches with this idea. But scholars like Lindblom (1959) opine that policy decisions are not made by rational choice but by incrementalism. In the 1970s Pressman and Wildavsky (1973) brought out a seminal implementation studies that highlighted the various organisational dimensions affecting policy outcomes. Contrary to that Allison (1971) is of the opinion that organisations are not necessarily rational actors; there are political and procedural influences in their choices.

Forest policies and implementation have so far not been analysed from this perspective. The role of FD has mostly been viewed in negative terms (Hannam 1999). But what leads to such a negative role of one of the oldest administrative mechanisms is not answered clearly. In explaining the evolution of forest policies and programmes, organisational influences have a substantial role to play. How and why such influences counts need to be looked into in details. Side by side, the role of forest bureaucracy in forest administrations calls for a closer scrutiny.

The Organisational Space vis-à-vis Indian Forests

There are two categories of stakeholders in the organisational space dealing with Indian forests – the first category includes organisations, and the forest bureaucracy that runs these organisations forms the second category. The important organisations involved in the affairs of Indian forests are the MoEF, forest department, civil society organisations based and working in India, international agencies including funding agencies. The MoEF is the 'nodal agency in the administrative structure of the Central Government (sic) for the planning, promotion, co-ordination and overseeing the implementation of India's forest policies and programmes' (Government of India 2013: 1).

The forest departments are part of the state governments and their stated functions are determined by a document of Maharashtra government. The three-fold specifications are protection, conservation and development of forests, scientific management of forests, and research, extension and education (Government of Maharashtra 2013). Thus, while the MoEF plays a key role in formulation of policy and design of programmes, it is the state level FD that implements the initiatives of the MoEF. Also, it is clear that the functions of FD are mainly related to protection (policing), scientific management and research and development, which minimises the scope for people-oriented programmes. Extension is the only stated objective that directly deals with people:

> To create awareness of populace for best land use, for raising, fuel, fodder, crops on available waste land not under active cultivation, promote farm forestry, social forestry, participate in watershed management carried out for integrated development of the area, eco-development works now being introduced to promote and motivate populace for joint forest management, create infrastructure for sustenance of the developed areas (Government of Maharashtra 2013: 3).

There are various other sister concerns of FD such as state forest development corporations, minor forest produce corporations, etc. that look after subsidiary (commercial) activities of the forest administration. Further research and academic institutions like Forest Research Institutes, Indian Institute of Forest Management, and Wildlife Institute of India are engaged in various scientific and managerial research, education and training works. Often, the findings of scientific research have been used by political and apolitical stakeholders. Such organisations and the individual actors associated with the academics have also taken a standpoint either matching with conservationist or livelihood or commercial perspective.

The civil society organisations or non-governmental organisations (NGOs) are a recent addition to the forest affairs in India. They had no official function until the national forest policy that brought in the concept of a facilitating role of NGOs. In the joint forest management (JFM) the NGOs mostly take up training and facilitating activities. Some have become service providers for soft activities (hard activities are policing and plantations that are done by the FD). The radical NGOs undertake advocacy that include campaigning for community's rights, mobilisation of community to take up the rights issues.

The international agencies like World Bank not only finance the forest development projects but also influence the forest policies. Bilateral projects like those financed by the Swedish International Development Agency (SIDA) are also of similar nature, while international NGOs like Oxfam and Greenpeace promote activism.

The forest-related bureaucracy is selected by an all-India service named Indian Forest Service (IFS). This is a cadre-based and extremely hierarchical personnel structure. Originally established in the 1860s, the IFS cadres have been the flag-bearers of the FD in particular and the forest administration in general. In 1966 the service was reorganised (Singh et al., 2007). The hierarchical behaviour of the forest bureaucracy can be attributed to the policing function that is oriented with a culture similar to police or armed forces having a strict hierarchical and authoritative system. In fact, the field-level officials to the rank of Rangers have a *khaki* uniform that looks like that of police personnel. At ministry level, both at state and centre, however there are secretaries who are not from IFS, rather they are from the Indian Administrative Service (IAS) cadre. At district level also the District Collector, who is an IAS officer, has the coordinating role for all the departments that includes FD.

Evolution of Forest Policies and Laws in India

Colonial Days

Before the British rule in India, forests were either under community control or under the kings who used it for hunting. At that time, the demand of forest produce was also not very high. Only after the industrial revolution started, and the British ran out of wood in its home and in South Africa, India became the source of wood that the British government needed to build rails and for other industrial use. In this context the British government issued various policies to make a way for increasing its control over the forests.

The first law was the Indian Forest Act of 1865, subsequently in 1878, 1894, and 1927 various acts or policies were issued. The objective of these laws was to restrict the rights of people and to bring in complete control over forests. In terms of implementation, Saravanan (2003) in a paper on colonial regime and forest policies mentioned that the district collector and conservator played key role in bringing in the tribal forests under colonial control.

However, Gupta (2005) mentions that the nationalised land under the control of revenue department were a roadblock for the FD; hence it wanted full control over the forest land. Thus the effort was to suggest for more and more power for FD. This is primarily the reason why the 1978 act brought more teeth for the FD despite opposition by the Brandis. Brandis was in favour of providing rights to community. But people like Baden-Powell wanted a greater control for FD (Guha 1996 in Gupta 2005).

There are multiple opinions, however, on the factors that led to alienation of community's rights. While Gadgil and Guha (1992) attribute it primarily to the commercial interests, Gupta (2005: 58) says that 'European theoretical concepts viewed all forest land belonging to crown'. This further led to use of various western concepts of property rights that made requirements like of permits for grazing. This increased the transaction cost of people but decreased that of the government; while the British saw it as a national property, people in India considered forests as commons (Gupta 2005). The scientific management focus of forestry has also been brought in by Richard Groves (cited in Weil 2006).

Post-Independence Forest Laws

After Independence the policy did not change much except for the passage of a new national forest policy 1952. This policy was scientific management oriented but retained the commercial intent. This probably was not under organisational influence. The Nehruvian policy looked for the state as a promoter of industries; private players were not significant enough. Thus industry interest was not much different from the public interest. Thus the MoEF/FD had a clear focus which earlier was missing.

The National Commission of Agriculture 1976 further highlighted the need for production forestry and it even considered the privileges of forest produces given to the rural people as free supply, and cited this as the cause of forest destruction.[1] To reverse this phenomenon, a mechanism like social forestry was suggested (Government of India 1976).

All these had devastating effects on forest cover. This was explained in policy circles as a result of 'decentralised' nature of forest regime. Forest was a state subject. When the country was under the infamous Emergency, the Congress government, through the 42nd Constitutional Amendment, brought forest into the concurrent list. The role of Indira Gandhi in taking up environmental issues has also come for special mention. She had a pro-environment attitude and during her tenure as prime minister many conservation-oriented legislations including Wildlife (Protection) Act, 1972, and Forest Conservation Act, 1980, were passed. She won the International Union of Conservation of Nature award for her initiatives (Singh et al., 2007). While the subsequent government reversed many provisions of the 42nd Constitutional Amendment, the position of forests in the concurrent list was not altered. This indicates that this issue had strong organisational back up, otherwise such radical changes would not cut across party lines (particularly in the exceptional political situation of late 1970s).

The passage of Forest Conservation Act, 1980, (FCA) was a contentious issue. It brought in some clauses that provided extremely high amount of power to the forest bureaucracy. In fact, the major opposition at that time was from within; departments dealing with industries knew that restrictions on forest land would put difficulties in construction of roads, rails and laying transmission lines. Further, industries also required a large amount of forest land as that was the easiest route for land acquisition. Informal sources say that the then Forest Secretary T.N. Seshan has played a crucial role in convincing other departments.

The FCA 1980 had tremendous impact: the rate of deforestation decreased immensely. Conversion of forest land for non-forest purposes decreased from 0.15 million ha to 0.016 million ha annually (TERI 1998: 102). But it also alienated the forest dwellers. There was an increased dispossession of tribal people and increased the hardship of them (Sachchidananda 2005) because of the cumulative effect of various forest policies that culminated after the FCA.

During post-1980s, there was discontent against the FCA, and subsequently against the government in the National Forest Policy, 1988, which for the first time in modern Indian history accepted the local people's participation in forest management. This policy was a result of 'deliberations among intellectuals, academicians, NGOs representing forest dependent communities' (Gupta 2005: 62) and government.

While the National Forest Policy, 1988, suggested a role for the NGOs that they can act as a catalyst to the JFM, the FD did not always accept them. They were part of various working group but the FD did not co-opt them out of genuine interest. Rather they were forced to bring in NGOs to look fair (Arora 1994). However, it is clear that the FD people lacked participatory skills and hence NGOs coming in a big way fulfilled this gap (Potter 1996). The latest policy in this regard is that the FRA brought in 2006 would recognise the rights of community over forest land. This was largely due to the influence of civil society and international donors.

Actors and their Roles in Forest Policy and Implementation

Indian Forest Service

One of the interesting features in the Indian forest history is the existence and abiding influence of IFS over matters pertaining to forest. The IFS was established in 1860s and it continued in the same form as existed after Independence. In 1966, it was reorganised to its present form. It continues to be an all-India service (similar to that of Indian Administrative Service, Indian Police Service). The identity of IFS has been seen as 'negative' in the participatory regime of forest management (Hannam 1999).

In general, members of the Indian Forest Service thought of villagers as beneficiaries to be spoken for rather than treated as equals, or alternatively saw them as 'the problem' or 'the destroyers of government forests' (Hannam 1999: 228)

Hannam takes the 'negative' view from IFS from Gadgil and Guha (1992; 1995). They are the same authors who narrated the positive approach of D. Brandis, the founder of the forest service in India. According to Gadgil and Guha (1992), the Brandis, the first Inspector General of Forests was not in favour of complete control to be exercised by state. During his visit to various parts of India he had observed the effectiveness of community-based approaches and hence, was strongly in favour of community's rights to be a better mechanism than state control.

A question arises as to how the IFS over a period of time could develop an anti-people image. Why the behaviour of IFS in particular and FD had undergone such a dramatic change over time? Weil (2006) discusses Groves' conceptualisation of IFS as proponent of scientific management, stating that this was the root of modern environmentalism. However, Weil has further added that by the 19th century the colonial state turned to commercial forestry and conformed to

Gadgil and Guha (1992)'s analysis. Further, in the early 19th century the standing of FD was enhanced because it provided better financial results (Weil 2006: 327). With better revenue contribution the credibility of the department was enhanced and hence it was natural that the forest officials would be in favour of commercialisation. After the Independence, the focus of scientific management reverted probably because of changing political and international scenario. However, the exact path of the change in focus is still not very clear.

Donors' Roles

Donor agencies have been quite influential. Lele (2002) pointed out that support of donors played a key role in promoting JFM. Even government orders have been issued under such pressures. Matt and Kerr (2007) says that in Tamil Nadu the FD introduced the JFM approach only where the externally funded projects was running. Although the JFM guidelines inculcated participatory approaches, but that did not mean that the FD had accepted this by heart. According to Saxena (1995) such contents were put because of World Bank's pressure. However, the influence of donors did not always have positive outcomes. Funded projects often did not have a post-project mechanism (Kumar 2002). Project-based approaches, often pushed by international funding agencies on the pretext of building efficiency in governmental operations focus on limited areas rather than having comprehensive and holistic interventions. It was revealed that these approaches increased pressure on non-JFM areas, while JFM-intervened areas were saved from degradation (Matta and Kerr 2007).

NGOs Role in Policy Sphere

As mentioned earlier, NGOs have played the role of activists or facilitators. While the facilitating roles of NGOs have been appreciated by FD officials, Matta and Kerr (2007) mention that they found the local trusts and religions bodies to be more effective. Further, when there is convergence of resources of FD and NGOs the outcomes were quite encouraging. However, the FD has never been in favour of the activist organisations and even those worked for policy advocacy. Korten (1992) says that such dislikes arise because the NGOs question the basic assumptions of government authority.

It has earlier been mentioned that in the formulation of National Forest Policy, 1988, NGOs played an active role. Many NGOs contributed significantly to implementation of JFM. But the role of NGOs in highlighting the need of FRA has particularly drawn our attention. When in 2002, the Supreme Court of India issued a directive to evict all encroachments, the FD started a nation-wide drive towards eviction of forest dwellers. Many NGOs, however, came forward and stood by the people. Finally, the MoEF relented and recognised the rights of forest dwellers. Ultimately, the Ministry of Tribal Affairs was made the nodal agency for drafting the FRA Bill. Even after this there were several campaigns allegedly carried out with support of forest bureaucracy to exaggerate the negative consequences of FRA including that of abetting climate change (Gopalakrishnana, undated). This must be noted that NGOs are not a homogeneous group and there are NGOs that support the other side too. However, in general, the tone of NGOs has been pro-people.

Other Organisations

After the 73rd Constitutional Amendment the panchayati raj institutions were provided more authority over local resources including forest produces. However, the FD officials favoured independent institutions for JFM rather than integrating it with the panchayatiraj system (Matta and Kerr 2007). The Ministry of Tribal Affairs played a key role in drafting the FRA, but it did not have the forest bureaucracy by its side and that probably was responsible for its neutral or pro-tribal image.

The research agencies have also been associated with forest-related policy discourses. The remote sensing establishment, for example, brought in the issue of decreasing forest cover. Organisations like Forest Research Institutes have primarily focussed the production or conservationist point of view. Universities also have various disciplines – the social science disciplines have generally taken a pro-people stance, while the scientific disciplines have focussed more on conservationist approach.

The Identity Question

Tribal identity in India is one of the important contemporary issues. Much of the changes in forest policies have been, no doubt, propelled by the emergence of tribal identity and recognition of tribal rights. But this issue is not the focus of this paper as the policy changes have rather bluntly favoured the tribal communities. It would have been more desirable to look into the reasons why such changes were not recognised by the policy implementors.

While the forest bureaucracy, as discussed above, has evolved to be a hierarchical and headstrong entity, there have been parallel changes in policy space to progressively recognise the tribal rights. These two things do not go hand in hand. Recognising tribal rights and handing over the control of forest management to them is definitely going to decrease the power of forest bureaucracy. As discussed earlier, the FD has earned its identity of self-sufficient organisation, which has strengthened its legally backed role of protector of forests. Consequently, when the FD encountered the tribals, who were the traditional users of forests and were in demands of forest rights, they later were dealt with in an antagonistic manner.

Béteille (1967; 1998) discusses various aspects of tribal identity that include habitation (hills and forests), culture and language. But the FD identifies them as an impediment, as a challenger to its own identity. In order to maintain its own identity as the protector of forests in India, the FD has sought to strengthen its hold again and again irrespective of the policy changes in favour of the tribals.

Thus, for the sake of maintaining its own identity, the FD and the forest bureaucracy have tried to oppose the pro-tribal forest policies time and again. This is an interesting proposition because the organisational space is only supposed to be the implementer of forest policies rather than pursuing its own ends. Without making a case for it, this proposition demands serious attention from all quarters.

Concluding Remarks

Based on the discussion made in the above sections, it can be concluded that organisational stakeholders have their share of influences in forest policy formulation and its implementation. While the FD is the agency to implement forest policies, it is also responsible for resisting attempts to shift emphasis from conservation to people-oriented regime. In pursuing the objective of maintaining its own identity of self-sufficient and headstrong organisation, FD has blocked the path of proper implementation of pro-tribal forest programmes and policies.

This shows that the Weberian view of neutral bureaucracy does not work in the present situation. Organisations do have their own preferences in determining policy directions. The organisational culture of FD also must be seen in this context. The IFS as a strong and powerful bureaucracy has its own interest in legitimising its interests. Ultimately, it transpires that public interest is not one-directional. The national interest vis-à-vis forests, has been viewed from various perspectives – conservation, livelihoods, and commercial. No wonder, the bureaucracy would like to stick to the position that helps its own power structure. This pattern of behaviour matches with Mishra's observation that bureaucracy often tries to align the policies to meet its own interest (2010).

Allison (1971) points out that the organisations go by their standard procedures and that they need not necessarily match with the national or public interest. The Forest Department and associated agencies are one of the oldest administrative agencies. It would be hard to define them in terms of rigid implementation of policies, particularly when it contradicts some of their standard procedures. Putting the blame squarely on FD would be illogical. The FD has to work on a contradicting platform. What happens when the policies are not clear and how does a bureaucrat decide? Lipsky (1980) points out that the street level bureaucrats have their discretionary powers and they have to manage according to the local requirements. According to Etzioni (1960), the state public goal is often different from the private goals that the organisational actors adhere to. Hence, such realities must be kept in mind while designing policies, particularly those looking for a paradigm shift.

The following propositions and research questions come out of the above discussion that would be relevant for future research and its implications:

Firstly, organisational influences on forest policies are deeply entrenched in its cultural traits. Hence, it would be naïve to consider the FD as simply implementation of any policy regime. Before such policy regimes are changed, there must be sufficient structural changes in the existing arrangements. For example, while explaining the link between ecology and society, it has been pointed out that one cannot be overstressed at the expense of the other. Secondly, when faced with contradictions, the actor would tend to go for convenience rather than striving for rational decision. The increment list view of policy has been highlighted since long. But this has to be recognised with all seriousness. Thirdly, the issue of cultural changes and how the original policy thoughts of the founders of FD were diluted have been touched upon in this paper. But more in-depth analysis of how the FD has evolved over time needs to be taken up.

Kauffman (1955), while looking at the administrative behaviour of forest service in the United States, had pointed out that there were centrifugal forces in the organisations and it needed specific structural and normative efforts to bring together the organisations to a common platform. Any long-term change in the administration of forests should be backed by associated and consistent efforts to bring structural and cultural changes in the organisational space itself. Probably that would help in bringing a smooth transition from a hierarchical bureaucracy to a more people-oriented bureaucracy.

Note

1. So clearly is this stated that I fall short words to put in my own terms. This sentence is paraphrased from the original as given in Government of India (1976: 25).

References

Allison, G.T. 1971. *Essence of Decision: Explaining the Cuban Missile Crisis*. Boston: Little, Brown and Company.

Arora, D. 1994. 'From State Regulation to People's Participation: Case of Forest Management in India', *Economic and Political Weekly*, 29 (12): pp. 691–698.

Béteille, A. 1967. 'Race and Descent as Social Categories in India', *Daedalus*, 96 No. 2: pp. 444–463.

Béteille, A. 1998. 'The Idea of Indigenous People', *Current Anthropology*, 39, No. 2: pp. 187–192.

Etzioni, A. 1960. 'Two Approaches to Organisational Analysis: A Critique and a Suggestion', *Administrative Science Quarterly*, 5, No. 2: pp. 257–78.

Gadgil, M., and R. Guha. 1992. *This Fissured Land: An Ecological History of India*. New Delhi: Oxford University Press.

Gadgil, M., and R. Guha. 1995. *Ecology and Equity: The Use and Abuse of Nature in Contemporary India:* London: Routledge.

Gopalakrishnan, S. (undated). The Forest Rights Act and the Resource Struggle for India's Forest Rights Act. http://www.academia.edu/251471/The_Forest_Rights_Act_and_the_Resource_Struggle_in_Indias_Forests. Last accessed 30 January 2014

Government of India. 1976. *Forestry,* National Commission on Agriculture: Part IX. New Delhi: Government of India.

Government of India. 2013. *Annual Report: 2012–13.* New Delhi: MoEF.

Government of Maharashtra, 2013. *Maharashtra Forest Manual 2013*, Vol. I (Draft for Approval).Online: http://www.mahaforest.nic.in/fckimagefile/05-MFM-Vol%20I%20_Draft%20for%20approval_.pdf. Last accessed 18 January 2014.

Gupta, K. 2005. *The Political Economy of Forest Management: Importance of Institutions and Social Capital*. New Delhi: Associated Publishers Pvt. Ltd.

Hannam, K. 1999. 'Environmental Management in India: Recent Challenges to the Indian Forest Service', *Journal of Environmental Planning and Management* 42 (2): pp. 221–233.

Kauffman, H. 1955. *The Forest Ranger: A Study in Administrative Behavior.* Washington DC: RFF Press.

Korten, F.F. 1955. 'NGOs and Forestry Sector: An Overview'. *Unasylva*,171: pp. 3–10.

Kumar, S. 2002. 'Does Participation in Common Pool Resource Management Help Poor? A Social Cost Benefit Analysis of Joint Forest Management in Jharkhand, India', *World Development*, 30, No. 5: pp. 763–782.

Lele, S. 2000. 'Godsend, Sleight of Hand, or Just Muddling through: Joint Water and Forest Management in India', *Natural Resource Perspectives*, No. 53.

Lindblom, C.E. 1959. 'The Science of Muddling Through', *Public Administration Review*, 19, No. 2: pp. 79–88.

Lipsky, M. 1980. *Street-level Bureaucracy: Dilemma of the Individual in Public Services*. New York: Russel Sage Foundation.

Matta, J.R., and J. Kerr. 2007. 'Barriers beyond the Partners: Bureaucratic and Political Constraints to Implementing Joint Forest Management in Tamil Nadu, India', *Environment, Development and Sustainability*, 9: pp. 465–479.

Mishra, P.K., and S. Raghavan. 2008. 'Feasibility of Tropical Pine in Koraput, Orissa', *The Indian Forester*, 134, No. 4: pp. 542–548.

Mishra, P.K. 2010. 'Dilution Process of Policy Implementation Strategy: An Analysis of Changes in the Guidelines for Watershed Development Programmes in India', *International Journal of Rural Management*, 6, No. 2: pp. 243–263.

Pressman, J.L. and A. Wildavsky, 1973. Implementation. Berkely CA: University of California Press.

Potter, D. 1996. 'Democratisation and the Environment: NGOs and Deforestation Policies in India (Karnataka) and Indonesia (North Sumatra)', *Journal of Commonwealth and Comparative Politics*, 34, No. 1: pp. 1–37.

Sachhidananda. 2005. 'Impact of Forest Laws on Livelihood System with Particular Reference to Tribal Customs and Natural Resources in Schedule V Areas'. In *Dispute Resolution, Tribal Customs, and Forest Laws (A series on Self-governance for Tribals, Vol. II)*. Edited by S K Singh. Hyderabad: NIRD.

Saravanan, V. 2003. 'Colonial Commercial Forest Policy and Tribal Private Forests in Madras Presidency: 1792–1881', *Indian Economic Social History Review*, 40: pp. 403–423.

Saxena, N. 1999. *Towards Sustainable Forestry in the UP Hills: Draft for Comments*, Moussorie: LBSNA, 1995. Cited in Hannam 1999.

Singh, M.P., J.K. Singh, R. Mohanka, and R.B. Shah. 2007. *Forest, Environment and Biodiversity*. New Delhi: Daya Publishing House.

Sharma, B.D. 1989. *The Web of Poverty*. Shillong: North Eastern Hill University.

TERI. 1998. *Looking Back to Think Ahead*, New Delhi: Tata Energy Research Institute.

Weil, B. 2006. 'Exploitation and Cultural Change in the Indian Forest Service, 1875–1927'. *Environmental History*, 11, No. 2: pp. 319–343.

CHAPTER 11

Making Forest Dwellers Deprived

Examining Implementation Process of Forest Rights Act, 2006 in India

BIDHAN KANTI DAS

The forest cover in India is not improving despite implementation of Wild Life Protection Act 1972 (WLPA; modified in 2002) to conserve forest biodiversity by creating national parks and sanctuaries. In fact, after more than 37 years of launching the 'Project Tiger' in 1973 with 1827 tigers (as per Tiger Census 1972), tiger population has dwindled to 1411 in 28 tiger reserves (Bijoy 2011). In addition, there are other acts and rules that specifically aim to conserve forest resources, of which mention may particularly of the Forest Conservation Act, 1980.

Historically, relationship between tribals and forests was characterised by co-existence, where tribals were considered to be integral to the survival and sustainability of ecological system. This symbiotic relationship was acknowledged and crystallised as customary rights over forest products. These rights were not recognised and recorded by the government while consolidating state forests during colonial period as well as after Independence. This led to insecurity of tenure and threat of eviction, leading to alienation of tribals from their ancestral land. This historical injustice was further exacerbated by WLPA 1972 and FCA 1980. Due to historical forest rights deprivation, there exists a strong co-relation between forests, tribal habitation and poverty (Poffenberger et al., 1998).

However, to undo this injustice, some inclusive measures were initiated, like Joint Forest Management (JFM), 1990, guidelines under National Forest Policy 1988, Panchayats (Extension to the Scheduled Areas) Act (PESA) 1996, etc. But the introduction of the 'Scheduled Tribes and other Traditional Forest Dwellers (recognition of forest rights) Act 2006', popularly known as the Forest Rights Act (FRA) 2006, is perhaps the most important step that challenges the 'Eminent Domain' of the state, intends to undo historical injustice over land rights, and tries to empower forest dwellers for their own governance. The present study tries to examine how far the legal enactments have actually translated into reality at the implementation level.

The main question is, how far and to what extent the tribals and other forest dwellers could get their rights established, particularly in relation to FRA 2006? An attempt has been made here to reveal how rules and procedures framed by forest bureaucrats and conservationists actually lead to denial of rights to forest dwellers and tribals. For this, FRA 2006 will be the case of analysis.

Forest bureaucracy always sees 'forest' as a national property and believes that forests can be saved only through 'command and control' approach. They also believe that FRA 2006 will destroy dwindling forest resources in India, and undo whatever success that was achieved through implementation of WLPA 1972 and other forest conservation acts and rules. Based on this assumption, the present study tries to identify what actually is happening in the field. It tries to answer such a question as who are the real destroyers of the forests: forest bureaucracy or tribals. Lastly, an attempt is made to find why the forest bureaucracy is so keen on denying the rights to forest dwellers. Why does the forest bureaucracy believe that forests can only be saved without human interference? For this, various secondary materials, government records, status reports of some NGOs, etc. have been analysed.

The paper is organised as follows. The following section traces the events that led to emergence of Forest Rights Act. It also discusses some major provisions under the act. The third section deals with analyses of the implementation status of FRA across India based mainly on secondary data. The fourth section shows how conservationists and forest bureaucrats are denying access to rights provided under FRA by subtly changing the rules framed for implementation of the act. The last section discusses the possible causes for poor implementation of FRA.

Tracing Historical Roots of the Forest Rights Act

Historically, tribals and other forest-dependent communities in India have been deprived of rights over forest lands. They have been systematically excluded from their original habitat through some legislative measures in both pre- and post-Independence India. The application of these measures has been expropriated and the right to live in and use the forest as a livelihood and as grazing land, has been negated (Sivaramakrishnan 1999; Bijoy and Raman 2003; Ghosh 2007), thereby contributing to the marginalisation of millions forest-adjacent and forest-dwelling communities (Sarin 2003).

The forest rights deprivation started in the 19th century under the British regime, when the British started reserving and restricting forest use for commercial exploitation for continuous supply of timber for railway sleepers and ship-building and through legislative measures, such as the Indian Forest Act 1927 (Springate-Baginski et al., 2009). This reservation involved appropriation of customary forest lands of tribals through a 'settlement' process. The Imperial Forest Department created 'reserved forests' in areas where the timber was valued highly, extinguishing rights. The areas where forests were perceived as less valuable, the 'protected forests' were established, where some 'privileges' were conceded (Springate-Baginski et al., 2012). As a result, conflicts, repeated agitations and uprisings intensified, which were ruthlessly suppressed by the administration (Grove et al., 1998; Sivaramkrishnan 1999; Pathak 2002). Despite resistance of colonial policies, policies in independent India have not been changed. Rather, state forest policies and land annexation processes continued as per 1927 Indian Forest Act. In fact, in many cases the condition of tribals and forest-dependent communities has worsened, as 'due processes of settlement of rights were generally forgotten in the post-Independence takeover of remaining feudal private forests' (Springate-Baginski et al., 2012). However, administrators of both colonial and post-colonial India have taken some legislative measures to provide local rights over forest use. For example, the Indian Forest Act 1927 (particularly Section 28 providing for 'village forests'), the Indian Constitution, specifically Schedule V and VI for protection and governance of forest resources by tribal communities; the Ministry of Environment and Forests (MoEF) guidelines of 18 September 1990 for resolving conflicts with tribals and other forest dwellers related to forest land as well the national Forest Policy 1988; and the PESA 1996, which provided for self-governance based on their customs and traditions in Schedule V Areas, including management of community resources and ownership of non-timber forest products (ibid.). These provisions, however, were not properly implemented due to apparent resistance from highly centralised, bureaucratic forest department in India.

The policy-makers and administrators in independent India continued to follow the legislative and management structure, including the Indian Forest Act 1927, of colonial administration in managing forest resources. The post-colonial governments failed to resolve tenurial conflicts of colonial regime (MoEF 2004). Instead, the forest area increased from 40.48 million hectares in 1951 to 69.63 million hectares in 2008 (Kashwan 2013). But forest people who have been living in these areas long before the Imperial Forest department came into existence, still live on and cultivate these forest lands (Sarin 2005). Researchers have identified various reasons like blanket declaration of legal forests under IFA 1927 (Sarin 2005; Kumar et al., 2005), non-recognition of customary land use such as shifting cultivation and hunting-gathering, poor settlement of forest rights (Kumar et al., 2005) and administrative confusion over the status of land (Ghosh 2007; Kumar et al., 2005). Similarly, various policies and legislative measures between 1960s and 1970s have been introduced for curtailing the rights over major non-timber forest products (NTFPs), which constitute an important part of the livelihoods of forest-dependent communities. A more stringent exclusionary measure has been taken to stop interference on the forest reserve through introduction of Wildlife Protection Act 1972. In India; over 65 per cent of the Protected Areas (PAs) were characterised by human settlements and resource use (Kothari et al., 1989). A recent estimate suggests that there were 3.7 million people living within the protected area network in India (TTF 2005). They are deprived of all sorts of service provisions and access to resources. Similarly, enactment of the Forest Conservation Act 1980 provided legal provision to disapprove forest land for non-forestry purpose. The MoEF

issued a series of circulars in 1990 under Forest Conservation Act (FCA) 1980, to address the problem of non-recognition of rights on forest land, but the efforts were mostly unsuccessful (Sarin 2005). Despite this legal provision, forest lands have been diverted for mining and large-scale industrial projects, resulting in forced displacement of forest-dwelling people. According to MoEF (2004), 9.8 lakh hectares of forests have been diverted for 11,282 projects since 1980, out of which over 1.6 lakh hectares are for mines alone. In 3 years, about 300 mining projects have led to over 20,000 hectares of forest being cleared. According to Centre for Science and Environment, between 2007 to 2011, MoEF granted 2,04,425 hectares of forest land for mining, industrial and other development projects. Only 1.7 per cent of forest lands diverted during the period were related to 'social services, rehabilitation and human settlement' (Kashwan 2013). In the absence of land titles, forest-dependent communities failed to get compensation. On the other hand, hundreds of thousands of families, whose ancestors lost their rights over property usage, including residences, cultivations, a variety of customary rights and access to forest products, due to several legal measures, continue to be regarded as 'encroachers' on their own lands in the forest department records (Gadgil and Guha 1989; MoEF 2004). In addition, FCA severely curtailed the ability of forest-dependent communities to claim rights to the pre-existing cultivations and homesteads. In many cases, entire villages – located inside the erroneously demarcated boundaries of forest lands – were recorded as 'forest villages', which naturally came under the jurisdiction of forest administration (Shah 2005). As a result, communities were deprived of essential services like drinking water, health, education, all-weather roads and governmental development schemes from civil administration (Kumar and Kant 2005; Springate-Baginski and Blaikie 2007).

These systematic intervention of institutional regimes results in exclusion of the forest people from forest resources that leads to widespread poverty and causes marginalisation of such people. It is further reinforced through the dynamics of inter-regional and intra-regional inequities (Baviskar 1994). An estimate suggests that of about 300 million people living below poverty line in India, about 200 million people are partially or wholly dependent on forest resources for their livelihoods (Khare et al., 2000). The World Bank estimated that about 84 per cent of the tribal groups live in forested landscapes and are forest dwellers (2006). So, legal recognition of pre-existing forest land cultivations and homesteads, as well as access, protection and management of forests, is vital for improving socio-economic condition.

The growing crisis of forest loss despite forest legislations, emerging violent conflicts between forest department and local people and the huge diversion of forest lands for industrial and development projects, led to consideration of some concessions. At the end of the 1980s, the forest department launched joint forest management policy as a strategy to involve local people's help in the protection of their faltering plantation efforts based on Arabari experiments in south-west Bengal. According to a mutual agreement, local people were informally allowed access to NTFPs (with some reservations), a share of revenue from forest department's timber felling, and sometimes wage labour opportunities (Springate-Baginski et al., 2012). This model was finally endorsed in the National Forest Policy, 1988, which rapidly spread with donor encouragement and was formalised nationally in the 1990 JFM Order of the MoEF. But the Order suggests that JFM agreements were ad hoc administrative decrees, without any legal basis. Due to lack of legal protection of rights, the forest departments (FDs) of states unilaterally alter benefit-sharing mechanisms, by issuing new executive orders (Springate-Baginski and Blaikie 2007). In effect, FDs are capturing major share of forest productivity, which is attributable to the participating local people (Vernon and Fehr 2011). Further, the FDs have used the JFM programmes as instruments to further expand their authority by, firstly, imposing their management plans on village forests, and secondly, generating funding support from donor agencies and even expanding their staffing and salary structures (Springate-Baginski et al., 2009). Though conflicts have reduced and forest wealth has improved to a certain extent, benefits for livelihood sustenance are still meagre, which is even negligible for women and the poor among the marginalised groups. This discourages the people about JFM at the village level. In the project-based JFM programme, people's interest continues till availability of wage labour continues and diminishes after the project ends. In fact, a World Bank study concludes that participants of JFM were 'reduced to mere labourers, hired mainly to plant trees' (World Bank 2005). Though more than 1,00,000 forest protection committees have been formed in India, less than half remain active, primarily due to disillusionment. Many researchers argued that in most cases the state forest departments used international aid for JFM programme to reinforce and even expand the de jure forest boundaries demarcated during colonial times (Sundar 2001, Springate-Baginski and Blaikie 2007). Such attempts by the state forest departments reached an unprecedented level in 2002.

The first real drive for the FRA came in the year 2002 when the MoEF issued a directive on 3 May 2002 for forest departments to evict all so-called 'encroachers' ineligible for regularisation by 30 September 2002 (MoEF 2002). This order identified an area of 12,50,000 hectares under encroachments spread across eight states. The MoEF admitted in 2004 that between May 2002 and August 2004, people occupying an estimated 1,52,000 ha of forest land had been evicted (PIB 2004). More than 3,00,000 families of tribal and non-tribal forest dwellers had been forcefully evicted (CSD 2003; Dreze 2005). Media reports estimated that evictions would eventually cover about 10 million tribal and non-tribal forest dwellers (Kaur 2002). More than a hundred villages were burnt in Madhya Pradesh, eight people were killed in police firings, and 40,000 families were left homeless in Assam. The forest departments employed elephants to crush mud-thatch houses in Assam, Maharashtra and Kerala (CSD 2003). The FDs and police force fired at women and children participating in anti-eviction agitations (Dréze 2005). This led to a massive uproar and protests, and the MoEF had to intervene to stop the process. The large eviction drive created mass-scale mobilisation of forest-dependent communities into popular movements across the country. It resulted in a loosely united campaign of various civil society activists and organisations across 10 states coalesced into the Campaign for Survival and Dignity (CSD). The CSD became a key player and interlocutor for the forest rights issue at the national level.

The forceful eviction became the major political issue in 2004 parliamentary election as the major political parties promised legislations to recognise the rights of tribal and forest-dependent communities to gain support (MoEF and MoTA 2010). The CSD and other organisations working on forest rights mounted pressure on the newly elected government led by the United Progressive Alliance to fulfil its promises. The new central government administration formed the National Advisory Council (NAC), which recommended the government to pass a law to provide land rights and other user rights to forest dwellers (Kumar and Kerr 2012). The prime minister asked the Ministry of Tribal Affairs (MoTA), instead of the MoEF, to prepare a draft bill to recognise rights of forest-dependent communities after a meeting on 19 January 2005 at the Prime Minister's Office. It was also decided that a technical support group would be created to help MoTA to draft the bill (Kumar and Kerr 2012). This was a major shift, as a result of protests from various forests rights organisations like the CSD and the National Forum of Forest People and Forest Workers. Then it took years of heated debate and oppositions between various stakeholders like CSD, conservation NGOs and the forest bureaucracy for finalisation of Forest Rights Bill, which was finally passed in the Parliament in December 2006.

The stakeholders have clearly divided themselves into two broader alliance groups. One alliance group strongly favoured the status quo based on conservation ideas, while the other wanted to undo historical injustices on tribals and forest-dependent communities (Sarin and Springate-Baginski 2010; MoTA and MoEF 2010). The related government departments – MoTA and MoEF – were in conflict on ideological ground and the problem was sorted out by the prime minister himself (MoTA and MoEF 2010). Civil society organisations and promoters of rights advocated better deals for forest dwellers based on arguments of democratic rights, poverty alleviation and improved incentive for conservation, whereas the pro-conservation alliance based its campaign on the ideas of wildlife and nature conservation (Bose 2010). It has been argued that the powerful conservationist lobby unleashed a major 'media misinformation campaign' (Kumar and Kerr 2012). In fact, data and information provided by parties for and against the bill varied to a great extent. The proposed bill, it is argued by the 'against' group, could lead to a loss of 15 per cent of India's forest cover while the pro-rights group argued that it dealt only with 2 per cent of India's forest land (Bose 2010). But intense pressure from pro-rights groups and their political ramifications in following elections in 2004 meant that the act was finally passed in the Parliament in 2006. However, the act and rules under FRA were strongly contested by both the 'for' and 'against' groups. It is argued that the FRA is a much diluted version of what was proposed initially (Sarin and Springate-Baginski 2010).

Figure 11.1

Forests, Tribal Habitation and Poverty Concentration: Strong Co-relation

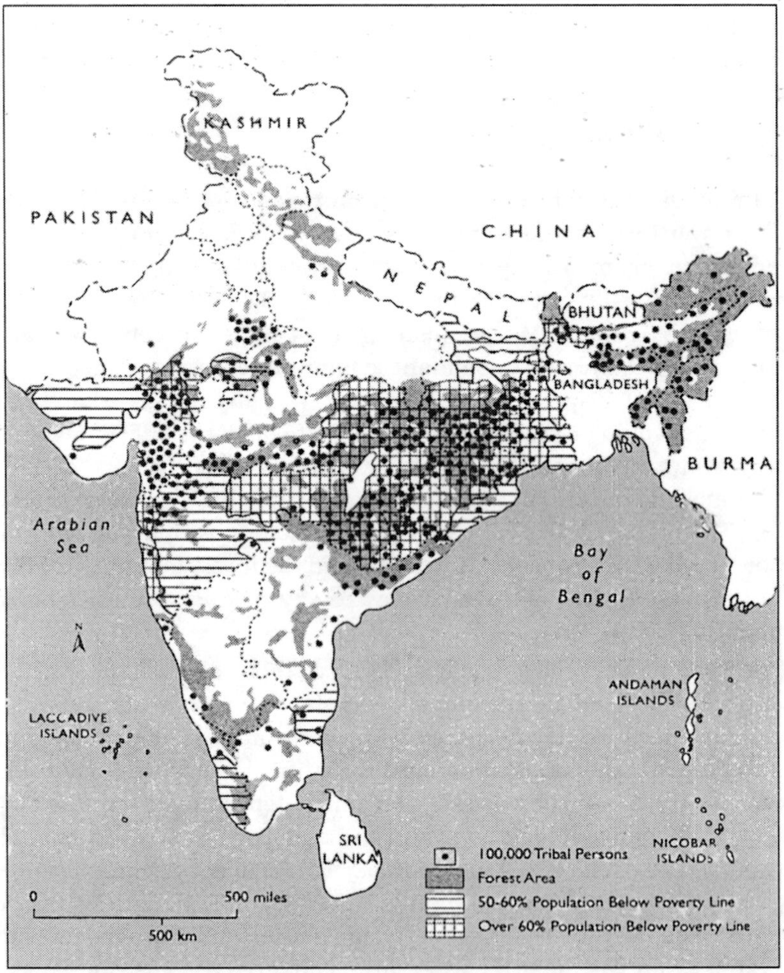

Source: Poffenberger and McGean 1998.

Major Provisions of the Act

The FRA seeks to address the historical injustices that have been done to forest-dwelling Scheduled Tribes and other traditional forest dwelling communities in the creation of forest lands in India. The act in its preamble categorically states its aim:

> 'To recognise and vest the forest rights and occupation in forest land in forest dwelling scheduled tribes and other traditional forest dwellers who have been residing in such forests for generations but whose rights could not be recorded (and); to provide for a framework for recording the forest rights so vested and the nature of evidence required for such recognition and vesting in respect of forest land' (Government of India 2006).

Under this act, members of Scheduled Tribes can claim rights, provided they have been residing in or dependent on forests prior to 13 December 2005. In addition, other traditional forest dwellers can also claim rights provided they have been residing in the forest for at least 75 years prior to 13 December 2005. The rights conferred are heritable but not alienable or transferable. The act contains various rights broadly categorised as:

- *Land rights:* Right to hold and live on forest land as an individual or community and to cultivate the land as a livelihood;
- *User rights:* Right to collect, own, use and dispose of minor forest products that have been traditionally collected within or outside village boundaries by forest dwellers; community rights such as cattle grazing on forest land; community rights to fishing and collecting other products from water;
- *Right to protect and conserve*: Right to protect, regenerate, conserve or manage any community forest resource that the community has traditionally protected and conserved for sustainable use;
- *Right to rehabilitation package*: Right to relocation and rehabilitation if evicted or displaced from forest land without providing legal entitlement to relocation or rehabilitation before 13 December 2005.

As per Section 6(1) of FRA 2006, the rights determination process is to be initiated at the community level by the Gram Sabha (village assembly), effectively overriding JFM committee. The final rights determination and preparation of a record of rights is to be vested on sub-divisional and district level committees with representation of both government officials and members of elected local self-government institutions (Section 6[3] to Section 6[9], FRA 2006). So, it is a multi-layered process of various authorities. It is the Gram Sabha that initiates the process to determine the nature and extent of individual or community forest rights, though the power of the final decision on the validity of a claim lies with the district-level committee headed by district magistrate (Dash and Kothari 2014). The implementation rests on discretion of the state-level implementing agencies.

Analysis and Discussion

FRA Implementation Status

Number of Claims Actually Accepted: Disparity in State level

Analysis of individual claims reveals that about three-fifth of the total individual claims have been accepted across India (Table 11.1). But it varies across states. The percentage of individual title distribution is lowest in Karnataka. Similarly, individual title distribution in relatively larger states with high forested landscapes is only about 40 per cent. In Madhya Pradesh, only one-third of individual claimants got land titles. However, relatively smaller states like Kerala and Tripura have performed better compared to larger states like Andhra Pradesh, Chhattisgarh, Gujarat, Maharashtra and West Bengal. The only exception is Odisha where three-fifth of individual claimants got title deeds (Table 11.1). So, overall there is high rejection rate across India with variation among states.

Table 11.1

State-wise Distribution, Extent of Rejection of Individual and Community Claims (as on 31.1.2015)

States	*Individual Claims*			*Community Claims*		
	No of Claims Received	*No of Titles Distributed*	*% of Rejection*	*No of Claims Received*	*No of Title Distributed*	*% of Rejection*
Andhra Pradesh	4,00,053	1,67,263	58.19	10,959	2,107	80.77
Assam	1,26,718	35,407	72.06	5,193	860	83.44
Chhattisgarh	8,17,809	3,36,590	58.84	N/A	N/A	N/A
Gujarat	1,82,869	68,769	62.40	7,182	3,856	46.32
Karnataka	2,56,104	7,604	97.03	4,575	96	97.90
Kerala	36,140	24,599	31.94	1,395	4	99.72
Madhya Pradesh	5,52,142	1,79,700	67.45	40,501	39,245*	03.10
Maharashtra	3,44,834	1,45,469	57.82	6,074	1,869	69.23
Odisha	5,97,222	3,41,999	42.74	12,500	3,474	72.21
Rajasthan	69,123	34,189	50.54	652	65	90.03
Tripura	1,82,340	1,20,418	33.96	277	55	80.15
Uttar Pradesh	92,512	17,654	80.92	1,123	834	25.74
Jharkhand	42,003	15,296	63.58	N/A	N/A	N/A
West Bengal	1,37,068	51,069+	62.74	3,241	108	96.67
Total	38,36,937	15,46,026	40.29	93,672	52,573	56.12

* 20635 claims ready for distribution + 16904 ready for distribution

Source: Ministry of Tribal Affairs, Govt. of India, 2015.

Figure 11.2

Year-wise Distribution of Land Titles Under FRA 2006

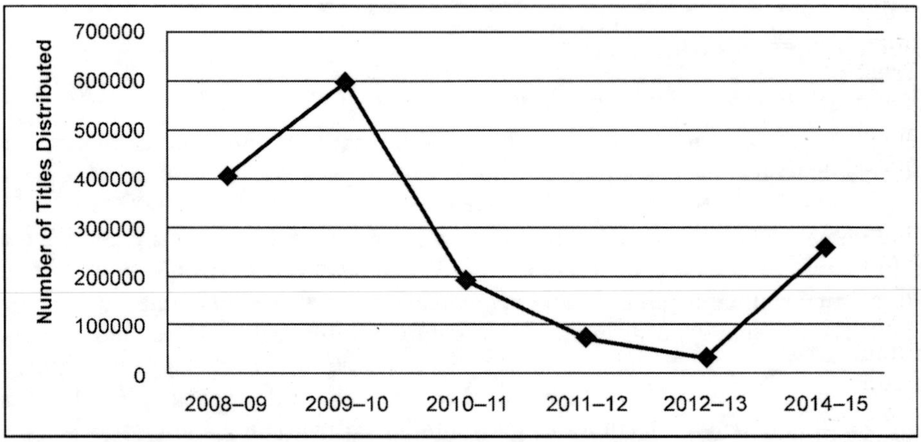

Note: Number of land titles of 2014–15 also includes 2013–14

Year-wise distribution of land titles revealed that title granting was at its peak in 2009–10, and drastically dropped in 2010–11. It further declines in the following years. But the granting of land titles increased to some extent in 2014–15 (Figure 11.2). The implementation of the act started in 2007 and got its momentum between 2008 and 2010. During this period, it is argued that major forest-bearing states went to general elections (Down to Earth 2013).

The Asian Indigenous Tribal Population Network (AITPN) has identified factors like Forest Rights Committee (FRC) formation at Panchayat level rather than Gram Sabha (habitation/village) level in several states, predominance of forest officials and obstruction caused by them during process of verification and decision-making at various levels, denial of proper hearing of claimants for their cases, systematic denial of reasonable opportunity to file petitions against the rejections before higher authorities, and non-communication of rejections to the claimants denying the right to appeal (AITPN 2012). Moreover, there is severe shortage of trained staff at local level in departments like tribal affairs and forest. The concerned departments have taken the implementation of FRA as an additional responsibility, which has led to slow progress and rejection of claims (MoEF and MoTA 2010). Others identified differences in objectives, attitudes and perceptions of concerned departments, leading to lack of coordination and high rate of rejections (Sathyapalan 2010). Low acceptance of claims might be due to high rejection of claims submitted by the 'other traditional forest dwellers', as they have to prove continuity of settlement for last three generations under the act. It is difficult to prove 75 years of settlement in most cases. In fact, claims of other traditional forest dwellers have not been considered for recognition in West Bengal (author's personal observation). In Odisha, it is one of the main reasons for rejection of two-thirds of the claims (Jena 2010).

Forest Land Distributed: Claim Versus Reality

During finalisation of the bill between 2004 and 2006, the conservationists, environmentalists, wildlife biologists and forestry administration vehemently criticised and opposed the bill on the plea that it would cause irreversible damage to wildlife. They claim that this act would result in handing over of 50 million hectares of the country's 67 million hectares of forests to tribals and other traditional forest dwellers (Saravanan 2009). A senior advisor of Wild Life Trust of India argued that empowering villagers to claim forest land would pockmark the heart of the tiger country and there simply won't be any forest anymore (Basu 2007). Some others pointedly called it a 'sell out to vote bank politics' (Munshi 2005).

On the other hand, MoEF, has expressed similar apprehension. It has objected on several counts. Firstly, giving power of land claims to Gram Sabhas would lead to local vested interests gaining control; secondly, the goal of bringing one-third of the country under tree cover under National Forest Policy 1988 would become impossible if 2.5 hectares of land is distributed to each forest dweller; thirdly, de-notification of vast areas of forest lands and elimination of legal protection for forest cover will have catastrophic effects on the ecological balance; and fourthly, more than 60 per cent of India's forests will be transferred to 8.2 per cent of its population (Dang 2005; Munshi 2005).

However, forest rights activists argued that the act would not distribute land, but only recognise their long occupational rights and give titles to them (Bhatia 2005). Secondly, existing legal protection for forest cover would not get eliminated, because the act categorically stated that forest rights holders would not only refrain from 'any activity ... that adversely affects the forest and the biodiversity in the local area', but also try 'to stop any activity which adversely affects wildlife, forest and biodiversity, whoever responsible'. Thirdly, degradation of forest cover, it is argued, is solely attributed to the timber mafia, land grabbers, *mahajans* (moneylenders), and mining and diversion of forest lands for non-forestry uses (Sarvanan 2009). It is estimated that 33.3 lakh hectares of natural forests were cleared and replaced by plantations between 1951 and 1979. Afterwards, forest authorities had diverted 9.81 lakh hectares of land for non-forest uses, particularly for 11,282 development projects, but completed only 7.3 per cent compensatory plantation (Krishnaswamy 2005).

The claims by conservationists and counter-claims by pro-rights activists are not based on empirical evidences. In fact, there is a lack of systematic study regarding magnitude of forest land claimed and distributed under FRA across states of India except one (Kashwan 2013). Any systematic analysis will help to examine the gloomy picture portrayed by conservationists and forest administration about the potential impact of the FRA. Analysis of the report of the MoTA data revealed that only 30.48 lakh hectares of forest land out of 449.47 lakh hectares of total forest land (less than 7%) in 14 major states of India has been distributed (Table 11.2). If we consider state-wise distribution, it is revealed that Tripura distributed highest percentage of forest lands. Among the larger states, Andhra Pradesh has performed better in land distribution compared to Madhya Pradesh, Chhattisgarh, Odisha and Gujarat. On the other hand, large states like Karnataka, Jharkhand and West Bengal failed to distribute even one per cent of their total forest lands (Table 11.2). The performance in respect of land distribution in states like Odisha, Karnataka, Chhattisgarh, Madhya Pradesh, Jharkhand and Maharashtra is very poor, though these districts have either larger forest areas or higher tribal concentration.

Table 11.2

State-wise Distribution of Forest Land (Individual and Community) Distributed Under Forest Rights Act 2006

States	*Total Forest Land (sq km)*	*Total Forest Land Distributed (sq km)*	*Percentage of Total Forest Land Distributed*
Andhra Pradesh	46,389	5,894.42	12.7
Assam	27,673	314.07	1.13
Chhattisgarh	55,674	2,836.93	5.10
Gujarat	14,619	44.52	3.04
Karnataka	36,194	147.86	0.41
Kerala	17,300	133.62	0.77

Cont'd...

...Cont'd

Madhya Pradesh	77,700	7,110.40	9.15
Maharashtra	50,646	4,231.40	8.35
Odisha	48,903	2,672.61	5.46
Rajasthan	16,087	210.53	1.31
Tripura	7,977	1,685.70	21.1
Uttar Pradesh	14,338	566.86	3.95
Jharkhand	22,977	152.49	0.66
West Bengal	12,995	71.45	0.55
Total	4,49,472	30,480.04	6.78

Though FRA has the provision for recognising rights for land parcels of up to four hectares to each legitimate claimant, the average size for which titles have been granted is only 1.4 ha in 2012. It has, however, increased to 1.97 ha in 2015 (MOTA 2012, 2015). Still, the average size of land granted is less than half of the 'four hectares' stated in the act. The average size of lands granted for legitimate claimants is maximum (just less than 3 hectares) in Maharashtra. Notably, most of the states have granted less than one hectares on an average to each legitimate claimant (Table 11.3). Village level data from Gujarat and Andhra Pradesh also reported similar findings (Kashwan 2013). The average area of forest land claimed at village level is less than two hectares per household.

Table 11.3

District-wise Distribution of Average Land Granted for Each Claimant

States	*No of Titles Distributed*	*Total Forest Land Distributed (hectares)*	*Average Size of Land Granted (hectares)*
Andhra Pradesh	1,67,263	5,89,442	3.52*
Assam	35,407	31,407	0.89
Chhattisgarh	3,36,590	2,83,693	0.84
Gujarat	68,769	4,452	0.06
Karnataka	7,604	14,786	1.94
Kerala	24,599	13,362	0.54
Madhya Pradesh	1,79,700	7,11,040	3.96*
Maharashtra	1,45,469	4,23,140	2.91
Odisha	3,41,999	2,67,261	0.78
Rajasthan	34,189	21,053	0.62
Tripura	1,20,418	1,68,570	1.40
Uttar Pradesh	17,654	56,686	3.21*
Jharkhand	15,296	15,249	1.00*
West Bengal	51,069	7,145	0.14
Total	15,46,026	30,48,004	1.97

* No separate data on individual and community available

It is argued by conservationists that forest-dependent people can have the opportunity to claim land of sizes near to the allowable limit of four hectares, because Forest Rights Committee (FRC) at village level has significant autonomy in making claims under the act (Kashwan 2013). But state-level as well as village-level data does not support the argument of vote bank politics of land grant programme put forward by conservationists (Munshi 2005). However, the sudden spurt in distribution of land titles during the poll eve of 2009–10 was an exception (Figure 11.1). The fact is that forest dwellers would not invest resources for clearing forests to get a meagre amount of land. Moreover, they have to face penal proceedings for clearing forest lands (Kashwan 2013). So, it may be concluded that villagers did not try to take advantage of the autonomy that was provided under the act. Even the elected representatives of higher level committees largely did not misuse their position for large-scale clientelistic land grants. In Madhya Pradesh and Chhattisgarh, forest officials admitted privately that the number of claims and the area of forest land claimed under the FRA were much lower than apprehended (Kashwan 2013).

Denying Community Forest Right Claims

The provisions like access rights to minor forest products, protection and management rights of forest resources under community forest rights (CFRs), etc. under the act have a potential to change the top-down centralised governance system of forests to enable greater decentralisation and site specificity. It provides collective livelihood security to communities (Desan 2013).

The analysis of the report of MoTA revealed that though individual title distribution is relatively higher, the performance of community land distribution is very poor across India. In fact, about three-fifth of all community forest claims have been rejected till 2015 (Table 11.1). There are about 1,70,000 villages have forests within their boundaries, covering about 32 million hectares. It is expected that there should be at least one community claim per village. But only 93,000 community claims have been received, of which 52,000 claims have been recognised till date across India (Table 11.1). Moreover, government agencies misinterpreted community rights and recognised claims only for development projects like health and education centres, roads, transmission lines, etc. but not for use and management of forest resources (Desan 2013).

The analysis of state-level data provides wide diversity in accepting community forest claims. Karnataka has performed worst in the category compared to other larger states. Conversely, in Madhya Pradesh, almost all the community claims have been accepted. On the other hand, only 20–30 per cent of community forest rights have been accepted in larger states like Andhra Pradesh, Maharashtra, Odisha and West Bengal. Interestingly, though smaller states have performed well in individual land distribution, they failed to accept community rights claims (Table 11.1).

In Chhattisgarh, only 250 community rights were processed out of 2,14,918 total claims in the state, and none of them were rights over non-timber forest products (NTFPs). An NGO, Samarthan, from Bhopal, reported that community claims were not approved in areas that have dense forests and high concentration of tribal population in Chhattisgarh and Madhya Pradesh. The Chhattisgarh government started processing community claims only after the tribal affairs ministry ordered it in July 2008; even then the rights did not include NTFPs (Down to Earth 2010). Though tribals ranked NTFPs as the number one community asset based on dependence for their sustainable livelihoods, only 7.3 per cent of claims granted in Chhattisgarh gave community rights, while in Madhya Pradesh, it is about 23.6 per cent (ibid.).

The scholars identified some reasons for abysmal status of community forest claims. It is argued that forest administration is not interested in recognising community claims, since the forest department potentially loses larger amount of land compared to individual claims. Secondly, there was confusion in the interpretation of the provisions of the FRA on the various types of community forest rights (CFRs), the procedure for claiming them, and how the claims should be mapped and processed. However, in September 2012, FRA rules were amended making some significant clarifications, like defining CFRs and making clarifications that support decentralisation of NTFP governance. Under Section 3 (1) (i) of CFRs, it also provides a standard 'claims and titles' format for recognition of CFRs (Desan 2013). Thirdly, there is a lack of awareness about the provisions of the act among most of the lower level forest officials who are supposed to process the CFR claims. For example, a forest officer of Darbha in Jagdalpur district of Chhattisgarh said, 'The directive from senior officials was to go to forest villages and collect signatures on forms that identify agricultural land and dwellings; we were not told about MFP' (Down to Earth 2010). Forest administration is not interested to accept rights over NTFPs as it is its major source of revenue. Most states have nationalised certain NTFPs like mahua, sal seeds and flowers, tendu leaves and certain gums. According to the forestry statistics of India, the produce accounts for 50 per cent of forest revenue. These states trade these products through cooperatives and corporations as against rights of forest people provided under FRA and the Panchayat (Extension to the Scheduled Areas) Act (PESA). After the Supreme Court banned tree felling in forest areas without working plans, NTFPs have emerged as the main source of revenue for forest departments. In fact, most forest departments earn more from NTFPs than timber. For example, Andhra Pradesh gets Rs 82 crore per year from NTFPs, while timber generates Rs 43 crore only. In Chhattisgarh, the tendu capital of India, MFP accounts for 60 per cent of forest revenue (Down to Earth 2010). Fourthly, Ashish Kothari and his colleagues have cited dominant political system as the major cause. The political objective of the FRA is to re-establish rights over forests and customary territories to local communities and to establish community governance system of forest resources. This is completely undermined, according to them, by the national government as the act is reduced to 'beneficiary scheme', which aptly suits the current political and development discourse governed by the neo-liberal economic agenda.

Subversion of Provisions under the FRA: Depriving Forest Dwellers

There are several instances of procedural changes in implementation of FRA by concerned state-level agencies across the country. These changes eventually subverted or denied the rights of forest-dwelling people enshrined in FRA.

Firstly, the act recognised Gram Sabha (GS) at the village level is the basic unit. The sole responsibility and authority has been vested in the Gram Sabha to identify and verify individual livelihood rights and community rights and use of sustainable resources, as well as to protect forests and biodiversity to maintain ecological balance for strengthening conservation regime. Section 6(1) of FRA states:

> The Gram Sabha shall be the authority to initiate the process for determining the nature and extent of individual or community forest rights or both that may be given to the forest dwelling STs and OTFDs within the local limits of its jurisdiction under this Act by receiving claims, consolidating and verifying them and prepare a map delineating the area of each recommended claim in such manner as may be prescribed for exercise of such rights and the Gram Sabha shall, then, pass a resolution to that effect and thereafter forward a copy of the same to the sub-divisional-level committee.

Under Rule 3(1), the Gram Sabha will constitute a FRC to execute those rights provided in the Act. The Gram Sabha shall elect 10–15 members – of which one-third should be STs – to the FRC. In practice, FRCs were not constituted in several states at village level; rather, they were recognised at panchayat level. In West Bengal, several orders were issued by the Backward Class Welfare Department as well as the Panchayat and Rural Development Department in 2008. The order replaced the term 'Gram Sabha' by 'Gram Sansad' for the implementation of the act. Moreover, it was stated that FRCs could be formed at Gram Sansad level with representatives from the local forest and land revenue department as permanent invitees (Jha 2010). Another order by the Panchayat and Rural Development Department stated that FRC will act as a functional committee under Gram Unnayan Samiti (GUS). The chairperson and the secretary of GUS shall act as the chairperson and the secretary of the FRC and the officers from the district's Panchayat and Rural Development Department shall be permanent invitees in the FRC (ibid.). This is a blatant violation of the act. It has tremendous implication in denying rights of forest dwellers over forest resources. The Gram Sabha, as the act says, is the village assembly, comprising all the members of the village, whereas Gram Sansad is a body constituted with all the voters at gram panchayat level under the West Bengal Panchayat Act 1973. The gram panchayat may comprise several villages based on size of the adult population. The role of Gram Sansad differs from Gram Sabha. Gram Sansad acts as an organ of a panchayat to identify beneficiaries and distribute benefits of various governmental schemes, not to settle various rights and nurture community forest rights and management of forest resources. So, equating Gram Sansad with Gram Sabha is a blatant violation of the spirit of the act. This attempt actually leads to settling of land rights as a part of formal function of PRIs and thereby undermines the potentiality to spread awareness about rights and responsibilities of forest governance at the community level.

Similarly, equating FRC with Gram Unnayan Samiti is another case of violation of the act. As per the act, FRC will elect a chairperson and a secretary from its members. But the orders mention that the members of the GUS will select the members of FRC and GUS chairperson and secretary shall work as the chairperson and the secretary of the FRC. So, the chairperson of the GUS will become chairperson of FRC of a Gram Sabha, not considering whether he or she has any relationship with the forest (Jha 2010). Moreover, though officials are not allowed to incorporate the FRC under the act, the orders of the department. reflect dominance of bureaucrats. This eventually leads to quasi-representative committee, working under the pulls and pressures of village-level politics (ibid.). This sort of deliberate violation of rules is also observed in other states. In Andhra Pradesh, Gram Sabha has been interpreted as Gram Panchayat (which encompasses more than one village or hamlet). As a result, there is a serious problem in implementation. The Gram Panchayat, which is much larger than a village, cannot focus on the specific needs of the rights-deprived forest villagers (Reddy et al., 2011). In effect, villagers were not properly informed about the FRA and many could not apply for their claims. Secondly, Section 6(3) under FRA 2006 stated: 'The State Government shall constitute a sub-divisional-level committee (SDLC) to examine the resolution passed by *Gram Sabha* and prepare the record of forest rights, and forward it through the SDO to the district-level committee (DLC) for final decision'. And any person aggrieved by resolution of Gram Sabha can file an appeal before SDLCs within 60 days from the passing of resolution under 6(2) of FRA and challenge the decisions of the SDLC within 60 days before DLC under Section 6(4) of FRA'. But Rule 14(3) of 2007 states that SDLC may either allow or reject or refer the petition to concerned Gram Sabha for its consideration, which is a clear violation of the act. Moreover composition of SDLC reveals domination of the bureaucracy as representatives, rather than persons from STs and other traditional forest dwellers. Besides, Rule 1 and Rule 15(1) of 2007 stated that resolution of Gram Sabha and SDLC is to be communicated to the claimants on the day resolution passed. In reality, it does not happen, which is against natural justice.

Notwithstanding bureaucratic shortcomings of the rule-framing process for operationalisation of the act, forest administration has made deliberate attempt to deny rights provided under the act. Firstly – as already mentioned – the forest administration is reluctant to recognise community forest rights and has thereby tried to impede the process of vesting community rights. This is because forest administration does not want to lose control over forest governance. Secondly, several national conservation organisations, conservationists and foresters vehemently criticised the act and challenged its constitutional validity in the Apex Court of India (Sethi 2008). The Bombay Natural History Society, a conservation group, sued the central government arguing that enactment of the FRA violated the Constitution of India (Kashwan 2013). Wildlife activists also criticised the provisions for community forest rights. A member of the National Wildlife Board, Valmik Thapar, is against the philosophy of participatory conservation, calling it 'utopian'. Rather, he is in favour of strict protection measures 'which would further reinforce exclusionary conservation measures' (Kashwan 2013). In Andhra Pradesh, several initiatives have been taken to obstruct the implementation of the act at the state level. Several state governments – including that of Andhra Pradesh – filed several writ petitions against the implementation of the act between 2007 and 2008, arguing that this will lead to degeneration of forests, and the people will misuse the act (Reddy et al., 2011). However, the Andhra Pradesh High Court dismissed the objections of writ petitioners and granted clearance for implementation and issue of final rights titles (Reddy et al., 2011). Thirdly, several state forest administrations authorise extra statutory bodies under the control of forest departments to disempower the Gram Sabhas in controlling and managing their own forests provided in FRA. For example, the AP forest department also violated the provisions of the act by issuing administrative order in August 2008, to misinterpret the provisions of community rights under FRA, in order to deny community rights to forest villagers and to appropriate those rights for forest department local bodies. Vana Samrakhsan Samitis (VSSs), ad hoc administrative bodies, were created under the control of forest administration, to implement JFM schemes and to claim community rights (ibid.). In this way, the government deliberately misinformed the communities. The VSS is a selected committee constituted for project implementation. So, this is an evidence of deliberate attempts to obstruct implementation process on the part of forest department staff, at a strategic level by using JFM committees to usurp community rights (Springate-Baginski et al., 2012). Similarly, the West Bengal Forest Department issued an order renaming all forest protection committees into JFM committees under JFM programmes. Considering provisions of FRA, the resolution states that 'Joint Forest Management Committees shall be constituted for the purpose of development of degraded forests and forests prone to forces of degradation' (Jha 2010). The resolution deliberately violated the provision in Section 5 of the act that clearly mentions that power is handed to the Gram Sabha and local communities to conserve, protect and regenerate forests. The FD and other state authorities are expected to help the Gram Sabha in management and conservation of forests. Moreover, the resolution also contradicts the various rights stated in Section 3 of the FRA. For example, it curtailed ownership rights for MFPs in all forests including national parks and sanctuaries. It is reported that officers from the Cooch Behar Forest Division (Wildlife III) are pressurising people to form new JFM committees with the threat of withdrawing money allotted for development purposes (ibid.). In fact, there is no space for collaboration between FD and forest dwellers under the act. So, the FD is desperate to retain control over forest resources by creating JFM committees without any legal standing. Fourthly, the amendment of the WLPA 1972 – in 2006 – provided that critical tiger habitats are inviolate areas that must be identified on the basis of scientific and objective criteria, in consultation with an expert committee [Section 38V(4)]. Section 38 V (5) (ii) of the act goes on to require that prior to the relocation of any person from a tiger reserve, it must be established with the community's consent that human activity is causing irreversible damage to tiger populations. In reality, the National Tiger Conservation Agency (NTCA) under MoEF hurriedly released an order to notify Critical Tiger Habitats (CTHs) on 16 November 2007. The order stipulated a process of constituting a two-member expert committee headed by a chief Wildlife warden in consultation with the respective field directors of tiger reserves to delineate CTHs within 10 days of the receipt of the order (Bijoy 2011). Notably, forest rights rules were enacted by January 2008. For this, consent of Gram Sabha was not taken at all. It is a deliberate violation of WLPA 1972 (amended 2006). Consequently, forest dwellers have been deprived over the rights over large tracts of land in the name of CTHs, provided under FRA 2006.

Now the question arises – why is the forest administration, various conservation groups and wildlife biologists have consistently been arguing against devolving various rights to forest dwellers as observed in making of FRA, as well as denial of rights, particularly community forest rights, vested in the FRA, thereby impeding the process of implementation in the ground level? Current scholarship identified various reasons for not resolving long-standing conflicts and engaging local people in the management of forest resources. Researchers like Prakash Kashwan tried to analyse the forest administration's reluctance in devolution of power to local people in governance, by linking political and economic interests as observed in Asia, Africa and elsewhere (2013). He has identified three factors behind forest administration's desperate attempt to retain exclusive control over material resources of the forests, which constitute about 23 per cent of the country's total geographical area. Firstly, MFPs are the major source of revenue for forest departments. The FRA threatens the state forest department's control over MFP trade by vesting the right to collect and sell MFPs on local people (Down to Earth 2010; Sethi 2011). The text of the Minor Forest Produce (Ownership of Forest Dependent Community) Act 2005 reflects the very intention to retain control over MFP trade. The text defines 'ownership' as 'the right to collect and process the Minor Forest Produce in a manner prescribed by the State/Union Territory Government ...' That means forest departments are the ultimate authority for recognising 'forest dependent' people and which products would be considered as MFPs. Secondly, the control over forest territory is essential for maintaining the deep-rooted forest bureaucracy and its powers. By means of revenue generation from and supervision of one-fourth of total geographical area, forest officials are in a position to have a greater say in policy-making (Kashwan 2013). Thirdly, the forest department argued that revenue generation is tightly linked with the so called participatory JFM programme. The FRA provides statutory power to community rights whereas JFM lacks legal standing. The MoEF in its policy statement promised to transfer control of JFM committees to locally elected leaders in 1990s. But after two decades of implementation of JFM programme, local-level forest officers are still controlling the JFM committees and their bank accounts (Kashwan 2013). Even the share of forest income of forest protection committees is meagre, though they were successful in protecting forests under the JFM. In some cases, participating communities received no benefits. The large chunk of the revenue goes to state forest departments (Springate-Baginski and Blaikie 2007). In effect, the forest-dependent people are among the poorest in the country, contributing to 'environmental public goods without receiving adequate returns for the hard work and valuable time they invested' (Kashwan 2013).

In addition, one of the major obstacles in devolving power to local people in forest governance is the forest departments' historically rooted technical and cultural knowledge system, through which they control the production of and access to forest knowledge. In the last 150 years, the Indian Forest Service (IFS) has produced a distinctive internal culture and knowledge system of reproducing forestry management objectives and activities like survey and reserve of forest tracts, forest management plans, silvicultural operations, etc. for continuous flow of timber and actual field management of forest resources (Blaikie and Springate-Baginski 2007). Forest managers believe this knowledge system as 'modern', scientific and authoritative. 'Scientific forestry' has become the mantra of forest administration. Issues of local people's socio-economic needs, biodiversity and wildlife protection have historically been ignored in training courses on how to work with local people in managing forest resources. Moreover, forest managers always see 'forest' as a national property. So, they believe that the state agency has the exclusive right to control over forest protection, production and management (Gadgil and Guha 1992). In fact, at the policy level, there is no basic change between pre- and post-Independence periods. As per eminent domain law, the state is the sole owner of all forest resources. The National Forest Policy 1952 stated that exclusion of local communities from the benefits of forest management is legitimised for the larger interest of the nation. So, local people have no role in the management of forest resources. However, later forest policies have changed to include local people for forest management. The forest managers, who are habituated with the pre-eminent status that they enjoyed historically in matters relating to controlling forest resources, have received a jolt, since the FRA challenges their authority. Therefore, they find it difficult to accept the FRA's provisions.

Conclusion: Need for Reform

It is widely accepted that the forest property rights are critical for the well being of the forest-dependent communities, a necessary condition for empowering them to contribute to conservation goals (Bawa et al., 2011; Kumar and Kerr 2012). In post-Independence India, various policies and legislative reforms have not resulted in necessary community control over forest resources. In fact, there has been no real devolution of power and authority over resources, including transfer of land from the state to local people (Murombedzi 2001). Researchers argued for a process that gives communities control over their resources through tenure reform. It is based on the assumption that local communities have greater interest in sustainable resource use than governments or corporations (Brosius 1998) and that communities will develop a sense of proprietorship over forest resources and wildlife with devolution of power. The legislative enactment of forest rights provisions is a historic step in independent India that challenges states' eminent domain of forest governance and control. The FRA provides tribals and other forest-dwelling communities access to land they have been cultivating and forest resources they have been collecting (Government of India 2006), and marks a radical step towards decentralised governance of forest resources.

It is observed that implementation of the FRA has undergone a process of selective interpretation excluding many of the important and empowering provisions of the rights. They include non-recognition of Gram Sabha at village level as the unit of governance of forest resource use; poor implementation of CFRs or non-acceptance of CFRs deliberately linking with JFM; and declaration of all national parks and sanctuaries as 'Critical Tiger Habitats' under Tiger Amendment Act instead of 'Critical Wildlife Habitats' under the FRA. In addition, various state FDs denied the claims of 'OTFDs', or have put them on indefinite hold. This is because the state forest departments have decided to grant rights only to STs (like in West Bengal), or are insisting on proof of three generations of occupation of the land.

The FRA implementation process has deliberately been obstructed by the state forest administration, as is evident from continuance of various laws and policies that existed before the implementation of the FRA. In some cases, some new orders have been introduced to deny community rights under FRA. In most cases it is the forest department which interprets their rights provided under FRA and prescribes what suits them best. It is applicable to occupational rights of forest land or demarcation of critical wildlife habitats or equating development inputs with community rights or ownership of MFPs. Despite deliberate obstructions, the implementation of FRA is showing some positive results. It has granted forests and forest land rights, leading to livelihood security for a significantly large number of forest-dwelling people. Livelihood security has been increased due to land rights in pre-existing cultivation area and access to forest products, and the forest dwellers are realising a better income from them through value addition. The land titles make the forest communities eligible for services and benefits under various anti-poverty programmes. In addition, it had also improved the social status as observed in Odisha (Sarap et al., 2013). Tribal communities are claiming their rights over the major ecosystem areas, like Dongria Khond, Juang in Odisha; Soliga in Karnataka ; Maldhari in Gujarat; Baiga in Madhya Pradesh; and Maria in Maharashtra. CFRs are also claimed in several protected areas like Badrama and Karlapat sanctuaries in Orissa, Bilgiri Rangaswamy Temple Wildlife sanctuary in Karnataka, Madhmalai sanctuary in Tamil Nadu (Dash and Kothari 2014). In Gujarat, several villages in the districts of Dang and Narmada have formed protection committees even before securing CFRs. Villagers in Gadchiroli district in Maharashtra have evicted outside encroachers for their CFRs, and moved to take control over several wetlands forcing the government to withdraw fish contracts to outsiders (ibid.). Moreover, it has also enabled local communities to resist some very high profile mining and development projects that would have threatened biodiversity and wildlife. Suspension of the Vedanta Alumina project at the Niyamgiri Hills in Odisha due to sustained protest by the Dongria-Khond community, POSCO steel plant in Odisha, paper mill felling of bamboo in Vidharva in Maharashtra and government timber logging in Baiga Chowk area in Madhya Pradesh are glaring examples.

It is noteworthy that the FRA only provides secured rights for lands that they are cultivating for years, but does not allow clearing of existing forests and grant collective forest rights, which are likely to be co-related with better conservation outcomes (Kashwan 2013). Centralised control of forests and other ecosystems, in the form of national parks and sanctuaries, has often resulted in adverse effect on livelihoods of local people (Saberwal et al., 2001; Adams and Hutton 2007). The outright rejection of basic rights provided under the FRA by forest administration and wildlife activists reflects a strict adherence to dominant exclusionary models of conservation. They ignore the potential for achieving convergence of recognition of forest rights and nature conservation (Kashwan 2013). More fundamentally, this is also a denial of the fundamental rights of the subsistence-based forest-dwelling communities (Sikor et al., 2010).

But conservation agencies and the forest bureaucracy are strongly resisting reforms to the existing framework for forest conservation and governance. The state implementing agencies are not interested in enlightening the forest-dwelling people about the implications of FRA provisions to the forest dwellers. While implementing process, state agencies, particularly forest administration, consciously stressed on individual rights rather than community forest rights. Clearly, the objective of the FRA, which was to restore customary areas to local communities and to establish community governance, has been diluted by the state apparatus to the extent that the Act is reduced to a 'beneficiary scheme' like 'patta' or land distribution scheme. During awareness campaign on FRA, the government agencies intentionally chose to publicise individual land rights, but were completely silent about more powerful and crucial component of community rights to the forests. Most state implementing agencies are not prepared to give much time to the process. They only paid hurried field visits. It actually prevented forest dwellers to make themselves aware about the implications of FRA. Nevertheless, providing CFRs to forest dwellers could act as major empowering tool in addressing historical injustices.

To make FRA a success, there is an urgent need to initiate changes and reforms at the forestry organisation. There is an urgent need for the change in current system of governance. The first step is to devolve power to the local communities. Alignment with the existing policy and bureaucratic norms is, however, important for successful implementation (Hodges and Durant 1989). Various existing laws like the Indian Forest Act, the Forest Conservation Act, policies (National Forest Policy, JFM), programmes (afforestation, projects), institutions and the forest service have to change their priorities to align with FRA for proper implementation. In Madhya Pradesh and Odisha, participatory governance policies helped faster implementation of FRA than other states with restrictive policies (Sampath 2010). Besides, there should be clear-cut guidelines on the governance and management of CFRs specifying relative powers, roles, and responsibilities of communities, the FD, and other stakeholders operating at the village, district, state and national level. There should be coordination between various stakeholder departments with the of Ministry of Tribal affairs functions as a nodal agency. In addition, intensive awareness programmes involving various stakeholders like local communities, forest department, revenue department, non-governmental organisations about their roles and responsibilities as well as potential and implications of FRA need to be undertaken. Successful implementation of the FRA across different forest resource areas in India, as well as areas inhabited by the poor and marginalised tribal communities, will definitely ensure improved livelihood and restore conservation governance. After all, conservation governance is intricately connected with the improvement of livelihood of forest-dependent tribal groups and the success of it depends a lot on their participation into the process.

References

Adam, W.M., and J. Hutton. 2007. 'People, Parks and Poverty: Political Ecology and Biodiversity Conservation', *Conservation and Society*, 5: pp. 147–183.

Asian Indigenous and Tribal People Network. 2012. *The State of Forest Rights Act: Undoing of Historical Injustices withered*. New Delhi: AITPN.

Basu, P. 2007. 'Tigers Pitted against Tribes by Indian Forest Law', National Geographic News. National Geographic Society. Online http://news.nationalgeographic.com/news/pdf/99299653.html. Last accessed 29 September 2014.

Baviskar, A. 1994. 'Fate of the Forest: Conservation and Tribal Rights', *Economic and Political Weekly*, 39.

Bawa, K.S., N.D. Rai, and N.S. Sodhi. 2011. 'Rights, Governance, and Conservation of Biological Diversity', *Conservation Biology*, 25: pp. 639–641.

Bhatia, Bela. 2005. 'Competing Concerns', *Economic and Political Weekly*, 40, No. 47: pp. 4890–4893.

Bijoy, C.R., and K. Raman. 2003. 'The Real Story: Adivasi Movement to Recover Land', *Economic and Political Weekly*, 38, No. 20: pp. 17–23.

Bijoy, C.R. 2011. 'The Great Indian tiger show'. *Economic and Political Weekly*, XLVI: pp. 36–41.

Bose, I. 2010 'How did the Indian Forest Rights Act, 2006 Emerge?' IPPG discussion paper 39, University of Manchester.

Brosius, J.P., A. Tsing and C. Zerner. 1998. 'Representing Communities: Histories and Politics of Community-based Natural Resource Management', *Society and Natural Resources*, Vol. 11, No. 2: pp. 157–168.

CSD. 2003. *Endangered Symbiosis: Evictions and India's Forest Communities. Report of the Jan Sunwai* (Public Hearing). New Delhi: Campaign for Survival and Dignity.

Dang. Himraj. 2005. 'The End of Conservation', *Seminar*, 552: pp. 50–54.

Das, T., and A. Kothari. 2014. 'Forest Rights and Conservation in India'. In *Rights and Responsibilities.* Edited by Holly Jonas, Harry Jonas and SM Subramanian. Natural Justice and United Nations University. Malaysia.

Desor, S. (ed). 2013. *Community Forest Rights under Forest Rights Act: Citizen's Report* 2013. New Delhi: Kalpavriksh and Vasundhara with Oxfam India.

Dreze, J. 2005. 'Tribal Evictions from Forest lands'. New Delhi: National Advisory Committee, Govt. of India.

Down to Earth. 2010. How Governments Subverting Forest Right Act. *Down to Earth*. Online http://www.downtoearth.org.in/print/2187. Last accessed 10 February 2015.

Gadgil, M., and R. Guha. 1992. *The Fissured Land: An Ecological History of India*. New Delhi Oxford University Press.

Ghosh, S. 2007. 'Commons Lost and "Gained"? Forest Tenures in the Jungle Mahals of South West Bengal'. Working Paper No. 7. Norwich: Overseas Development Group, University of East Anglia.

GOI. 2006. 'The Scheduled Tribes and Other Traditional Forest Dwellers (Recognition of Forest Rights) Act, 2006', No. 2 of 2007. New Delhi: The Gazette of India, Government of India.

Grove, Richard H. 1995. *Green Imperialism: Colonial Expansion, Tropical Island Edens and Origins of Environmentalism, 1600–1860*. New Delhi: Oxford University Press.

Guha, Ramachandra and Madhav Gadgil. 1989. 'State Forestry and Social Conflict in BritishIndia', *Past and Present*, 122: pp. 141–77.

Hodges, D.G., and R.F. Durant. 1989. Professional State Revisited: Between Scylla and Charibdis. *Public Administration Review* 49: pp. 474–485.

Jena M. 2010. *Law on Forest Rights Fails to Deliver*. http://ipsnews.net/news.asp?idnews=50652. Last accessed 12 May 2014.

Jha, S. 2010. 'Process Betrays the Spirit: Forest Rights Act in Bengal', *Economic and Political Weekly*, Vol. XLV: pp. 3324–27.

Kashwan, P. 2013. 'The Politics of Right-based Approaches in Conservation', *Land Use Policy*, 31: pp. 613–636.

Kaur, N. 2002. 'Targeting Tribal People: The Union Ministry of Environment and Forests Seeks to Clear 12.5 lakhs Hectares of Forest Land by Evicting its 10 Million Strong Tribal Population', *Frontline* 19: p. 21.

Khare, A., M. Sarin, N.C. Saxena, S. Palit, S. Bathla, F. Vania, M. Satyanarayana, 2000. 'Joint Forest Management: Policy, Practice and Prospects. Policy that Works for Forests and People'. Series No. 3. India Country Study. *International Institute for Environment and Development* (IIED), London: p. 142.

Krishnaswamy, Madhuri. 2005. 'One Step Forward, Two Steps Back', *Economic and Political Weekly*, 40, No. 47: pp: 4899–901.

Kumar, K., and J.M. Kerr. 2012. 'Democratic Assertions: The Making of India's Recognition of Forest Rights Act'. *Development and Change*, 43: pp. 751–771.

Kumar, S., and S. Kant. 2005. 'Bureaucracy and New Management Paradigms: Modelling Foresters' Perceptions regarding Community-based Forest Management in India', *Forest Policy and Economics*, 7: pp. 651–669.

Kothari, A., P. Pandey, S. Singh, and D. Variava. 1989. *Management of National Parks and Sanctuaries in India: A Status Report.* New Delhi: Indian Institute of Public Administration.

MoEF. 2004. 'Affidavit on behalf of Ministry of Environment and Forests, Government of India, in the Supreme Court of India', I.A. No. 1126 in Writ Petition (Civil) No. 202 of 1995, Ministry of Environment and Forests, Government of India, New Delhi..

Munshi, I., 2005. 'Scheduled Tribes Bill', *Economic and Political Weekly*, 40: pp. 4406–4409.

Murombedzi, J. 2001. 'Why Wildlife Conservation has not Economically Benefitted Communities in Africa'. In Hulme and Murphree (eds.). *African Wildlife & Livelihoods:The Promise and Performance of Community Conservation.* Oxford: Blackwell.

NCFRA, Manthan. 2010. 'Report National Committee on Forest Rights Act (NCFRA)'. The Ministry of Environment and Forests and the Ministry of Tribal Affairs. http://moef.nic.in/downloads/public-information/FRA%20COMMITTEE%20REPORT FINAL%20Dec%202010.pdf, New Delhi.

Pathak, A. 2002. *Laws, Strategies, Ideologies: Legislating Forests in Colonial India.* New Delhi: Oxford University Press.

PIB, MoEF response to starred question No. 284 in Parliament on regularisation of encroachments on forest land on 16.08.2004.

Poffenberger M., and B. McGean (eds). 1997. *Village Voices, Forest Choices: Joint Forest Management in India.*, New Delhi: Oxford University Press.

Reddy, M.G.K., Anil Kumar, P. Trinatha Rao, and Oliver Springate-Baginskie. 2011. 'Issues Related to Implementation of the Forest Rights Act in Andhra Pradesh', *Economic and Political Weekly*, 46, No. 18: pp. 73–81.

Saberwal, V., M. Rangarajan, and A. Kothari. 2001. *People, Parks and Coexistence.* Hyderabad: Orient Longman.

Sampath, S.K. 2010. An Enquiry into Perceptions, Adaptations, and Resilience in Madhya Pradesh'. MS thesis, Faculty of Agriculture, University of Padua, Italy.

Sarap, K., T.K. Sarangi, and J. Naik. 2013. 'Implementation of Forest Rights Act 2006 in Odisha: Process, Constraints and Outcome', *Economic and Political Weekly*, Vol. XLVII, No 36.

Saravanan, S.V. 2009. 'Political Economy of the Recognition of Forest Rights Act, 2006: Conflict between Environment and Tribal Development', *South Asia Research*, 29, No. 3: pp. 199–221.

Sarin, M., and O. Springate-Baginski. 2010. 'India's Forest Rights Act – The Anatomy of a Necessary but not Sufficient Institutional Reform'. http://www.ippg.org.uk/papers/dp45.pdf/. Last accessed on 4 September 2014.

Sarin, M. 2003. 'Forest Conservation is too Complex an Issue to be Resolved by Executive Fiat', *Down To Earth*, 15 July.

Sarin, M. 2005. 'Why the ST (Recognition of Forest Rights) Bill 2005?' *Economic and Political Weekly*, 40, No. 21: pp. 2131–34.

Sathyapalan, J. 2010. 'Implementation of the Forest Rights Act in the Western Ghats Region in Kerala', *Economic and Political Weekly*, 155: pp. 65–72.

Sethi, N. 2008. 'PIL Challenges Validity of Forest Act', *The Times of India*, 21 February.

——. 2011. 'Now, An MSP For Forest Produce'. *The Times of India*, ******* **Date?**

Shah, Mihir. 2005. 'First You Push Them in, Then You Throw Them Out'. *Economic and Political Weekly*, 40, No. 47: pp. 4895–4899.

Sikor, T., et al. 2010. REDD-plus, forest people's rights and nested climate governance. *Global Environmental Change*, 20: pp. 423–425.

Sivaramakrishnan, K. 1999. *Modern Forests: Statemaking and Environmental Change in Colonial Eastern India*, New Delhi: Oxford University Press.

Springate-Baginski, O., and P.M. Blaikie (eds.). 2007. *Forests, People and Power: The Political Ecology of Reform in South Asia*. London; Sterling, VA: Earthscan.

Springate-Baginski, O., M. Sarin, and Gopinath Reddy. 2012. 'Resisting Rights: Forest Bureaucracy and the Tenure transition in India', *Small scale Forestry*. DOI: 10.1007/s11842-012-9219-x.

Springate-Baginski, et al. 2009. 'Redressing 'Historical Injustice' Through the Indian Forest Rights'. Research Programme Consortium for Improving Institutions for Pro-Poor Growth. School of Environment and Development, University of Manchester, UK.

Sundar, N. 2001. 'Is Devolution Democratization?' *World* Development, 29: pp. 2007–2023.

TTF. 2005. *Joining the Dots: The Report of the Tiger Task Force*. New Delhi: Government of India, Union Ministry of Environment and Forests.

Véron, R., and G. Fehr. 2011. 'State Power and Protected Areas: Dynamics and Contradictions of Forest Conservation in Madhya Pradesh, India', *Political Geography*, 30: pp. 282–293.

World Bank. 2005. 'India Unlocking Opportunities for Forest-Dependent People in India (In two volumes)', Volume I. Main report, 'Agriculture and Rural Development Sector Unit South Asia Region'. New Delhi: The World Bank.

World Bank. 2006. *India: Unlocking Opportunities for Forest Dependent People.* New Delhi: World Bank.

PART V

Governance and Tribals

CHAPTER 12

Tribe, Political Party and Local Self-Government

An Ethnography on the Santals in Rural West Bengal

DAYABATI ROY

The changes in the rural society of West Bengal, have probably been more spectacular in the Indian context, particularly during the last three decades. During this period, 'rural West Bengal has been subjected to extensive governmental intervention in the form of land reforms and democratic decentralisation. This made West Bengal's rural political economy ... distinctly different from the rest of the country' (Bhattacharyya 2002: 59). But, the question arises how far this extensive governmental intervention could affect the lives of the marginal people of the province. The question becomes more pertinent when the same scholar states, or rather concludes, in the same article that 'as our fieldwork showed, the poor – especially the Dalit and the Tribal population – felt increasingly alienated from the institutional politics of party-society. Indeed, if institutions cannot innovate ways to accommodate the poor – as was done during the implementation of land reform laws – the atrophy of party-society may create space for various 'forbidden forms of claim-making' (Samadddar 2000) that have little regard for the existing democratic norms.' (ibid.). Against the backdrop of Lalgarh Movement signifying 'a fight against age-old deprivation and humiliation and for the assertion of dignity and the rights of the people' (Bhattacharyya 2010: 17), this ethnographic research finds that the hierarchical division between the ruling elites (the dominant castes and classes) and the marginal social categories, here the Santal tribe, still continues, though in a complex form, in the functioning of grass-root democracy in rural West Bengal. The Santal people of the rural areas still feel marginalised and deprived in the dominant caste Hindu-class power structure and try very often to organise themselves around their own ethnicity-based organisation.

But the question arises whether the tribe as a social category takes of late a new shape and recreates a new kind of political consciousness as consequences of implementation of myriad of development policies including the affirmative action programme like reservation initiated by the state institutions. This question seems to be immensely important since any affirmative answer to this question requires re-contextualisation and re-conceptualisation of tribe. The definition of tribe pronounces that, as the scholar argues, 'one of the marked features in terms of which tribes in India came to be conceptualised is geographical and social isolation from the larger Indian society' (Xaxa 2011: 2). In addition, by virtue of the fact that the tribal people live in isolation from the larger Indian society, as the definition asserts, tribal groups enjoy autonomy of governance in terms of their own laws, traditions and customs (ibid.). But it cannot be denied that after a series of efforts on behalf of successive governments towards the development and welfare of the tribal people since Independence, the latter today do not stand in the same position as they were earlier. The majority of the people belonging to almost all tribal groups in India are now more or less intricately linked with the state institutions and various political parties, and hence could not be governed strictly in terms of their own laws and ethos. The extent of the entanglement between the tribal people and the state domains is so intense that, Partha Chatterjee argues, the autonomous domain of the subaltern groups seems no more in existence. A closer observation of the everyday politics of a tribal group might be a better way to understand and gauge the actual state and dynamics of this entanglement. The notions on the actual state and dynamics of the entanglement of the tribal group with the state and political parties could determine whether we require re-conceptualising and re-defining the tribe in the present context.

The Ethnography

The research is mainly based on an ethnographic field work[1] in a village Kalipur.[2] Kalipur is a remote multi-ethnic village in Hooghly district and is inhabited predominantly by a Scheduled Caste (SC) and Scheduled Tribe (ST) population. Among the 259 families in the village, the number of SC families is 106 and that of ST is 61. Besides, there are Other Backward Classes (OBC) families with six, minority group (Muslims) with 50 and general caste with 36 in number. Mahishya is the dominant caste among the general castes in the village who could earn prosperity in the field of agriculture during the Green Revolution period. Since 1978, both the village and the gram panchayat had been completely dominated by the Communist Party of India (Marxist) [CPI (M)] party that won the last panchayat elections (2008) uncontested. The present study has its focus on the CPI(M) and the type of entanglement it had with the tribal group in the village over the decades. Pakhi Murmu, the tribal leader belonging to the Santal community,[3] had been active in the CPI (M) since the 1960s when the party began to organise the peasant struggles to get an entry into the village. In fact, he was the main organiser of the ST-SC people on behalf of the party during those turbulent days, and subsequently became the panchayat member in 1978 on behalf of the CPI (M). Then he left the CPI(M) for some time, tried to organise the Revolutionary Socialist Party, India (RSP), another Left front partner, in the village and came across a frequent harassment in series of events that followed. Finally, he again came back to the fold of the CPI (M). He was found actively organising the ST people in the village during the period of my field work. The trajectory of his political life had made him one of the most important characters in the village that needed a closer study.

Pakhi Murmu resided just on the bank of a tank. He was allowed to reside on the land by the tank owner by virtue of his most likely connection with the dominant party. Some other families also stayed nearby and the area was known as Santalpara, i.e. the hamlet of Santals. This area was located at a distance from the main Adivasipara, i.e. the hamlet of tribal people. As habitation space in the Adivasipara became inadequate for housing the burgeoning population, a section of tribal people began to shift to this side of the road and construct their own settlements over time. Most of the houses were muddy thatched structures while only a few have asbestos or tin sheets on their rooftop. Pakhi's house had asbestos on the roof, thanks to the welfare scheme Indira Awaas Yojana (IAY).[4] It was a two-room incomplete house. One room was meant for the cows and the other for Pakhi and his wife was separated by a half-built wall. Sitting in his room, which was quite dark even at 10 am, we started talking. We could not clearly see each other. I sat on the bed of Pakhi that had still the unruffled mosquito net on it. Some food was kept on the floor. Pakhi's wife had cooked in the morning and gone to work in the field.

Pakhi Murmu began to talk in a low voice, 'I have lost everything for the party. My life has been spoiled after joining in politics.' But why he was feeling like this at a time when their party was in power both at the state level and in the local panchayat? The party organisation was also quite strong in the village. Pakhi Murmu replied:

> The party is no more ours. It has been usurped by the *bhadraloks* (upper caste gentlemen)[5] and the *baroloks* (the rich). The people, against whom we had to struggle once, have now become the party leaders. In this situation, how can our condition improve? It has remained as it is.

> Pakhi Murmu continued:

> We have built up the party, established it bit by bit. At that time hardly anyone worked for the party, which was new in the area. Since the regime of the United Front (1966–69), we the adivasis have organised a series of movements here. I was known as the only CPI (M) person in the area. We almost continuously struggled against the zamindars (landlords) for confiscation of ceiling surplus land,[6] for wage hikes and against all kinds of oppressions. We were beaten up, had to go 'underground' for long and even spent nights on the branches of trees. Police had issued arrest warrant against me. People in thousands used to gather in my exhortations. During those times the bagdis and duies, i.e. the caste groups belonging to SC category did not stand steadfastly behind us. Today the very same people have become leaders by virtue of being elected in the panchayat. After so much of pleading, I got only six asbestos sheets for the roof of my house. Earlier Khagen was an agricultural labourer. Now he has managed to improve his position in quick time.

How did he get attracted to the party? Pakhi Murmu began reminiscing about the old days:

> Those were the days of the zamindars and the reign of the Congress party. Suman Mukherjee, Bidhan Mandal and Pranab Banerjee, the CPI (M) party leaders, came to the village. We held discussions with them and began organising the people. I was then a very daring person and was also physically well built. I could convince people to join the party. So very quickly the organisation could get ground in the area. Village people used to say it was the organisation of Pakhi. So I became an eye sore to the zamindars. Many times they attempted to kill me and every time I could manage to escape. Zamindars, their agents and the police were all against us. But we succeeded in confiscating substantial amount of ceiling surplus land. Many landless peasants got land. I got 0.4 bigha[7] of land. Party decided the amount of land to be distributed to each one of us.

Pakhi Murmu went on:

> But I have never been a leader in the party. I am totally illiterate. As I could organise men and women in the village, leaders used to call me to resolve any dispute or organise any programme. Tribal people and other toiling masses used to follow me. When I became the panchayat member for the first time, Khetra Pal, the rich peasant of the village and his associates targeted us. But there was tremendous opposition and even the women resisted them.

It appeared from Pakhi Murmu's narration that he was the leader of 'rebellions' and rebellion was indeed a 'collective enterprise'[8] (Guha 1983: 115). Guha argues that 'it (rebellion) uses communal processes and forms of mass mobilisation, expresses mass violence in the idiom of communal labour and encourages communal appropriation of the fruits of pillage in many cases.' The assertion of the tribal people and also the SC people in Kalipur during 1960s and 1970s was in fact a rebellion of collective enterprise and mass violence. Pakhi Murmu was the key figure in that rebellion, and it seemed that he did not forget those days.

Pakhi Murmu remembered the past through those memorable incidents that had occurred in his life. Not unexpectedly, numerous conflicts took place during the early days of the Left Front government. Till then, the landowning community was so hostile that they could go to the extent of beating up a panchayat member of the ruling party. The tribal community spearheaded their movement against this landowning community probably in line of the legacy of the old tribal and peasant movement as described by Guha. Guha (1983: 336) claimed:

> So long as landlord authority continues to function as a significant element in the ruling culture and continue it will for long even after the genuine (as against spurious) end of landlordism in the economy and property relations all mass struggles will tend inevitably to model themselves on the unfinished projects of Titu, Kanhu, Birsa and Meghar Singh.

But did the landowning community become submissive by now? Pakhi Murmu answered:

> 'Khetra Pal and his associates are the new zamindars, the big farmers. Previously, the Kayasthas,[9] the Kars and the Mitras were the zamindars. They had their own *lathials* (people who fought with sticks). One side of the village was then covered by forest. We were residing near the forest. Due to our united struggle, the main Kayastha zamindar fled the village. They got decent jobs in Kolkata. Later on, when the government began to seize the ceiling land, the Kayastha landholders sold off most of their land at throwaway prices. The solvent Mahishyas, the middle and agricultural caste in West Bengal, mainly purchased those lands. Some Swarnakars and Benes, the Other Backward Castes in West Bengal also purchased some of their land. Some among the Mahishyas became prosperous as they used to cultivate on their own. They are now the big landowning people in the village. Their sons are entering the CPI (M) party. The CPI (M) party now looks like the old Congress party.'

How can the rich people find a place in the Communist party? This seemed to be a puzzling question to which Pakhi Murmu had no answer. He had fought against the zamindars drawing on the unity of his community. Pakhi Murmu said, 'In spite of being a panchayat member, I continued to the struggle against them on different social issues. Not only in this village, I used to visit other villages as well to mobilise people in struggles. The leaders used to do office works sitting in the panchayat office.'

His account was so vivid that events of the past got enlivened through it. Even now he seemed enchanted with the converse of struggle and was keen to judge his party and its leaders on the basis of success achieved through struggles. He was the hero of those struggles that had been instrumental in entrenching the CPI (M) party in that locality. He could not forget the memories of those struggles that had provided them some rights, recognition and social prestige in the village. Now when the party had shied away from those types of struggles, people like Pakhi seemed to have lost importance in the party. Here lay the crux of his ambivalent relationship with the party. Pakhi had been the panchayat member for only one term, i.e. for five years. Pakhi narrated,

> 'Sanatan Tudu became the next panchayat member. But I remained at a distance and my job was to organise the people and unite the poor. At that time, the wage of the day labourers was very low. It was only Rs 5.00 plus 750 grams of rice. That was in the year 1986–87. Pakhi initiated the wage increase struggle after consulting the party leaders. The struggle continued for 20 days.'

Pakhi went on:

> They tried to bring agricultural labourers from outside the village. We resisted the attempt. All the agricultural labourers' families were united in the struggle. But the *babus* (the landed gentry) were not ready to concede to our demand. Then Sanatan Tudu on behalf of the CPI (M) party tried to deceive the struggling agricultural labourers. He proposed and endorsed the terms of the landowners. Ironically, the party leaders backed him. He could mislead a section of the struggling people. We, the adivasis, remained steadfast till the last, but the SC people were persuaded to withdraw their struggle.

Pakhi's statement again validated Guha's formulation on peasant insurgency; Guha stated that 'even when solidarity between ethnic groups triumphed over separateness for a time, it weakened soon under pressure from their common enemy': here the common enemy was the landowning community and perhaps even the CPI (M) party to some extent at the later stage of the wage increase movement (Guha 1983: 331). But it was also true that the tribal leader Sanatan Tudu 'deceived' the movement fighters and forsook the interest of his own ethnic group. Thus the ethnic groups, in the post-colonial period, non-existent as an organic community as compared to their counterparts in the colonial times, and were rather more or less fragmented due to factors like the deep penetration of the political parties into the ethnic communities. But were the movements of the ethnic groups in the colonial period really devoid of fragmentation or differentiation? The scholarly study of Bandyopadhyay (1994) on the Namusudra movement in Bengal, 1872–1947, showed ample evidences of differentiation or fragmentation in the said movement.

Pakhi's brother-in-law, who was present during this part of our discussion, commented, 'These SC people, particularly the Maliks,[10] are always agents of the babus. They always remain subordinated to the landed gentry. They are the double-dealers.'[11] Pakhi Murmu continued:

> The party then asked me to withdraw the struggle, but I refused to budge. This led to differences of opinions in the party. I proposed that we could stop the movement only against those landowners who were ready to concede to our demands. One evening a few local party people came to discuss the matter with me. But the discussion didn't yield any result as they were insisting on calling off the strike. At the end they attacked me unexpectedly and beat me up severely and then went away. That day on the occasion of a tribal festival, all my people were outside the village.

Pakhi Murmu filed a case against five CPI (M) persons including Bidhan Mandal, the local committee secretary of the CPI (M). The RSP arranged his court expenses and also met the cost of his medical treatment. In presence of the party members, he joined the RSP. In the year 1993, he contested the panchayat election on behalf of the RSP and was defeated by only a few votes. That means a considerable section of the village people had voted for Pakhi Murmu after he left the CPI (M) and joined the RSP. But the RSP organisation could not flourish in an isolated pocket. In Pakhi Murmu's opinion, such a village-level organisation could not be expected to survive for long, particularly when all the power of the panchayat was concentrated in the hands of the CPI (M). There was also tremendous pressure from the CPI (M) that a small organisation like the RSP could not withstand. So the tribal people under the leadership of Pakhi Murmu again came back to the fold of the CPI (M) party. How could they, the adivasi people, survive without the help of the panchayat, which was totally under the control of the CPI (M)? All these welfare schemes and projects in the panchayat were meant for them, the adivasis, the SC and the poor. How could they stay aloof from the panchayat and the party leading the same? This seemed to be the crux of his realisation after so many years of struggle. People like him and his community could not survive without the help of the political parties. Even if the party was not their 'own', of their own choice, they had to cling to it until a suitable alternative emerged to replace it.

Pakhi Murmu remarked, 'We have no other way but to join the CPI (M). We cannot live without the support of a party. And we cannot join the Congress or TMC-BJP, as these are the party of the landowners.' So he again approached the CPI (M) leaders and told them, 'We have nowhere to go. Hence, I have decided to work for the party again.' On the other hand, no party could ignore a person like Pakhi Murmu who could establish himself as an efficient organiser and a natural leader of his own community. Hence, the leaders of the CPI (M) once again accepted him in the party, but he could not cope with the present atmosphere prevailing in the party. Pakhi Murmu, a 65 years old, is still a strong built man. He said, 'Bidhan Mandal allotted a chair in the party office for me and for some time I used to sit on it. But I can't follow what they discuss these days. So I don't feel any more interest to go there.'

Pakhi Murmu said:

> People like me who had established the party through intense struggles remain deprived in the village. They never ask me what benefits are to be distributed, who should get those or who are to be included in the beneficiary committee. But most of the money spent in different schemes is meant for people like us, the adivasis. Funds that are meant for our development are misappropriated by the Maliks (i.e. the SC people to which the panchayat pradhan belongs). But even now whenever the party needs to mobilise the people, I am asked to take the responsibility. They cannot organise people for rallies and other party programmes.'

Pakhi's brother-in-law again commented, 'Pakhi did not get anything for the sake of dharma'.[12]

Noticeably, Pakhi Murmu, in his long narration, repeatedly spoke in terms of 'us' and 'they'. While the word 'us' was used to mean the adivasis in particular and poor and toiling people in general, 'they' meant sometimes the landed gentry, sometimes the party leaders, sometimes the SC people who were getting the bulk of panchayat facilities at the cost of others. He seemed to consider them, the adivasis, as the 'other' of the mainstream. The mainstream was once represented by the landlords and the Congress, then by the CPI (M) leaders and the landed gentry and finally, the 'opportunists' among the SC community. His feelings were not isolated ones, but were also shared by others in his community as was evident from the words of his brother-in-law. But people like Pakhi Murmu could not probably remain steadfast in their dharma in these days self-centred politics. They had to compromise with the organised domain to get necessary relief and other facilities provided by the state.

After Pakhi Murmu quit the CPI (M) party in 1983, Sanatan Tudu was selected as the next panchayat member from the tribal community by the party. In that very year he got membership in the party and was also elected as panchayat member for two consecutive terms. He used to cultivate 2 acres of land as a sharecropper, out of which he had grown potato in 0.66 acre of land last year. He resided with his wife in tin roofed house that had two rooms made of mud-walls. About Pakhi Murmu, he said:

> He was the first panchayat member of the village. But he could not complete the full term as he was in trouble due to pilferage of funds. He was caught red-handed. Then, Bidhan Mandal asked me to contest the local panchayat seat on behalf of the party.

To mention once more, both Parkhi Murmu and Suman Mukherjee, the erstwhile leaders of the CPI (M) party who had left the party, were accused by the party leaders of corruption in the panchayat activities.

> Sanatan Tudu was cautious when he said, 'Previously, Panchayat functioning was better as all were honest then. Khagen Malik is otherwise a nice person, but not everything is running well. I represent the village development committee,[13] Panchayat schemes are generally discussed there. But often we remain ignorant about some of the schemes. Earlier the number of schemes was not many and all the party activists were aware of them. Discussions among us took place freely about who would be the beneficiaries of these schemes. Now such things are discussed, but not everything is transparent. I once got Rs 500 as old-age allowance for two months. After that nothing has come and nobody knows why.'

A contemporary of Pakhi Murmu, Sanatan could not remember exactly when he came close to the CPI (M) party:

> I was in the party since the days of the United Front government. Pakhi and I worked together for the party. We led many struggles during those times and suffered a lot. Party leaders used to come from outside. Now I have become too old to carry out party responsibilities. I asked Bidhan Mandal to release me from the duties. He said that without me they couldn't run the organisation in the village. Hence, I have to continue with the responsibilities given to me.

He added, 'I have to attend the party meetings and rallies. Now I cannot attend all. But I work hard to gather people to make party meetings and rallies successful. Apart from these, I have to collect donations for the party, for the Krishak Sabha, for DYFI and even for Mahila Samiti.'

But why did he collect money even for the Mahila Samiti? His candid reply was, 'Can they collect money on their own? They only attend meetings and rallies occasionally. So we have to look after their works as well.' Earlier, as the narratives of social anthropologists working on tribal studies suggest, women in the tribal community in general 'were portrayed as having a better status than women in caste societies, with physical mobility, choice in marriage ... access to property and resources' and were regarded as independent not only in economic spheres, but also in all spheres of society and politics with their prominent roles in decision-making (Xaxa 2004: 353). But the tribal women in contemporary period seemed to have been losing their previous roles in social organisation, as the scholar argues, 'If one takes the case of tribes such as Santhals, one finds that the withdrawal of female labour occurs among those who live in a multi-caste village or its vicinity and where they form a small minority.' (ibid.: 350–351).

Sanatan Tudu's forefathers hailed from Birbhum district. Long back, they had migrated to the tea gardens in North Bengal in search of work and finally migrated to this place. At that time, the village was surrounded by jungle and the adivasi people were asked by the zamindars to clear the jungle and settle there. Sanatan Tudu used to cultivate the land of the old zamindar family of the village as a sharecropper. He was a registered bargadar.[16] Once they had led many struggles against this Kayastha family of Satya Kar. Sanatan Tudu said, 'But we have not conducted any struggle in recent past. During the Left Front period, generally a day's token or symbolic strike was organised every year for wage hike and Rs 1–2 was increased per year.'

It transpires that Sanatan Tudu, though associated with the CPI (M) party, was not much enthusiastic to be involved with the party affairs. He thought that the party leaders were not like before; they had now become self-seekers and were reluctant to organise labour movements against the landed gentry for wage hike. On the other hand, the local party committee of the CPI (M) required the people like Sanatan Tudu after Pakhi Murmu left the party to represent the tribal community both in the panchayat and at the party level. The opinion of Chand Murmu, a Village Education Committee (VEC)[17] member and the panchayat member of Madhupur,[18] might help to discern to what extent the tribal people in general got representation in the political sphere of the village. Chand Murmu, an agricultural labourer, said,

'I am not at ease in the panchayat office and other government offices as I am illiterate. I am in the VEC but don't attend the meetings regularly. In fact, my presence is not at all necessary. They don't need me. Only when they require my signature, they come to me.'

Chand Murmu was only aware that some elderly persons in adivasipara were entitled for old-age allowance. But he did not know, or were rather reluctant to know the amount of allowance in a year they were entitled to. He got enraged and said, 'We badly need electric connection in our hamlet. Despite our repeated requests, the party leaders did not pay heed to the issue. They don't care what we say. They act according to their own wish.'

Haren Hembram was the tribal *morhol* (chief) of Kalipur and his post was now largely ceremonial. He was an agricultural labourer and in dearth of work throughout the year. He had been associated with the party since its beginning in the village. But he said, 'After CPM came to power, Pakhi left the party weakening the party's base in our community. We also became inactive to a great extent since then. Since then those who were active in the Congress party sneaked into the party. They have now become the leaders of the party. How could the party work for the masses? The old CPM has changed. It no more remains the same party as it was earlier.'

Haren Hembram then began recollecting the past days:

> After quitting the CPM, Pakhi and Mukherjee (the erstwhile (CPI)M party leader of the village) set up contacts with the RSP party and brought the same to our village. We all joined the new party. The CPM doesn't allow other parties to exist. So it began to put down the new party. This led to severe conflicts and clashes in the village. Even tribal people of one para got divided and fought

> with their brethren from another para. At the end, we found it useless to fight among ourselves. Moreover, we realised that we won't be able to continue with the RSP party; so we left it. But we needed a party that could provide us some sort of support (*Kintu party to ekta korte habe. Ekta abalamban to darkar*). Hence, we again came back to the CPM party. This party has done a lot for us, for the poor.

Though Haren received some benefits from the panchayat in the form of loan to purchase goats and cattle, he had strong reservations about supporting party leaders. 'I don't support any of the present leaders. I just attend some meetings of the party and nothing else. Moreover, neither do we have much time nor do we have enough education to be involved in party activities' he said. The tribal people of the village had selected Haren as the morhol. In earlier days, the morhol used to adjudicate in all squabbles and in social and religious matters of the tribal people. Particularly in matters connected with marriage, *sraddha* (last rite) and other festivals, morhols used to play vital roles. Still, the tribal people had their own morhols for each of their hamlets. What had been their roles in the present day?

Haren replied:

> At present the morhol has no role as such in adjudicating the problems arising in the tribal society as the party has become all in all (*sarbesarba*). Even problems arising in the conjugal life are sometimes settled by the party. This leads to more problems very often as they don't know or bother to follow the norms of the tribal community. But, in any case, we have to follow their decisions.

When the party's adjudications were not in line with their community norms, what did they do? Haren Hembram replied, 'We have no other way but to follow the rules of the present regime.'

Conclusion

It transpired that the tribal people of Kalipur had been trying hard to cope with the changing situation. The tribal community had been the main base of CPI (M) in its early days. The RSP, another constituent of the Left Front, also tried to establish itself in the area drawing on the support of the same tribal group. But the attempt failed and instead, the tribal people had to come back to the fold of CPI (M) once again. Since then the tribal people had been maintaining a dual relationship with the party with no other alternative available to them in the present situation. While they were apparently associated with the party, they seemed to be also maintaining a distance from the present activities of the party. They adhered more to the past orientation of the party than to its present variant. They seem to be aggrieved with the new leadership of the party. Culturally, they have been sanskritised to a great extent by forgoing their traditional rituals and festivals and instead adopting to the Hindu rituals like the pujas.

Pakhi Murmu apparently belonged to the ruling party and had been an ardent activist of the party. But he carried the rebel in him all through, castigating the pro-rich activities of the party and dissociating with all the anti-labour actions of the party. When he was a panchayat member, he never felt interested to sit in the panchayat office and instead spent his time organising people in peasant struggles. Now after rejoining the party, he was offered a seat in the party office, but he refused to sit there. He was reluctant to earn the prestige of being associated with the upper caste leaders of the party. Instead he remained a humble organiser of the ST people in favour of a party that he didn't believe to represent his community and class interests. He believed that the subalterns could not live today without the support of an organised party. He knew through his long experience that whatever rights and benefits the subalterns had achieved in recent times was because of the relentless struggles under a political party. Without the support of the party, those struggles would not have been possible. Though that party had of late turned pro-rich, obstructing their movements against the landed gentry and hobnobbing with their erstwhile 'enemies', he had no other alternative but to associate himself with the same party that appeared to him still better than the then main opposition parties in West Bengal. At the same time, he thought that as most of the panchayat schemes were meant for the development of his community, it would not be wise for his community to stay away from the party to run the panchayat and should try to garner as much benefits as possible for the community that had struggled most for bringing this party into power. Though Pakhi was associated with the ruling party most of the time during the last 30 years, he had refused to accept the party's elitist turn during this period. He even tried to oppose the party, sometimes from within and on other occasions from outside.

This was also an instance of subaltern entanglement with the elite domain, but the defiance in him against the elitist party had been more prominent all through his interactions with the party since its ascendancy into power in the state. A prominent subaltern historian has observed that the 'two elements that together constitute the subaltern mentality' are 'submissiveness to the authority in one context' and 'defiance in another' (Bhadra 1997). In the case of Kalipur these two elements of subaltern mentality were reflected in the actions and thoughts of the two leading subaltern persons. If Khagen Malik, the Bagdi panchayat member of the party, was an epitome of subaltern submissiveness to the organised domain, Pakhi provided an example of defiance by refusing to be directly entangled with the elite domain.

The difference in the mentality between these two subaltern leaders seemed to have their origins in the histories of evolution of the two communities as also in the divergent process of their interaction with the organised domain. The tribal community was in the forefront of peasant struggle in the late-1960s that had challenged the authority of the old landlords. Again this community, under the leadership of Pakhi Murmu, waged a number of movements against the rich farmers in the early period of LF rule. The tribal community had gained some rights and tried to assert those through these struggles. Ultimately it fell apart with the mentor party when it was not ready to side with their struggle and rather opposed it in the later period. During all those struggles, even in the 1980s, the subaltern assertion was at its peak, when the biggest landowner of the village Khetra Pal had to beg Pakhi Murmu for his life, when the landed gentry offered bribes to Pakhi for a compromise that he had refused, when Pakhi and his community earned the support of all and sundry in the area. During the labour strike in 1986, the party leaders asked him to call off the strike, but he and his community defied the party directive and as a result his own party men beat him up. That was the peak of their defiance vis-à-vis the organised domain. It was also indicative of their desire to assert the relative autonomy of the subaltern consciousness in them.

At the surface level, an overview of the political situation of Kalipur might reveal the complete subordination of the SC-ST communities to the organised domain, or the hegemony of a single party for being in the saddle of power for long 30 years. But the undercurrent of discontent among these subaltern communities was more than evident in my ethnographic work. If domination exists as a form of governance, the subaltern response would probably be both subordination and resistance or defiance. Both the elements of subaltern consciousness could make their presence in this village. This may occur in other villages facing similar situation. As the political process pursued by the state had not always been democratic, leaving very little space for ventilating opposition views and organising opposition parties, it perhaps failed to a great extent to bring the lives of the subaltern people under its ideological hegemony. Though the rural poor had to gather at the party and panchayat offices to get their share of doles, this was more a case of patron-client relationship than one of equal rights of citizenship. So only the people likely to receive benefits assembled in gram sansad meetings or in party rallies. Most of the people seemed to have lost interest in the functioning of the panchayat. A study conducted by Moitree Bhattacharya (2002) in two villages of *Bardhaman* district has made similar observations.

But the tribal people in the post-Lalgarh scenario[19] seem no more inclined to follow the decisions of the 'party' in all spheres of life. The tribal people of Kalipur, who since long have been in search of an alternative party to represent their interests in the organised domain, have reportedly joined the Jharkhand Disham party (JDP) en masse. The JDP which is meant to represent the tribal community has become a strong force in Dhaniakhali block[20] just before the parliamentary elections in 2009. This development is significant as it shows how the integrity of a community can transcend local boundaries and gets consolidated across a large part of the state against the government and the dominant ruling party, attaining the capacity to substantially influence the dynamics of the organised domain of politics. Here the community bonding proves to be more effective than the party affiliations in determining the political behaviour of a social group spread over a large area. There is, however, no guarantee that this trend will continue uninterrupted.

To sum up, the present study reveals three main features regarding the lives and life-world of the Santal tribe in a plural situation marked by party politics. One, while the village people belonging to Santal tribe are connected with the party politics for the sake of safeguarding their everyday life, they do keep, at the same time, a distance from the party to an extent. Two, the tribal people, here the Santal people, do mostly aspire for the benefits from distribution programmes of the state institutions though most of them maintain that the delivery of these benefits are far from their satisfaction. Three, notwithstanding their discontent and apathy, the everyday lives of the Santal tribe are now more or less determined by the rules and prescriptions of the state led politics or they directly come within the purview of the elite domain. In this changing context, it may be concluded that the tribe as a social category needs to be re-conceptualised and re-defined on the basis of the findings and insights gained from revealed by the recent researches accomplished primarily to explore the social and political dynamics of various tribal groups at the grass-root level. But, the grass root itself calls for a relook. Any attempt to redefine or reassess tribe in the present context has to be multi-dimensional. The present case is a pointer to the fact that party politics is making rapid inroads into tribal life so much so that their basic tribal identity gets skewed and distorted at times. It seems that 'entanglement' involving tribal groups, state and political parties rarely goes to the advantage of the former.

Acknowledgements

Initial versions of this paper were presented in the ADI workshop on 'State, Society and Marginality' held on 21–22 November in the University of Copenhagen, Denmark, and also in the IDSK workshop. I am thankful to all participants of both the workshops for their comments and especially to Professor Peter B Andersen, Professor Amit Prakash and Professors Marine Carrin, Abhijit Guha and Rajat Kanti Das for their useful comments and suggestions.

Notes

1. The ethnographic field work has been carried out in the period between 2006–2008 as a part of the author's doctoral dissertation titled's 'Changing Pattern of Politics in Two Villages of West Bengal, India.
2. Kalipur is a fictitious name of the study village. The ethnographic research has been conducted in the year 2006–2008 as a part of doctoral dissertation.
3. The Santal are a Dravidian tribe found in the western part of West Bengal, north Odisha and Santal Parganas of Bihar. In West Bengal, the Santals of Bankura, Birbhum, Malda and West Dinajpur districts are believed to be migrants from Bihar. Santals are now mostly agriculturalists. Their native language is of the Kolarian stock. See also Chaudhury S 1967.
4. Indira Awaas Yojana or IAY is a central government (Ministry Rural Development) funded social welfare programme to provide housing for the rural SC-ST and poor people belonging to BPL category in India. Under this programme, Rs 45,000 in the plain area and Rs 48,000 in difficult areas is given to each beneficiary for constructing houses. It is important that houses are allotted in the name of the woman or jointly in the name of husband and wife.
5. The terms bhadralok and chhotolok are commonly used in Bengali parlance to mean people belonging to the higher castes and lower castes respectively. The former applies to the educated higher caste people, who consider themselves as *bhadraloks* or gentlemen and the latter means the uneducated lower caste people. More often than it, it is the bhadralok who uses the term *chhotolok* in derogatory sense, Here *bhadra* means gentle, *lok* means people and *choto* means substandard.

6. Even after the promulgation of the Land Ceiling Act during the Congress regime, the rural gentry used to retain much of the above-ceiling land through evasive transfers to relatives, friends and fictitious persons. This latter category of land was popularly termed as '*benami* land'. After the installation of successive United Front governments in West Bengal in the late–1960s, a peasant movement broke out in many parts of West Bengal principally to reclaim these benami lands so far held by the landlords through their connection with the administration and the political leaders in power. The CPI (M) became popular among the poor in the countryside by leading this movement.
7. Bigha is a unit of measurement of land in West Bengal. One bigha is generally 0.1338 hectare or 0.3306 acre.
8. Guha borrowed the term 'collective enterprise' from Lefebvre who used it to describe the peasant revolts in France in 1789. See Guha 1983.
9. Kayastha is one of the higher castes in West Bengal.
10. Malik is a sub-caste of Bagdi caste group. Bagdi belongs to Scheduled Caste category.
11. See also Ruud 1999. Ruud describes how and why a particular jati, here Bagdi, is being preferred by the local CPI (M) and consequently political allegiance is shaped. In Kalipur, the trajectory of Bagdi participation in the CPI (M) may corroborate of Ruud's story
12. Dharma may be translated as religion in English. But in India, the word carries some deeper connotations. For example, dharma is in broader sense a duty or morality in life that should be followed irrespective of one's race and religion. Dharma also implies fighting against injustice and struggling for achieving justice. In the two great Indian epics, Ramayan and Mahabharat, the fight between what was just and unjust was described as dharma.
13. By enacting 'The West Bengal Panchayat (Amendment) Act in 2003, the West Bengal government conceived the idea of Village Development Committee (VDC), i.e. Gram Unnayan Samiti. The objective of VDC as a village level functional body constituted by the selected members of the village is to ensure 'active participation of the people in implementation, maintenance and equitable distribution of benefits.' See Bandyapadhyay 2003.
14. Krishak Shabha is the peasant organisation of the CPI (M). DYFI, i.e. Democratic Youth Federation in India is the youth front of the CPI (M). Mahila Samiti, i.e. Ganatantrik Mahila Samiti or Democratic Women's Organisation of the CPI (M).
15. See Guha (2003: 130). He states that the tribal women play a prominent as well as an equal role both in *hool* and *shikar*. Hool means rebellion and shikar means hunting.
16. Bargadar is a sharecropper who can be defined as a type of tenant who borrows land from the landlords or other landholding classes for cultivation on the terms of giving a particular share of the crops produced on the land to the landowner and agrees to share a fixed proportion of the produce with the owner. The Left Front government in its initial days had launched the 'Operation Barga' programme' to register the names of the bargadars so that they could not be evicted by the landowners. The stipulated share of crops is three-forth for the bargadar and the rest to the landlord.
17. The VEC, i.e. Village Education Committee is a recent policy initiative of the central government meant to implement decentralisation of governance in the sphere of education, envisages that the local communities would govern the affairs of primary education themselves.

18. During my field work Madhupur was a separate gram sansad and Madhupur had its own VEC, though Kalipur primary school was meant for both villages. But the meetings of two VECs were jointly convened. During the panchayat elections of 2008, two villages, Kalipur and Madhupur, were merged and formed
19. In the Lalgarh movement of 2008 the tribal community of the state has mobilised, in an unprecedented show of solidarity, against the police repression on the tribal community, particularly on their women folk. Since then throughout the state the tribals, especially of the Santal community, have started joining different political formations, such as the Jharkhand Disam Party in Dhaniakhali, which suddenly rose from the ashes to challenge the authority of the so far all-powerful ruling party in the area.
20. In Dhanikhali the tribals constitute 13.9 per cent of the total block population. The report of tribal mobilisation in JDP in the Dhaniakhali block was published in *The Times of India*, dated 6.5.2009.

References

Bandyapadhyay, D. 2003. 'The Caucus and the Masses: West Bengal Panchayat (Amendment) Act, 2003', *Economic and Political Weekly*: pp. 4825–4827.

Bhadra, Gautam. 1997. 'The Mentality of Suabalternity: Kantanama or Rajdharma'. In *Subaltern Studies Reader:1986–1995*. Edited by Ranajit Guha. New Delhi: Oxford University Press.

Bhattacharya, Moitree. 2002. *Panchayati Raj in West Bengal.* New Delhi: Manak Publication.

Bhattacharya, Harihar. 1998. *Micro Foundations of Bengal Communism.* New Delhi: Ajanta Books International.

Chatterjee, Partha. 2004. *Politics of the Governed: Reflections on popular politics in most of the world*, New Delhi: Permanent Black.

——. 1984. *Bengal: 1920–1947, The Land Question*, Kolkata: K.P. Bagchi.

Chaudhury, S., et al. 1967. 'Study of Blood group and Haemoglobin Variants among the Santal Tribe in Midnapore district of West Bengal, India', *American Journal of Physical Anthropology,* 26, No. 3: pp. 307–312.

Corbridge, Stuart., et al. 2003. 'Making Social Science Matter–1', *Economic and Political Weekly,* and 14 June, Vol. 38, Issue No. 25, 21 June 2003.

Ghatak, Maitreesh, and Maitreya Ghatak. 2002. 'Recent Reform in the Panchayat System in West Bengal', *Economic and Political Weekly*: pp. 45-58.

Guha, Ranajit. 1983. *Elementary Aspects of Peasant Insurgency in Colonial India*, New Delhi: Oxford University Press.

Roy, Dayabati. 2008. 'Whither the Subaltern Domain? An Ethnographic Enquiry', *Economic and Political Weekly.*

Samaddar, Ranabir. 2008. 'Prescribed, Tolerated, and Forbidden forms of Claim Making: Report on Social Justice III'. Kolkata: Mahanirban Kolkata Research Group.

Xaxa, Virginius. 2004. 'Women and Gender in the Study of Tribes in India', *Indian Journal of Gender Studies*, 11: p. 345.

Xaxa, Virginius. 2011. 'Tribes and Social Exclusion', Occasional Paper, No. 2, Social Inclusion Cell: CSSSC-UNICEF.

CHAPTER 13

Conceptualising Tribal Autonomous Rule in Tripura

A Study with Reference to Tripura Tribal Area Autonomous District Council as Seen From a Historical Perspective

DIPANNITA CHAKRABORTY

Independence and autonomy are the two complementary concepts that need to be expanded to all spheres of life in order to enjoy freedom without sacrificing the essentials of meaningful traditions. In regions where diversities exist in racial, ethnic, lingual, cultural domains, this concept of self–rule within a constitutional framework can enable a community to take its own decisions regarding administration of its own area without being 'guided' or 'pressurised' by any other community or other power agencies. In other words, it is a process of extending democracy to the grass-root level by creating a sense of independent authority and endowing the people with responsibilities. This principle of democratic decentralisation ensures more community participation as the latter is institutionally and statutorily involved in managing their own affairs and decision-making process.

After Independence, India discarded the British policy of isolation and non-interference and replaced it by policies of integration and development, laying much emphasis on preservation of culture and upholding the spirit that believed that the tribal people should develop along the lines of their own genius. The Constituent Assembly had set up an advisory committee to deal with matters relating to the tribal people, to build an autonomous administration in the hill areas and preserve their traditional way of life as also safeguard their customs and culture. The North-Eastern region of India is not only rich in terms of natural resources, it is also the abode of numerous tribes of various ethnic affiliations, as a result of migratory waves from time immemorial. To tackle the problems unique to this region and also to preserve the democratic traditions and cultural diversity of its people, the Sixth Schedule was conceived by the

framers of our Constitution. The idea is to give regard to their traditions without tampering their essential rights and in the process each state may use its own nomenclature for systems of governance, which will have local acceptance and also enable them to deal with the changing world.

A Glimpse of Tripura

Tripura, earlier known as Independent Tipperah and also Hill Tipperah, is a tiny state in the North-Eastern region of India with an area of 10,491 square km. A single dynasty ruled this kingdom and exercised absolute control over an area abounded with hill tribes. Geographically, the state was divided into two parts, the hills and the plains, and was categorised as a first division princely state of India as the rulers had an independent hand in internal administration with their own laws, army and police. The plains of Tripura were occupied by one Jagatram Thakur following a conspiracy, and Nawab Shuja-ud-daulah of Bengal renamed the plains of Tripura as Chakla Roshanabad (an area of 589 sq miles of plain land) in 1733. The kings remained independent in the hills while they became zamindars under the Bengal nawabs in respect of the plains, though not exactly a zamindari raj, the king of Tripura had a dual identity and the princely state got divided into two distinct parts (Mackenzie 1979 and 1981). Consequently, for centuries, cut-off from the outside world by the protective hills the kings maintained all their traditions and customs in their independent territory. The earliest reports, those of the political agent A.W.B. Power stated that even in 1872 the population of the state could be divided into two categories – the inhabitants of the hills and those of the plains. The hill tribes were mostly the Tipras, Jamatiyas, Noatias, Reangs, Halams and Kukis, the Chakmas, Mogs; while the plainlanders were the neighbouring Bengalis and Manipuris. During the 1940s, following serious communal disturbances in the erstwhile East Pakistan there had been a huge influx of refugees, and the immigration of plainlanders changed the profile of the state completely (Imperial Gazetteer of India 1905). Partition also led to sacrificing of 70 acres of cultivable land under the Chakla Roshanabad. In the meantime, on 15 October 1949 the state of Tripura acceded to the Dominion of India following the Tripura Merger Agreement. In 1956 the Territorial Council was formed as a step towards popular participation in a democratic government, and ultimately on the 21 January 1972 Tripura gained statehood by an act of the Parliament [The North-eastern areas (Re-organisation) Act 1971].

Rationale and Background

A long-cherished dream of the indigenous people of Tripura in the form of known tribes was believed to have been fulfilled by creation of Tripura Tribal Area Autonomous District Council (TTAADC) in 1985, certain administrative and legal authority was handed over to the council that aimed at working towards safeguarding the tribes' rights in respect to land acquisition, use of forest land, social customs, economic development, primary education, etc. It is therefore obvious that the issues of autonomy of indigenous tribes of the state and the associated problems will be the focal attention of the scholars in future.

But this issue has not been able to draw attention of the scholars to any noticeable extent. Only few research articles have tried to highlight the issue.

Hebel Koloy's (2001) article 'Experience of Autonomous District council in the North East India with Special Reference to Tripura State' is a critical review of the work of TTAADC prior to the formation of the village committees. Subir Bhaumik (2005) dealt with the formation and working of the ADC in the state and the insurgency problems highlighting the tensions and weaknesses as well as the impact of autonomy arrangement on the leadership. Bhattacharya (2005) focused on the political treatise of terror activities and politics of autonomy movement in the State. The problems and prospects of TTAADC was identified by Basu Majumder (2004) in her article, 'Tripura Tribal Areas Autonomous District Council: Problems and Prospects'. This paper is a research article and an important narrative on the administrative structure of the TTAADC in the earlier days, which has made a sincere attempt to point out the inadequacies of the ADC during the initial years. In her other article 'Democratic Decentralisation and Tripura Tribal Areas Autonomous District Council: A Review', Basu Majumdar deals with the relevant details of decentralisation process in the State.

J.J. Roy's (1997) article entitled 'Working of Autonomous District Council in Tripura' identified the general weaknesses in the implementation of the Sixth Schedule wherein he had raised the land related issues. Bhaumik and Bhattacharya's (2005) article 'Autonomy in the North East: The Hills of Tripura and Mizoram' makes a comparative analysis of autonomy movement in the two states.

In this background, the present study focuses on the issue of tribal autonomy movement in Tripura since pre-merger period. To be very specific, the study covers creation of TTAADC and its working during all these years with special emphasis on how the tribes have actually availed of the opportunities. It also seeks to examine the contributions of administrative measures and welfare activities in wiping out socio-economic disparities. For example, the land scarcity problem is dealt with through proper management of forests, thus increasing the net cropped area. Tripura being a border state with an equally large marginalised plainlander population, it is worthwhile to see whether this self-rule has created any schism among the people. The ultimate question is whether TTAADC is able to satisfy the aspirations of the tribal people in Tripura and at the same time wipe out any sense of alienation. The study also attempts to find out to what extent the autochthons can exercise their free will in improving of their status in the development process.

To get a clear picture encompassing all these parameters, a case study of Padmabil Block, Khowai, is attempted. The block falls entirely under the ADC area and has 15 villages. The total tribal population of the block constitutes around 95.01 per cent of total population, while there is a marginal population of few 'other' category people residing in the area. Moreover, the block is historically recognised for initiating the much popular 'Jana Shiksha Andolan', which has changed the educational and cultural scenario of the state and has played a pioneering role in bringing the two segments of population on an equal footing.

Towards Autonomy

Tripura was ruled by the tribal traditional monarchy whereby the chiefs of the Tripuri tribe subjugated the other tribes, viz. Kuki, Halam, Reang, Jamatiya, and established their authority, though giving enough freedom to the latter in social control mechanism. However, with the ushering of modern administration during the late-19th century the kings 'invited' the neighbouring Bengal nationals. Gradually the indigenous masses, who had assumed that the king was one of them, turned distant from him and, though they looked up to him with awe and respect, did not always display wholehearted loyalty. Often the king seemed to overlook their demand for controlling famines, introducing poverty alleviation programmes, but continued to invite and pamper the plainlanders. Revolts, skirmishes, uprisings followed leading to further estrangement of relations between the king and his tribal subjects. The king tried to wean away the tribals by introducing them to settle paddy cultivation, tea cultivation, but the autochthons did not show much interest.

To pacify them, Maharaja Bir Bikram decided to bring certain reforms in administration by spreading education and also introducing the Grama Mandali Act in 1940. The 'mantra' of ethnic identity caused a furore in the political arena of the state since the population belonged to diverse racial groups. With the merger of Tripura with Indian Union in 1949, the indigenous people looked forward to their socio-economic upliftment. But those were the days of mass immigration following the Partition. Population grew by leaps and bounds and the newcomers were settled in the 'tribal areas', at times even in the secluded corners of the state (Table 13.1) The growth of population was higher than the national average in the years following Independence. The decade 1951–61 shows a tremendous growth rate (78.71%). Though this alarming rate of population growth slowed down the pace of development, the administration was not bothered because the new migrants could happily put these lands to proper, use which were left fallow so long due to the reservation of the tribes against settled cultivation.

Table 13.1

Population Growth in Tripura

Year	*Population*	*Growth in Percentage*
1951	6,39,000	—
1961	11,42,000	78.7%
1971	15,56,000	36.3%
1981	20,53,000	31.9%
1991	27,57,000	34.3%
2001	31,99,203	16.0%
2011	36,71,032	14.7%

Source: Census of India, Various Issues.

Thus was broken the last remnants of their isolation. It was noticed that over decades the tribal population was dwindling; from a percentile share of 50.09 in 1941 it went down to 28.45 in 1981 as is evident from Table 2. Now when a demand for protection of the tribals' right to land has been raised, it is worth remembering that as early as 1952 Sri Dasaratha Deb, ex-Member of Parliament had suggested to Prime Minister Jawaharlal Nehru that '... some area or areas of Tripura shall have to be set aside for the tribals alone and no other persons should be allowed to settle there.' The Tripura Rajya Gana Mukti Parishad also submitted a memorandum to the prime minister on 10 September 1955 in wich they demanded that khas land around tribal habitations be declared as reserved areas for rehabilitation of the tribal communities.

Table 13.2

STs and Other Categories of Population in Tripura

Year	*ST Population (%)*	*Others (%)*
1901	52.80	47.20
1911	48.20	51.80
1921	56.37	43.63
1931	50.26	49.74
1941	50.09	49.91
1951	36.55	63.45
1961	31.53	68.47
1971	28.95	71.05
1981	28.45	71.55
1991	30.95	69.05
2001	31.05	68.95
2011	31.60	68.40

Source: Census of India, Various Issues.

In 1960–61, the scheduled areas and Scheduled Tribes Commission was entrusted under the chairmanship of U.N. Dhebar, with the task of finding towards finding a solution to the ongoing tribal discontent. The commission recommended setting up of tribal development blocks on an experimental basis. However, such blocks did not function up to the exception of the tribal people and were deserted by as rampant exploitations continued in these areas with the rehabilitation of plainlanders who were 'settled' on these lands. The presence of 'outsiders' in their land made them feel deprived and discriminated against and a growing sense of self-consciousness, identity crisis and non-fulfillment of basic needs led to transformation in their behavioural pattern too. A large number of tribesmen were reported to be seeking refuge in neighbouring forest areas of Assam, even Myanmar and Bangladesh. By this time the population profile of the state had undergone a sea change; it turned into a mixed area with some tribal dominated areas. Demand for implementing the Fifth Schedule was raised but to no avail. Hanumantaiya Commission Report on

North-East tribal problems demanding the implementing of the Sixth Schedule to tribal compact areas now intensified. A new elite leadership was created in the form of *Tripura Upajati Samiti* (1967) and an emphatic demand for 'land, language and local autonomy' was made on its behalf, which became the chief bone of contention. Land for shifting cultivation was dwindling, agricultural yield too fell and land they had once tilled were not found in the registered official records. But cry for restoration of land went unheeded. Even the Tribal reserves were abrogated by an ordinance on 28 February 1974 to accommodate the displaced people who came to seek refuge here in the aftermath of the Bangladesh Liberation War (1971). A third amendment was made to the existing TLR and LR Act of 1960 and 'Tribal Schedule Area' was formed in 1975. Yet the demand for autonomy did not get a priority, which led to terrorist activities. These reached its climax in a contemptuous bloody massacre of non-tribals in Mandai on 6 June 1980. The state was violently jolted out of its stupor. The state government acted hastily and passed the ADC Act of 1979 providing practically all the safeguards and power to the tribal communities under the Constitutional provision of Seventh Schedule, on 18 January 1982. Thereafter, to introduce internal autonomy in tribal compact areas and to protect the socio-cultural fabric and economic interests of the tribes of the state, the long awaited TTAADC Act was passed under the Sixth Schedule of the Constitution replacing the 39 months old ADC under the Seventh Schedule. Thus, the Tripura Tribal Area Autonomous District Council came to effect on 1 April 1985.

Tripura Tribal Area Autonomous District Council – Myth or Reality!

The TTAADC was formed with three objectives: (i) to provide autonomy to tribal compact areas; (ii) to protect the socio-cultural-economic interests of the tribal people of the state; and (iii) to bring about all round development of the territory demarcated as ADC. The formation of TTAADC was met with much enthusiasm and was spontaneously accepted by the people. The ADC was given a free hand in allotment, occupation or use of scheduled land or management of any forest land which was not reserved, and it was given the right to regulate and control shifting cultivation as well as money-lending operations. The hitherto withdrawn tribesmen came out of their seclusion to get a share of their own governance.

Initially, an area of 7,132.56 sq km was brought under the jurisdiction of the TTAADC, i.e. almost 68 per cent of the total area of the state and where more than 60 per cent of the population was essentially of the tribal stock. Around 462 moujas were included within the tribal area, which accommodated 19 tribes in the same district council, a unique feature in the North-East. It was indeed a landmark achievement in realising the long-standing demands of the tribals of the state. The council consists of 30 members out of which 26 are from for tribes and two are unreserved, (since there are non-tribals residing in these areas too), who are elected on the basis of adult franchise, and two are nominated by the Governor of Tripura. The TTAADC is vested with two types of power, legislative and executive. Administration of TTAADC and its subordinate offices are managed from its headquarters in Khumulwng, West Tripura. The council is headed by its chairman who is chosen by the elected members of the council.

Executive functions of TTAADC are managed by the chief executive member, who is supported by nine more executive members. He is also responsible for day-to-day administrative functions.

The Seventy Third Amendment Act in April 1994 has virtually revolutionised the concept of democratic decentralisation and conferred constitutional status to the rural local self-governing institutions. The Village Committee Act 1994 passed by the TTAADC was aimed at establishing and developing local self-government and to make better provisions for administration of villages into well-developed and self-sufficient units. One of the important achievements of the district council during the period is holding the election of local bodies at village level and formation of elected village committee in February 2006. For the first time in the history of Tripura election to 527 village committees was held in 2006 as a mark of which has helped in ensuring community involvement in decision-making. At the grass-root level, there are 527 village councils functioning today. TTAADC has been working to implement various state plans, central plan and centrally sponsored schemes to ensure overall economic and social development of the people. As a result of this election, responsible elected village committees came into existence in place of nominated village committees. These village committees derive their power and responsibilities under Section 20 and 21 of Tripura Tribal Areas Autonomous District (Establishment of Village Committee) Act 1994. The district council also vested power and duties with the elected village committees for the implementation of the developmental schemes of the state government and the central Government.

Land Question and the TTAADC

Land, the most valuable endowment of nature, has been the most precious possession of the autochthons of the state and the loss of it meant loss of their self-esteem too. The establishment of the TTAADC was intrinsically related to issues connected with land; question of the state, priority was given to land-reclamation schemes, soil conservation, shifting cultivation and rehabilitation of landless tribals. It needs to be kept in mind that the influx of neighbouring plainlanders into Tripura was on a much higher scale in comparison to any other North-Eastern states, and they depended on agriculture as their only source of livelihood. Earlier, they had reclaimed these lands and transformed the same for settled cultivation, but now as land got demarcated into ADC and non-ADC areas these had to be surrendered, and this made land question more problematic. The Tripura Land Revenue and Land Reform Act (1960) was amended for the third time in 1975 wherein it was made clear that the tribesmen had to sell their land only to members of their community. But the fellow tribesmen were hardly in a position to buy such land. ADC is now trying to reform the land problems in the state and restore those lands which were given away to new settlers.

The Land Records and Settlement Department of ADC has been is given the task of distributing land to the landless residing in the ADC area. Even for allotment of khas land within the area concurrence of ADC is required. The 'Achievement Report' revealed that in the initial years 35,718 landless were allotted land, and of these, 2678 belonged to the 'other' category; also 4,251 jhumiyas were rehabilitated in 48 projects relating to pisciculture, animal husbandry, etc. State based or national rural employment programmes were also implemented in these areas. Social forestry and rubber plantations were encouraged too, which could ensure a decent living to the residents of the ADC areas who had to depend on land.

As can be seen from the recent Reports (2012–2013), the net cropped area has increased manifold (1,48,381 ha) as also the gross cropped area (2,10,701 ha) with a high cropping intensity mark of 142 per cent. The villagers are trained in the latest available cropping method and they are now aware of the use of market technologies, bio-fertilisers, increasing production through improved seeds, nutrients. Tribal people who have been allotted land or khas land are advised to reduce the intensity of shifting cultivation, which is proving to be ecologically very harmful. To provide sustainable employment using land the as the resource base, tribesmen are encouraged to take up rubber plantation in non-forest land. They are also asked to raise rubber nurseries to reduce transportation expenditure.

The village committees are playing a strong role in this aspect. They can identify the really needy families of the area who may be a tribal or a non-tribal even and enable them to get the benefits earmarked for them since they reside in the ADC areas. The objective of the TTAADC for initiating local self-government and to make provisions for administration of village into a well-developed self-sufficient unit seems to be getting into the right direction.

The Forest Rights Act and TTAADC

Forests are an essential component feature in the land question of the state yet it becomes a problem where population requires space for rehabilitation as well as development. Most of the tribes depended upon the forests for collecting fuel wood, dry leaves, fruits, etc. or even for activities connected with *jhuming*. Their religion and traditions were also woven around the forests. As long as land was abundantly available such traditions were ecologically viable but rampant destruction of the forests led to dwindling of forest cover sooner than expected. 'Jangal Abadi' schemes had to be imposed, which hit the tribal economy many a time, a the forest areas had to be 'opened up' for rehabilitation purposes or practising shifting cultivation or even to collect forest products. The National Forest Policy (1952) emphasised a balanced and complementary land use and left it to the states to promote and protect the forests. In Tripura though the process of afforestation had started almost simultaneously with deforestation, forest cover receded at a regular pace. From a decent cover of 8,956 sq km in 1951–52 it receded to 5,920.30 sq km in 1981–82 due to unchecked growth of population and opening up of forest areas.

The Scheduled Tribes and Other Traditional Forest Dwellers (Recognition of Forest Rights) Act, 2006, was passed in the Parliament on 13 December 2006 and came to force on 29 December 2006. The act recognises the rights, responsibilities and authority of the forest-dwelling scheduled tribes and other traditional forest dwellers for sustainable use, conservation of biodiversity and maintenance of ecological balance. It also recognises their rights on ancestral land and their habitat. The act addresses the main aspects of land occupation, recognises and vests the occupational rights of an individual or a family or a community on the date of commencement of the act, but restricts the area under occupation to an extent not exceeding four hectares. Members of a forest-dwelling community have the right to hold and live in the forest land or use it for self cultivation for food security and livelihood. It also lays emphasis on the right to make use of minor forest produce including all non-timber forest produce of plant origin, e.g. bamboo, cane, coconut, honey, medicinal plants and herbs of various types. In light of above specifications, the act offers a wide opportunity to address the long-standing insecurity of tenurial and access rights of the forest-dwelling scheduled tribes and other traditional forest dwellers.

The aim of the state in implementing the FRA is to provide sustainable livelihood opportunities to the forest dwellers while retaining their symbiotic relationship with the forest and ensuring their socio-economic development as well as retaining the ecological balance. Out of the total geographical area of 10,491.69 sq km forest constitutes 6,294.26 sq km. Presently, most of these lands are being utilised for subsistence of the livelihood of several ethnic groups of Tripura. But the traditional practice of ecologically disturbing fragile system of agriculture, i.e. shifting cultivation (jhum) is still being followed by them, though with reduced propensity.

Under the provision of the act, Government of Tripura has already identified 1.17 lakh tribal families and allotted 1.78 lakh hectare of land among them. A large part of this area shall add to the existing 2.55 lakh hectares of cultivable area of the state. The land allotted to the forest dwellers of the state under the ST and OTFD (FRA) Act, 2006 is spread over 40 blocks. A three-year implementation programme is initiated too (2011–2014) wherein 25,000 ha is allotted for agriculture, 35,000 ha for horticulture, vegetable, etc. 34,500 ha for bamboo cultivation, and 10,000 ha for fodder-based crops. On the basis of reconnaissance survey of area under Forest Dwellers Act, 2006 it has been estimated that nearly 15–20 per cent and 25–30 per cent area can be brought to relocate their dwelling and also allowed rights under sustainable eco-friendly use for agricultural crops, vegetable, bamboo cultivation and other horti-plantation crops. The joint forest management (JFM) activities also aims at regenerating forest resources, meeting the local needs, sharing expected benefits and also reducing dependency on forests. At present the TTAADC controls a substantial forest area of the state as can be seen from the following data:

Table 13.3

Status of Forest in Tripura and TTAADC

Category	*Tripura (sq km)*	*ADC (sq km)*
Reserve Forest	3,588.20	3,129.57
Proposed Reserved Forest	663.70	114.29
Unclassified Govt. Forest	2,040.80	1,966.63
Protected Forest	1.60	0.75

Source: Office of the Department of Forests, Government of Tripura.

As it is seen from the Table 13.3, the total forest area under ADC is quite considerable covering 5,211.24 sq km out of 6,294.30 sq km. Most of the reserve forest comes under ADC jurisdiction and the essential forest dwellers who are mostly marginal farmers are now cultivating fruits, vegetables to ensure sustainable economic development. Anganvan Prakalpa, planting trees of commercially viable species, or those which are fast-growing species, raising rubber seedlings, etc. are carried out under the RKVY and MNREGA schemes. The annual reports of the TTAADC shows that 4,750 ha land has been brought under vegetable cultivation and 2,400 ha under fruits using the FRA, and there are 4,515 beneficiaries involved. The three newly created forest divisions, namely, Khumlwng, Bir Chandra Manu, and 82 Miles areas are catering to such forest dwellers, where scientific methods of forestry are introduced to ensure sustainable economic development to wean away the tribes from practising conventional primitive method of cultivation.

Education and Socio-Cultural Scenario

Education is a necessity, a tool for development and knowledge and is a renewable resource that can compensate for any inadequacy. The TTAADC has given emphasis on this factor since its inception in 1985. Initially, 1,374 junior basic (JB) schools were transferred to the control of the ADC, and under the SSA scheme more than 687 new JB schools were opened till 2009 along with four residential schools and one English medium school. Now the tribal students of the ADC area can have an access to quality education even in the remote corners of the state. These students are also entitled to house stipend, dress, attendance grant and also avail the mid-day meal programme up to class VIII. To reduce the drop-out rate, free text books are distributed, infrastructure developed and awareness spread among the neighbourhood to send the out-of –school students to school. Moreover, to raise the motivational level of the teachers, workshop-cum-training programmes are being organised. Also the students are trained in ICT methods, 100 schools are given K-Yan computers so that 5,000 students may be benefitted. Vocabulary workshops are organised. Kok-Borok dictionaries are being compiled to spread education in local language so that students do not drop out of the education system. The ICDS projects managed by the ADC regularly campaign for spread health and hygiene awareness among the rural people. The main objectives of healthcare services under TTAADC are to provide institutional healthcare services at the village level and popularise school-based health programmes

In order to develop the tribal culture and preserve their traditional art, a museum-cum-heritage centre, a tribal folk music college, a tribal cultural centre have been established. Efforts are made to revive their songs, musical instruments, traditional ornaments, costumes through Sahitya Sanskriti fairs. A small wing of science and technology department is established here with the aim of spreading scientific awareness among people of the remote corners of the state. To encourage the tribal youth to take up bio-entrepreneurship in fishery, agriculture, industry, positive steps are being taken.

Padmabil Block under TTAADC – A Case Study

To get an actual picture of the grass-root level work of the TTAADC, Padmabil block is chosen in the present exercise. The geographical area covers 81.625 sq km, which falls entirely under the ADC area having 15 villages. The total population is 44,787(male 22,243 and female 22,544) with a tribal population of 42,556, constituting 95.01 per cent, while there is a marginal population of few 'other' category people residing in there. The total available cultivable area is 4,603 ha while 3,601 is *tilla* (hilly) land and 7,449 ha is forest land.

On enquiry it was found that the a majority of the people depend upon agricultural activity and livestock rearing. Besides, commercial plantations in rubber, tea, fruits bamboo, teak and others are also undertaken. Almost all the major habitation areas are connected by roads and electricity has reached all villages. There are 51 JB schools, 47 SB schools, 6 high schools and 1 higher secondary school. Consequently, the literacy level has also risen in this area with only 96 illiterate persons in the age group of 15–50 years. Skill development training programmes are organised to impart skills among the youth of the region. Moreover, there are 45 continuing education centres.

There are 2,635 persons in the block who are forest right beneficiaries. Besides pisciculture, cultivation of other cereals, pulses, oilseeds are also very much encouraged and 614 ha are brought under irrigation. About 528 self help groups (SHG) are conducting regular workshops on lemon, bamboo, mushroom, pineapple cultivation.

Discussions with the chairperson and vice-chairperson of village committee revealed that almost all beneficiary schemes were being implemented here and the most important was the MNREGA and IAY schemes that had benefited a substantial number of inhabitants. A large number of SHGs are working here that are supported by the local people and administration and the youth are also benefitting immensely. Unyielding jhum is being discarded and new, improved methods of farming are being resorted to by the farmers of the block. Drop-out rates are brought lower and interestingly girls outnumber the boys and even avail higher learning opportunity. The usual story of lack of adequate funds remains, but there has been a sincere attempt to achieve the target even if the means are limited.

Concluding Remarks and Suggestions

The setting up of TTAADC empowered the indigenous tribes of the state and priority was given to their social, cultural and economic interests. In the initial period this 'Symbol of Hope' could hardly address the problems, many enterprising projects took a long time due to governmental procedures. Ignorance, illiteracy, and motivation for an improved economy remain a hindrance for tribes to take advantage of the new engagement. The ADC did not have a village council at the time and so could not show 'originality and innovativeness' and matters had to be disposed through time-consuming processes. Lack of adequate infra-structure, geographical isolation and recurring ethnic problems had severely impeded development work during those days. One should keep in mind that both the tribals and non-tribals of the state were equal partners in this long-drawn struggle for autonomy, but those non-trbals residing in these areas soon lost their rights over the land. Now they viewed the ADC promoting 'a narrow, selfish interest of the ruling class of exploiters in the tribal society'. It also needs to be borne in mind that in Tripura the ADC was built under the acceptance of the tribe as a generic and composite entity, a council for tribal areas rather than for a single tribe. Perhaps to deal with such administrative lacunae the Reangs, the Mizos, the Chakmas started demanding separate autonomy status. A schism was created between the two categories of people inhabiting the state; one could not take the risk of appeasing one segment at the cost of another. Hence, the state embarked upon a policy of improving the general standard of living of all people equitably and also to go ahead with achieving self-sufficiency in food production.

At present the TTAADC is getting funds from: (i) plan assistance from the state government; (ii) share of taxes from the state government; and (iii) transfer of funds. Meeting the salaries of staff was deputed to ADC by the state government in respect of primary education and for implementation of specific shemes. The village committees are set up with the objective to establish and develop local self-government and to make better provisions for administration of village into well-developed and sufficient unit. One of the important achievements of the district council during the period is holding the election of local bodies at village level and formation of elected village committee in February 2006 and again in 2010. As a result of this election responsible elected village committees came into existence in place of nominated village committees. One of the important aspects of elected village committee is the representation of women to the extent of 50 per cent of the total members, both in the village committee and as chairperson of those committees, apart from adequate representation of Scheduled Castes and Scheduled Tribes according to ratio of the population. The district council also constituted zonal development committees for each zone, sub-zonal development committee for ADC Villages of mixed RD block and TTAADC block development committee for 17 numbers. RD blocks, a which are exclusively within Sixth Scheduled areas, in which chairman and vice-chairman of the village committee have been included as members and MDC/MLA have been designated as chairman of the said committee. The ADC village committees are assisted by the village secretary of the village committee and as interviews have shown they are constantly on the vigil and help the local inhabitants to tide over their problems.

As was seen in villages of Padmabil block, introduction and subsequent implementation of a variety of economic measures like plantations, nursery raisings, horticulture, animal husbandry, piggery have undoubtedly aroused a new enthusiasm among the inhabitants. Funds are never ample but the reports show that more often than not the targets are achieved. The village committee has taken upon themselves the responsibility to initiate the development schemes for their village areas under the control and guidance of the executive committee. They look after the sanitation and conservancy of village areas, cleaning and maintaining of village roads and paths, construction and maintenance of rest house in the villages and maintenance of children, adult and women.

The ADC cannot manage all kinds of forests and often fails to motivate the inhabitants in preserving the same. The hilly terrain of the ADC areas render it impossible to carry out settled cultivation and often jhum is resorted to which destroys the soil nutrients and even lowers the yield. They are now given training in improved farming practices. Women empowerment and youth development programmes are encouraged through SHGs. It is expected that with the handing down of a few more rights, the ADC will be able to bring about a qualitative change in the lives of the people who live in such areas. No doubt, the major sources of revenue are still in the control of the state government and there are no Constitutional bodies in the council for planning or finance but, the state government is always ready for providing welfare grants to all its people, especially to those in the remote corners. A few suggestions may be made here: the district councils may be given more power as has been given to the Panchayat bodies by the 73rd and 74th Amendments; also all grants from the planning board may be made available directly to ADC and not routed through the state planning board departments such as rural development, agriculture. A few departments like land reform and revenue, health and family welfare, fisheries, forests need to be brought under the ADC control. Moreover, the customary laws need to be codified, which has always been a demand of the tribal people. There is also a demand that the police forces be formed from the members of local communities for better coordination of security for daily activities in ADC areas.

The State of Tripura has witnessed an abnormal spurt of population increase and creation of TTAADC cannot solve all the problems facing both the segments of the population as all the tribes could not be brought within its purview. Autonomy in its actual sense needs to come along with economic well being and this needs a monitoring cell to constantly review the welfare schemes of the government in an unbiased way. The benefits of welfare are to be reaped both by the tribal and non-tribal people of the state. Only then can the indigenous people will be in a position to exercise their free will. TTAADC is only an attempt in that direction, which in the recent times has been trying to give adequate representation to the tribes or ethnic groups of the state and is marching towards an inclusive growth with the aim of providing inclusive governance. From a tribe's own perspective, autonomy in this form may be a partial fulfilment to its craving for self rule.

References

Bhattacharjee, H. 1993. 'TUJS Alienated from Tribals', *The Statesman*, 11 July.

Bhattacharya, S.B. 2005. 'Autonomy in the North-East: The Hills of Tripura and Mizoram'. In *The politics of Autonomy: Indian Experiences*. Edited by Ranabir Samaddar. New Delhi: Sage Publications.

Bhaumik, Subir, and Jayanta Bhattacharya. 2005. 'Autonomy in the North East: The Hills of Tripura and Mizoram'. In *The politics of Autonomy: Indian Experiences*. Edited by Ranabir Samaddar. New Delhi: Sage Publications.

Basu Majumder, Chandrika. 2004. 'Tripura Tribal Areas Autonomous District Council: Problems and Prospects'. In *Decentralised Planning and Development: New Diretions.* Edited by Amalesh Banerjee. New Delhi: Kanishka Publishers.

Chakraborty, D., 2004. *Land Question in Tripura.* New Delhi: Akansha Publishing Co. Government of India, Administrative Reforms Commission, 1968 Report of the Study Team on the Union Territories and NEFA, New Delhi.

Government of Tripura. 1952. 'Forest Department Notifications No. 13', 29 April.

Government of Tripura. 1979. 'The Tripura Tribal Areas Autonomous District Council Act'.

Imperial Gazetteer of India, 1905. London: Oxford University Press, Vol. XIII. p. 122.

Koloy, H. 2001. 'Experience of Autonomous District Council in the North East India with Special Reference to Tripura State'.

Mackenzie, A. (1884) 1981. *History of the Relations of the Government with the Hill Tribes of the North-Eastern Frontier of Bengal.* Reprint, New Delhi: Mittal Publication.

North East Newsletter, Vol. XIII, No. 2 February. 2011.

Roy, Jagat Jyoti. 1997. 'Working of Autonomous District Council in Tripura in Autonomous District Council', In *The Autonomous District Council.* Edited by L.S. Gassah, New Delhi: Omsons Publications.

Report on Functioning, Structure of Local Governance in North Eastern Region with special reference to Autonomous District Councils/Autonomous Regional Councils, 2009, Submitted to Commission on Centre State Relations, Government of India by North Eastern Hill University, Shillong.

TTAADC, The Annual Reports of TTAADC, Various Issues.

Tripura Act, No. 12 Tripura Govt. pp 3–13 NEFA, Delhi, 1968, para 691.

Tripura Legislative Assembly Proceedings 15.12.67 Pvt Members' Resolution, A. Deb Barma and B.C. Deb Barma, pp. 2833.

www. law min.nic.in/ncrwc/final report/vi ch.9.html, Article 244–2. Last accessed on 21 December 2013.

PART VI

Emerging Areas of Tribal Studies

PART VI

Emerging Areas of Tribal Studies

CHAPTER 14

Salvaging a Common Descent and Lineage Between an Ex-'Criminal Tribe' of India and the Present-Day Gypsies of Europe

Weaving History and Spinning Tales on the Boundaries of 'Civilisation'[1]

SUBIR RANA

> The lyricism of marginality may find inspiration in the image of the 'outlaw', the great social nomad who prowls on the confines of a docile, frightened order.
>
> —Foucault 1991

> Travelling for profit is encouraged. Travelling for survival is condemned .... The globalized world is a hospitable and friendly place for tourists, but inhospitable and hostile to vagabonds. The latter are barred from following the pattern that the first have set. But the pattern was not meant for them in the first place.
>
> —Bauman 2002: 84

Introduction: Movement Metropole and the Criminal Tribes Act XXVII of 1871

Movement of people and livestock from one place to the other either in search of food, fodder and livelihood options was never uncommon in the ancient times and was a norm in almost all ancient cultures and societies. There was never any problem with non-sedentariness as itinerancy and ambulation were seen as endemic to the lifestyle and survival strategy of mobile communities like that of nomads, peripatetics and gypsies.[2] Moreover, not so long ago in the annals of history, roving bands of people and nomadic groups from Central Asia like the Huns, Tartars, Timurids and Mongols gave rise to 'nomadic empires.' According to Khazanov, most of the nomadic conquests were not a cause but rather a consequence of the weakness and disintegration of 'sedentary' states.[3] Chris Bayly informs us that large tracts of North India in the eighteenth century were already outside state control. After the decline of Mughal power, these areas were held under the sovereignty of loose federations of war leaders or titular heads, bands of herdsmen, 'plunderers', and other wandering groups.[4] The nomadic societies fitted well with the host societies and rather owed their existence to sedentary societies – a fact echoed by Khazanov and Casimir as well.

There were social, cultural and economic exchanges between the sedentary and nomadic communities. Casimir (2003) alludes to this historical fact saying that sedentary population lived in a symbiotic relationship along with different nomadic groups which at times overlapped due to the economic strategies devised by the groups. He gives the example of Banjaras in India who owned huge herds and functioned mainly as transporters, but at the same time were also attached with peripatetic entertainers. Not only this, but all great overland trade routes since antiquity and the Middle Ages were pioneered either by the nomads or with their participation. These social exchanges and interactions, cultural barters and encounters in later centuries got documented in oral traditions, works of art and in various cults and legends. Socio-economic engagements were largely peaceful owing to strict regulatory laws, and the various groups were integrated into larger regional systems through multiple criss-crossing ties. However, certain developments in other parts of the world in the 17th and 18th centuries were to have a strong impact on the itinerant and nomadic communities in specific and the Indian society in general.

The onset of the middle ages in Europe marked a rupture in the otherwise 'quiet' society. This period heralded a new era of scientific temper and new discoveries under the banner of enlightenment. European society was radically changing its social and political contours under the influence of these scientific undercurrents. Moreover, with the dawn of Industrial Revolution in England in the 18th century, the social landscape of societies and empires, kingdoms and colonies also altered, which later affected other parts of the western world. New cities armed with industries and factories started sprouting that required cheap labour for these industrial houses. Rousseau's and Locke's ideas of 'private property' having gained currency in the West led to its destruction and disrespect being akin to crime while undermining human life and dignity of the fringe population in the European society. This resulted in two island-like communities consisting of the opulent on one hand and the pauperised on the other. This led to the mushrooming of counter-society of the poor and oppressed on society's rim. An increase in crime and criminal activities in the wake of famines, impoverishment and hunger deaths was reported from all over Europe followed by a spate of diseases. Population was dwindling as living a healthy life became a precarious enterprise in the otherwise developed and progressive Occident.

According to Silvia Federici, Europe during the Middle Ages was witnessing migration, vagabondage and the rise of 'crimes against property' as strategies to fight impoverishment and disposession. This situation prevailed in Europe as well as in England owing largely due to the Enclosure Movement, capitalist accumulation and Price Revolution leading to the criminalisation of the working class. There were attempts by the government at desocialisation and decollectivisation attacking all forms of collective sociality and sexuality including sports, dances, festivals and other group-rituals. By mid-eighteenth century, movement of people especially on the periphery started being seen as strange and charged with suspicion, illegitimacy and criminality. The 'Bloody Laws' introduced in the 16th and 17th century Europe was to make vagabonds available for exploitation. This period witnessed nomads as being included in the register of disasters that listed, among others, cholera and plague. In 18th century France and England, a special category called 'dangerous classes' or for those who lived on society's rims came up in the official register. England passed legislations for harsh anti-vagabond laws prescribing enslavement and capital punishment in cases of recidivism. In many cases, physical torture accompanied by dismemberment and executions for being unproductive were also being taken as normal.

As mobility and flux, especially on the society's edges, was increasingly viewed as societal problem, rapid developments in the field of science and technology rendered nomadism and ambulatory practices as anti-state and therefore 'criminal.' The popularity of pseudo-science and the grand project of social engineering called 'Eugenics' as proposed by the biometrician Francis Galton,[17] the theory of Social Darwinism along with Lombroso's notion of hereditary criminality divided societies along racial lines.[18] In India, this was rendered possible through the colonial interest and anxiety to rule over the natives[19] and a giddy concoction of many pseudo-scientific theories, a heightened and racialised biology and a frantic *disciplinary* parade of anthropometry,[20] craniology, ethnology and anthropology. All these resulted in a grid like classification of the indigene into 'martial races,' 'criminal tribes,' 'nekmash,' 'badmash,' and 'effeminate Bengalis', etc.

The 18th century and the beginning of 19th witnessed an upsurge in criminal activities both in the metropoles and the colonies. France during late 18th century was a scene of terror and crime so much so that crime and criminals dominated popular culture, literature, statistical accounts, and documentary shows. Crime was a much talked about affair in people's lives in Europe at the turn of the nineteenth century since now the modus operandi of committing crime took a tangential turn. The lower classes who were equated with 'barbarians', 'savages', 'nomads' were now also branded as '*classes dangereuses*' or 'dangerous classes' and clubbed with the 'labouring classes' due to the brotherhood of poverty that they both shared. In the Indian hinterland, new kinds of crime and criminal activity like cattle theft or poisoning, vengeful arson, crop pilfering, counterfeiting, *megpunnaism* took roots. But it was thuggee and dacoity that ultimately became matters of serious concern for the empire as it challenged the very premise of the colonial law and order situation. So much so that a thug language called *'Ramaseeana'* was 'deciphered' by William Sleeman on the basis of which he listed various peripatetic communities as *thug-tribes*. It must be noted that even the defenders of the Crown were themselves part of these criminal activities. W.J. Hatch in his book *The Land Pirates of India* says, 'There is no doubt that for many years the police were hand in glove with the gangs rampaging round the countryside, and that they took part of the spoils of the robber bands.'

The reasons for crime and criminal activity showing a sudden swell was only natural as the colonial rule had created 'states of exception' within the colony. Speaking of the marginal population, a gradual elimination from their resources had pushed the tribals occasionally to lapse into criminality. 'Owing to their shrinking subsistence base, the tribal world took to plunder. Matters would become worse in a famine when they would descend from hills to loot villages which invited heavy reprisals.'[25] In fact, food prices during colonial India became the 'natural barometer of crime' and the 'the crime thermometer of India' went 'up and down with its harvests.'[26] Famine in India during the nineteenth century began to be regarded as 'the special famine crime.' Moreover, famines were managed by the British administration and acted as a pretext for helping the bigger grain merchants.[27] According to Meena Radhakrishna, repeated famine was one of the reasons advanced by the colonial administrators behind Indian criminality among other 'secular' causes like the introduction of the railways,[28] new forest and agricultural policies, etc. Bhangya Bhukya (2007) adds that dacoity was also a result of convicts having to commit a security after their release to pay the debts incurred to pay security.[29] However, in numerous cases, 'crime' was constructed to suit colonial policies and in many others they were matters of desperation to earn a living and subsist.[30] According to Arnold, these were complemented by the recurrent cycles of famine and draught which in turn were frequented by the trinity of smallpox, cholera and plague that caused 'tensions' in the empire in the nineteenth century. David Arnold says that the tendency of the dominant castes to assert their authority over lower castes and keep enemies at bay resulted in crime graph swelling up.[31] However, situation was not too good in the mother country as well.

England in the late eighteenth and nineteenth century was heading towards a socio-economic catastrophe and its colonies were in a state of unrest and rebellion. There was a 'moral pressure' on the empire to put a check on this escalating existential crisis that had reached the 'tipping point' due to the revolt of 1857 coupled by a growing fear from roving bands of armed cavalry men from Central Asia and mercenaries from Arabia who filtered into Hindustan and the peninsula through land and sea to engage in the buoyant military market.[32] Also movement of people in the guise of mendicants, fakirs, beggars and lepers had become easier and this had raised suspicion of the colonial authorities of an armed rebellion against the empire. The financial interests of the empire which incurred through a robust 'opium trade' in Central India and Rajputana after 1817–1818 necessitated that the circuits of traffic and trade be made safe from thugs or hereditary garrotters, dacoits, drifters, vagrants and such anti-social elements. The colonial administration also apprehended a nexus of the local zamindars and jagirdars with local subaltern communities to raid and target British authority.[33] Also a growing number of restless and unproductive populace who were neither taxable nor loyal to the empire, needed to be regulated. The empire was also facing the ire of peasants and tribal population who from time to time raised the banner of rebellion against unjust and oppressive agrarian policies. Nicholas Dirks gives the examples of Gujjars and Jats in eastern Uttar Pradesh who had posed problems for the administration due to their 'criminal propensities',[34] In some of these war-like efforts, the colonial state also sometimes faced defeat and therefore was apprehensive of another mutiny that would have engulfed the Empire completely.

Ranajit Guha has already mentioned that there were not less than 110 known instances of these protests and sporadic rebellions in a spread of 117 years ranging from Rangpur *dhing* to the Birasaite *ulgulan*. These rebellions, protests, jacqueries, revolts, uprisings, insurrections were staged by tribal communities and rural masses. According to Guha, 'insurgency' was particularly important as it referred to the consciousness that informed the activities of the rural masses such as jacqueries, revolt, uprising, etc. or to use their regional nomenclatures *dhing, hool, bidroha, ulgulan, fituri*, etc. To dispel this looming fear of another catastrophe, several legislations like the Indian Penal Code in 1860 and the Criminal Procedure Code in 1861 were enacted. Of these 'modalities of surveillance' an important piece of legislation called the Criminal Tribes Act XXVII of 1871 (CTA) was introduced, which marked a watershed in the history of crime, criminality and tribal history in India.

According to the CTA, crime was seen to be possessing genetic traits and thereby passed on from one generation to the other. Alongside this notion of 'hereditary criminality,' movement was turned into a criminal act with the colonial state acting as the 'panoptican.'Along with the beggars, vagrants, eunuchs and prostitutes, they also comprised the 'exterior castes' and the 'unproductive' population in the census report. The colonial state turned into a petentiary or a carceral state and the act inaugurated a new penal-scopic regime that declared almost two hundred tribal/forest and rural communities of India including wandering people, nomads, prostitutes, minstrels, beggars, mendicants and eunuchs as 'criminal tribes' (CT) or 'hereditary criminals.' The CTA was first applied to Northwest Provinces, Oudh and Punjab and later in 1911[35] a revised version was applied to the whole of India, which included the Bombay and Madras Presidencies. The CTs were enumerated as a separate social group from the 1911 census[36] and this act was further modified once again in 1924. This was done to provide greater judicial control and intrusion into the lives of the so called 'criminal tribes and castes.' According to Bhukya, the CTA was a reminder of Britain's own Black Act of 1723 passed by the Parliament under which hunters and paupers were to be hanged publicly and legally.[37]

Anti-movement legislations like the CTA that treated nomadism with its principal markers-mobility and itinerancy as a veritable threat to sedentary societies affected South Asia as a whole. It also hampered the movement of nomads by increasing the migration phases or forcing them to seek new pastures by hiking the grazing fees for the pastoralists. Europe witnessed mass persecutions and purging of wandering people, beggars, vagabonds, gypsies and nomads who inhabited the 'boundaries of civilisation' or the 'Zomia' as James Scott would put it. They comprised the 'abjects' or the 'subalterns' who were hounded by the colonial state and were treated as criminals and fugitives at large and who were directed by the state to be 'yoked' to lead a 'disciplined' and 'civilised' life.

The Nat as a 'Fourth World' Representative: 'Regimes of Circulation', 'Mobile Clusters' and 'Multiple Traditions'

The early historical and anthropological accounts regarding the identity of Nats were fraught with slipperiness for they were clubbed with many other smaller communities on a similar historical footing and occupational similarity. For all practical purposes, Nat became a leaky and porous category with crossovers and overlapping tendencies.[40] In reality, Nat was an *ocupational* (my emphasis) term which included a number of different clans who were grouped together merely on account of their common occupation of dancing, prostitution and performance of various industries.[41] This coalescing of many similar occupational and professional groups under one umbrella formation comprised a 'mobile cluster', i.e. the branching out of a particular ambulatory community into different professional groups who continued to live together in a symbiotic relationship with one another in one particular region. For example, Charans in the 17th century were a 'mobile cluster' who were engaged as animal husbanders, bards, merchants, farmers, genealogists, priests, guides for travellers and carriers of goods.

The Nats formed a rich talent-pool of indigenous knowledge systems and native skills. The Nats are known in the past as a community of tramping entertainers, peripatetic conmen, conjurers and charlatans in history besides carrying multiple other professional identities. This included herbalists, cupping artists, dentists and quack healers, tattooists, mat and basket makers, weavers, acrobats, jugglers, tricksters, thimble riggers, bards, genealogists, cattle herders, peddlers in daily wares, dancers and even prostitutes, etc. who together formed 'regimes of circulation.' There were interactions, exchanges and circulation of 'information, knowledge, ideas, techniques, skills, cultural production (texts, songs), religious practices, gods and even rumors'[42] among these different occupational groups at these 'contact zones.' These exchanges not only implied an ensemble of criss-crossing circulatory flows but changed things, men and notion that in turn ... shape(d) society.[43] This 'circulatory' nature of exchange translated in a more concrete and material form especially in the interstices and fringes of the Empire and entailed what Robert Redfield calls 'great tradition' and 'little tradition' possibly leading to 'multiple traditions'[44] or heterogeneity of cultures.

The Nats comprising of peddlers and itinerants, bards and conjurers were carriers of 'little tradition' and formed an important nodes and networks of exchange, communication and linkages at the micro level. To say that a peddler was only a mobile trader would amount to limiting the professional variability and diversification of his talents and skills. Professional boundaries were permeable ... identities multiple and intertwined[45] and there were cases of vocational overlappings and momentary crossovers (this did not however involve any dexterous or technical act) on certain occasions. 'In the Punjab countryside, cultivators and artisans could engage in part-time peddling activity and make up for the losses suffered in their traditional craft or when cultivators had time away from their fields.'[46] Moreover, 'in the vast network of peddling trade there were innumerable other small actors who forged countless links and because of which services and goods flowed within the rural world, connecting one village with another and likewise the town and cities to the country.'[47]

The Nats made their living by moving from one village to another and displayed skills of dexterity in village fairs and on festive occasions like marriages and other religious festivals. They were joined in by other variants of providers of entertainment and amusement offering a multitude of related services like the *Qalandars* who entertained with the monkey; *Bazigars* and *Madaris* with their tumbling, juggling and magic; *Jogis* and *Mirasis* who were genealogists and bards by profession; and *Faqirs* who played musical instruments. All these comprised part of a rich civilisational history and an illustrious cultural tapestry of the Nats, one that wove dexterity and spun tales on the boundaries of 'civilisation.'

While milling and traversing the villages, towns, urban centres and far-flung areas, these entertainers and performers, bards and peddlers, became vehicles of propagating the message of peace, brotherhood and harmony. They propagated the popular culture that bonded rural communities across regions, despite all their differences, strife and conflicts. In this way, the Nats connected different communities in the rural hinterland with the towns and cities and finally with the nation through their ballads, folk songs, drama and amusements.

Origin, Etymology and Myths: Tales of Blue Blood Origin

Nats have been one of the most active and widely spread itinerant communities in Indian history. Their adventurous peregrinations and ambulatory lifestyle can be gauged by the fact that the Nats were found in as far as Lahore and Baluchistan (the then undivided part of India). The origin of the generic word *'Nata'* can be traced to ancient India and finds mention in scriptures like the *Vedas,* Valmiki's *Ramayana*, Vatsyayana's *Kamasutra*, Manu's *Manusmriti*, Kautilya's *Arthasastra* and Bharat's *Natyasastra* besides Buddhist texts and Jain granthas. They also find a rich mention in the census reports and government documents of colonial and post-colonial times as well as in the personal memoirs, travelogues and works of colonial administrator-proto ethnographers. Through these important source materials, we are made aware of the social role of the Nats and their occupational profile as actors, dramatists, performers and dancers. These texts prove that the Nats had been in existence since 600 B.C. to 300 B.C., i.e. from the *Sutra* period.

The generic meaning of the word *Nata* comes from the root *nat* and has its different variations like *natati* (to dance), *natyati* (to represent anything dramatically, act, perform, imitate). The word *nat* however stands for an actor, dancer or mime and *nata* corresponds to jugglers, acrobats, buffoons, conmen and performers practising sleight of hand and exhibiting feats of agility. In the caste gradation, Nat has been counted among the seven *antyajanya* and were equivalent to the Shudras in the caste stratification from the past 250 years. In the *Smritis*, food given by Natas have been treated as impure and therefore not worth eating. According to the *Dharmasutras*, those dancers who traded their dancing and acting talents were treated as fallen and degraded.

The word *Narttaka* owes its origin to the root word *nat* and means a dancer who also performs extraordinary feats of strength and agility. The word *Nataka* means play par excellence, which shows worthy and exalted personages only and comprises all the elements of a dramatic composition.

Nati meant an actress, courtesan or a harlot and *Nataraja* or *Natesvara* symbolised the 'King or Lord of Dancers' that is Siva.[54]

During the Mughal period, it seems that the Nats enjoyed a position of eminence as trainers in music, dance and acrobatic performances and started claiming their ancestry to the Mughal court.[55] During this period, Nats were known among people as artists trained and well versed in the art of music and dance. Abul Fazl in his *Ain-i-Akbari*,[56] notes that the *Nats* were 'rope dancers' and they performed 'wonderful acrobatic feats' and played on the *tal*[57] and the *duhul*. A section of the Nat was called '*bahurupiya*' which derives from the word *bahu-rupi*, i.e. multiple-forms or one who practised the art of disguise. In some medieval texts, they are also shown to be theatre artistes or *nautee* or *nati*, i.e. instructors of musical arts.[58]

The obscure 'origin' of the Nats[59] and the multiple versions around it makes their historicity an enriching and engaging exercise. The oral tradition of the Nat traces their ancestry to the Rajput as well as Brahmins. Some of them still claim ancestory to the chivalrous Hindu ruler of Mewar in north-western India during medieval times. Maharana Pratap celebrate his birth anniversary with great pomp and show. Since Maharana Pratap was a Rajput, the Nats too follow the rules of purity and pollution within their own sub-divisions as well as castes that are ranked inferior to them like Chamar, Dhobi and Dusadh. Rajnats who claim positions be at the apex of the Nat social pyramid, were supported by kingdoms and principalities, landowning and the elite class who wanted to be entertained and therefore had a retinue of performers that included acrobats, jugglers, singers, bards, genealogists and also concubines.[60]

However, other myths of origin place them at par with the lowest in the social hierarchy that is the *antyajanya* or the lowest of the low. A common thread runs through all these myths and origin stories of peripatetic communities where tales of exile are followed by an act of transgression of norms: sexual promiscuity which is both acknowledged and suppressed: representation of birth as immaculate conception sanctifies the person born, imbuing him with mythic and divine significance.[61] The notion of a good past and a fall or decline from that due to a mistake or a curse is embedded in many other peripatetic myths. Just as the myths of origin of the Nats and its various versions render their intelligibility a bit muddled, so are the opinions centered around the community's link with the modern-day Gypsies in Europe.

Tracing Lineage, Descent and Affinity with the present day Gypsies of Europe

A great historical debate has been raging in recent time that has important bearings on the historical antecedents of the mobile and peregrinatory communities of India, viz. the nomads, vagrants Gypsies and vagabonds and their contemporaries in modern Europe. Academic debate centring around the theory of a common lineage and descent between the Gypsies of India and the modern Gypsies of Europe has been split up into two contending camps. While scholars like Angus Fraser, Ian Hancock, Captain David Richardson, Grellman and many others assert and claim a common ancestry with the Indian Gypsies, others like

Judith Okely and David Mayall, refute such a claim. However, it must be pointed out that there has been a strange and 'un-explained hesitancy' in accepting an Indian origin of the European Gypsies and therefore a common ancestry. Yet few others have even resorted to religious scriptures like the Bible to substantiate their viewpoint of an Egyptian origin of the Gypsies as these two similar sounding words[62] might be taken as a veritable proof of the origin of the present day gypsies in Europe.

This research takes into account those wide-ranging claims and counter-claims that deal with the terminology and 'true' identity of the 'Gypsy' from their land of origin and on their route to Europe. This section tries to engage with the claims of descent and lineage as well as historical continuum of the present Gypsies of Europe with the 'wandering tribes' or the 'Shudras' and so-called 'badmash' or the 'criminal tribes' of India like the Nats, Kanjars, Sansis and Doms, etc.

In the absence of a written history and a literate tradition, the history of Gypsy society lies fragmented as documents with the dominant non-gypsy or Gorgio or Gadje society.[64] At best, when such an effort was made by others by way of denigrating them especially in the Elizabethan times, it was put under a genre called 'rogue literature.'[64] Under these circumstances when there is a tabula rasa like situation, language then becomes the most indubitable proof of the ... genealogy of mankind; they add often physical certainty to historical evidence of ancient migrations, and of the revolutions of ages which left no written documents behind them.[65] Scholars, philologists, historians and linguists have sought to engage with these issues basing their arguments on philological and linguistic similitude between the two ambulatory communities. These ideational exchanges have raised some very important issues of translation, transmission and transformation of philological traditions from one continent to the other. However, in the recent past, matters have attained 'scientificity' as geneticists and natural scientists have collaborated in this pan-India 're-search' and found very striking results.

Sher Singh Sher in his book *The Sansis of Punjab* (1965) has tried to affiliate the modern day gypsies of Europe with the nomads and vagabonds of India specifically the Sansis of Punjab and Rajputs and Jats of North India by providing certain historical proof as also from the commonality in rituals and ceremonies from everyday life. According to him, the Gypsies of Europe are the descendants of the Indo-Aryans who entered North-West India in ancient times as wandering shepherds and hunters. He cites the case of Stephan Valayi, a Hungarian student of theology who in 1763 was surprised to find striking resemblance of vocabulary between a thousand Indian words with that of the Gypsies of Raab in Hungary. It proved that the language of Gypsies was an Indian language connected with original Sanskrit. After sometime, Rudigar, Grellman and Bryant added linguistic and historical supplement to this discovery. Sher Singh asserted that this breakthrough was placed at a more scientific footing by Pott when he published his two-volume work *Die Ziegeuner in Europa und Asien* (1844–45) which was followed by Miller, Alexander Paspati, Mklosich, Von Sowa, Ko Punicki and few others. John Beames, who published his three volume study titled *A Comparative Grammar of the Modern Aryan Languages of India,* regarded the language of the European Gypsies as one of the Aryan languages of India. M.de Goeje, a Dutch scholar asserted that the Jats and Zottes are related to them. Later, Sher Singh has named a battery of philologists like Pischel, Woolner, Macfie, Finck, Kuhn, Littmann, Sampson, Macalister, Ackerley and Gilliat-Smith who agree that much of the Gypsy language is of Indian origin, though in an altered form.

Some of the accounts suggest that the Gypsies were found outside India even before A.D. 1000. The Persian poet Firdausi in his *Shah Nama* wrote about the orders by King Bahram to import of ten thousand of both sexes from India. This event was also recorded by the Arabian historian Hamza of Ispahan where both of them called these people Gypsies. The Persian poet Firdausi used the Persian *Zott*, which is the regular Arabic pronounciation of Jatt or Jat of the modern Syrian word for the Gypsies. It is also learnt from Tabari that after Byzantine was conquered in A.D. 855, the Zott (Jat) inhabitants with their women, children and cattle were taken as prisoners to the Greek empire. There are many accounts that show that the Gypsies were in Europe in the 14th century. From 1417 onwards, there are authentic official and municipal records of the presence and movements of Indian Gypsies in different parts of Europe. According to these accounts, the Gypsies were not usually treated by the Gorgio society with respect and sympathy. In order to save themselves from outsiders and foreigners, they presented gifts to bishops, barons and emperors and got letters or recommendation from them to move from one country to another. In certain cases they also presented themselves as penitents and pilgrims who were exiled from their homes so that they could cross borders without any problem.

Speaking on linguistic similarity, Angus Fraser (1995) argues that if the three tests of evolutionary relationship, i.e. community of basic vocabulary, similarity of grammatical structure and regularity of sound correspondence are applied to Romani and certain Indic languages, all the findings suggest 'unity of origin.' According to Vesey-Fitzgerald, a British Gypsiologist, 'Roma were in India for an extensive period and could well be indigenous as depicted through a clear correlation between words in Romani and ancient Indian language of Sanskrit.' The idea that language could be used as a tool to trace the migratory route of Roma was popularised by Sampson (1923) and continues till date (Hancock 2002). Linguistic evidence suggests that Roma left India approximately 1000 years ago and spent a relatively short time in the Middle East. It has also been suggested that Roma did not move in one solid mass from east to west; rather, they pursued different trajectories over the years and not all of these ended in Europe. According to scholars, three migratory routes were taken: for Roma (the European Gypsy); for Lom (the Armenian Gypsy); and Dom (the Syrian and Persian Gypsy). Sampson (1923) argues that each nomenclature corresponds with the Sanskrit doma and the modern Indian dom which refers to a person belonging to the 'untouchable'. Dom jati composed of indigenous people of mostly Dravidian and Munda descent and who made their life full of singing and dancing.

Viorel Achim (2004) suggests that before the Gypsies set out on their wandering journey towards the west, they lived as a unified people somewhere in Northern India, they had an independent state and were not like nomads but worked in animal husbandry and agriculture. The Gypsies arrived in Europe as nomads who held together as a loose mass of people. The wandering that led them in this direction began approximately between the 5th and 10th century A.D. By the time they arrived in Europe, the gypsies knew nothing of their own origins. Around the end of the 14th century, they set out towards the west from the Balkans and the Rumanian principalities in larger or smaller bands. In contrast with the wandering peoples who had preceded them, they moved peacefully from one country to another. With their ragged, dirty and wretched appearance and their small amount of stock, it was a pity that they were feared as thieves and as deceivers by the local populace. What was unique about the Gypsies and their treatment by the host society was that unlike colonial subjects, the Gypsies were a 'domestic' and the 'internal other' who were held responsible for all the ills in the society including diseases and famines.

An effort to establish a commonality between the Nats of India and the Gypsies of Europe was made in the early nineteenth century. One of the earliest accounts of the Nats or Bazeegar was given by Captain David Richardson. Captain Richardson was compelled to inquire into the lifestyle of the Nats because of a dissertation by a German scholar H.M.G. Grellmann (1783) on the gypsies of Europe who according to him were the products of the wandering races of India and shared many similarities with the gypsies of Europe. Grellmann's ethnological study ended with an emphatic claim that the Gypsies were the descendants who came from Hindustan and formed the lowest of the low, i.e. pariahs, 'outcastes' or the Sudras in the Indian social gradation. Richardson's study premises itself on Grellmann's thesis along with his own observations and experiences as an administrator in India.

Richardson tries to establish a common link between the gypsies of Europe and the Nats who were the 'wandering race' of beings of India through various life traits like peregrination, argot (which in the case of Gypsies is undoubtedly a species of Hindustani and so is that of the Nats), similar professional engagements. He adds both have a captain or a leader, are considered as thieves and in manners of religion are equally indifferent with fooding habits being quite similar. Corroborating Grellman's insistence on a common vocabulary of the Nats and the Gypsies of Europe, Richardson further says that it is not just a mere coincidence of few words but the entire vocabulary differs not so much from the common Hindustani as provincial dialects of the same country usually do from each other. This aspect has been complimented in a big way by the nineteenth century British writer George Barrow in his book *The Zincalis: An Account of the Gypsies of Spain* (1907). Richardson gives the examples of various words in Hindi like *kanjars, jugg, khansama, burga and hooqu* and their Latin counterpart in modern times that got 'transformed' in due course of time to conjurers, jugglers, consumer, burgher and hooker. He later adds that the conjurers or jugglers who arrived in Europe around the 13th century introduced the viol of three strings which strikes an undoutable similarity with that used by the Bazigars. Finally, he says that even the word guitar is a borrowed term of the Hindustani sitar.

Richardson lists out a number of words both in the Gypsy and Hindustanee versions:

Gypsy	*Hindustanee*	*English*
Apra	Oopar	Above
Bebee	Beebee	Aunt
Pownee	Panee Brook,	drink water, tears
Cauliban	Kala-burn	Black
Chericloe	Chireea	Bird
Per	Peroo	Belly
Jamoval co pane drowei paneeja, e	Panee	A bath, water to bathe
Davies, devus	Dewus	Day to day
Rattie	Rat	Dark, night
Peola	Peena	To drink
Can	Kan	Ear
Dad	Dada	Father, grandfather
Jag	Ag	Fire
Peroe	Pyr	Foot
Valashte	Bilisht	Finger, a span
Por	Poora	Full
Mutchee	Muchee	Fish
Bootsee	Bahutsee	Great deal
Gur	Ghur	House
Shing	Seeng	Horn
Ballow	Bal	Hair
Tattoo	Tutta	Heat, hot
Yacorah	Ek Ghuree	An hour
Bocolee	Bhookha	Hungry
Shunalee	Soonaee	Hearing
Gecoa	Jee or Jeeoo, jeevika	Life, living
Liecaw	Likha	Letters
Riah	Rae	Lord
Rriena	Ranee	Lady
Dai	Daee	Mother, a nurse
Mass	Mas	Meat, or food, flesh
Tod	Doodh	Milk
Boot	Buhot	Much, numbers
Nack	Nak	Nose
Nie	Nuh	Finger nail
Nevo	Nya, nou	New
Bouropanee	Bura Panee	Ocean, sea, great water
Rashee	Rishee	Priest
Briskinee	Burkha	Rain
Doriove	Dureaa	River

Cont'd...

...Cont'd

Lolo	Lal	Red
Bauro-chairee	Buree chhooree	Sword
Pan and Pon	Buhin	Sister
Roop	Roopa	Silver
Starrie	Sitara, tara	Star
Dicken	Dekhna	Sight, to see
Loon	Noon	Salt
Banaw	Baloo	Sand
Chive	Jeebh	Tongue
Rook	Rookh	Tree
Dennam	Daant	Tooth
Chalk	Kaka, Chacha	Uncle
Panee	Panee	Water
Jaw	Ana, jana	To come, to go
Bouro Matchee	Buree Muchhe	Big fish
Kalico	Kalko	Yesterday
Tschor	Chor	Thief
Dori	dori	A band or string
Rajah	Rajah	A Lord or Chief
Ranee	Ranee	Princess
Raz	Raj	Principality
Banduk	Bundoog	A musket
Gan Jagga	Gaon, Juggah	A village or piace
Jammadar	Jemmadar	A Commander or Officer
Dur	Door	Far
Perdo	Poordo	To fill up, to accomplish
Cha, Chabben	Khana, Chabana	To eat
Ischummedele	Chooma detee	She kisses
Jungustri	Ungooshturee	A Ring
Are	Ard	Meal
Paka	Punkh	A wing
Sapa	Saboon	Soap
Aduito	Dotuh	Double
Tatip	Tapna	To warm
Surgawa	Soonghna	To Smell
Gewawa	Gana	To sing
Mongua	Mongna	To solicit
Pi	Peena	To drink
Medikkaha	Main dekhaa	I saw
Metschana	Puhchanna	To know

As cited in Deborah Epstein's *Gypsies and the British Imagination, 1807–1930*, a set of Romani words and their English translations appeared in

Joy Hoyland's *A Historical Survey of the Customs, Habits and Present State of the Gypsies* (1816):

English	*Gypsy*	*Hindi*
One	Yuk	Ek
Two	Duee	Do
Three	Trin	Teen
Four	Stor	Chaar
Five	Pan	Paanch
Ten	Dyche	Dass
Head	Charro	Sir
Eyes	Yoch	Aankh
Nose	Nack	Naak
Hair	Balo	Baal
Hot Day	Tai dewes	Tal is hot dewes is din
Ear	Kau	Kaan
Night	Raut	Raat
Fish	Morcho	Macchli
House	Kare	Ghar
Gold	Sonnekar	Sona
Horse	Gur	Ghoda

Hancock too speaks of a linguistic similitude to justify the theory of Indian origin of the present-day Gypsies of Europe on the basis of cultural repertoire and says that some groups in Hungary, Slovakia and Transsylvania maintain the Indian *bhirava* musical scale. There is some similarity between a type of mouth music known in India as *bol* and *bega* in Romani that consists of syllables imitating the rhythm of the table. The tribunal where internal disputes are settled, called the *kris (i)* in Romani has the same form and function as the Indian panchayat. The *pilivani* wrestling matches with oiled bodies or pehalvan is common both in India and Iran. Further, the Romani word pani meaning 'water' for example is exactly the same in Hindi, Panjabi, Nepali, Bengali, Marathi, Sindhi, Gujarati and fifty other Indian languages.[68]

According to Sher Singh Sher, the *Sansis* of Punjab (a Denotified Nomadic Tribe) and the Gypsies of India share a common strand. He gives various examples relating to taboos, marriage, social organisation, and there are many customs that they relate among the Gypsies of Europe.[69] He cites Latif, Russell and Archer who have used the word Sansi and Gypsy synonymously. Giving a historical proof, he says that the Sansi gypsies are known in Syria in connection with the love affair of Hazrat or Sheikh Sannan, which is widely read and remembered in Islamic literature. Baines Athelstane also mentions a close resemblance between the character and temperament of the Sansi women of Punjab and the gypsy women of Europe.[70]

In the recent past, in order to bolster and strengthen the argument of an Indian origin of the Gypsies in Europe, among numerous claims and counter-claims, genetic evidence in the form of DNA analysis and serum analysis have been deployed to verify these multiple claims. According to Sareen, 'The European Gypsies, who migrated from Northern India about 800–1,000 years ago, have been well studied serologically, mostly by ABO, MNS and Rh systems. The results indicate that their blood groups agree well with the warrior caste of northern India.'

The serological analysis by the geneticist Vijender Bhalla has identified 'a common ethnic substratum' in India that Romanies share with 'Jat Sikhs, Panjabi Hindus and Rajputs' (1992: 331–32)

More recent evidence is found in a report dated June 2001 from the Centre for Human Genetics at Edith Cowan University in Perth according to which:

> Analysis of slow-evolving polymorphisms has identified a single parental and a single maternal lineage of Indian origin shared by all groups (of Romanies tested.). These lineages belong to a small subset of the known genetic diversity of the Indian subcontinent. Thus, Roma descend from a small ancestral minority in the Indian subcontinent that has subsequently fractured into multiple population isolates within Europe.
>
> (Kalaydjieva et al., 1999: 15)

Taking all the proof provided either by way of linguistic and cultural similarities or by way of a genetic match by geneticists and serologists, it leaves one with little doubt that the Gypsies of modern-day Europe are the predecessors of the Gypsies and nomads of India. However, what has not been conclusively proven is the fact whether this genetic link is shared between the Nats and Doms and the Gypsies of Europe.

Conclusion

The Nat as an itinerant community earned its livelihood as tramping entertainers, charlatans, conjurers and conmen. However, street entertainment was increasingly becoming a problem in the colonies and therefore, the Nats were included under the ambit of the CTA XXVII of 1871 along with two hundred other tribal and ambulatory communities. In 1952, the so called 'criminal tribes' were 'de-notified' and now are labelled as 'Denotified Nomadic Tribes' (DNTs) The CTA was replaced by Habitual Offender's Act (HOA) in 1952.

The 'Gypsy Question' has been a highly contentious and sensitive one as it involved sorting a sizeable section of the European population on ethnic lines. During the *Third Reich*, the 'Gypsy Question' like the 'Jew Question' were clubbed together on account of the 'unpure,' 'unproductive' and therefore 'misfit,' aspect of their existence. This culimated in the *O Baro Porrajmos* or the 'great devouring' of human life of the vagabonds, gypsies and nomads that resulted in the extermination of millions of Roma.

The discourse on the issue of common origin and ancestry of the Gypsies of Europe with the 'wandering castes' and 'criminal tribes' of India is still rife and this has kept the debate alive and enriched due to different interjections from time to time. The importance of the matter has drawn the attention of social and natural scientists from all academic backgrounds including Gypsologists from many countries including prominent Romani intellectuals like Ian Hancock and others like Judith Oakley, David Epstein, David Mayall, Grellmann, Barrow, Richardson, Marsden and many others.

Is it that the Gypsies of Europe though found misfits and unacceptable by the mainstream society in Europe were still viewed as the 'domestic' and the 'internal other' and which kept them as a separate and unsullied stock? However, amidst all these arguments, it is of particular importance to see how language and cultural traits become a bridge that spans the 'missing' ancestral link of the nomadic races and Gypsies of India with that of the present day Gypsies of Europe. Moreover, going by the conclusive scientific validation from serologists and geneticists from India and also from other parts of the world of a genetic link between the two ambulatory communities, the burden of proof seems to weigh more towards those who have been defying a common link between the two communities.

Hancock approves of an Indian origin of the Roma Gypsies and places them in conjunction with the warrior caste, i.e. the Rajputs of India. However, the serological results analysed by geneticists in the recent years prove a resemblance to the Jat stock (who also belonged to an ex-criminal tribe) along with others like Punjabis and Rajputs as well. The linguistic proof and other similarities shared between the Nats and the gypsies of Europe have already been presented here. What remains to be seen is whether any conclusive evidence can be provided further by social and natural scientists in order to establish or disprove the practice of 'untouchability' and the so called 'hereditary criminality' between the two peripatetic communities.

Notes

1. This article, a part of my doctoral thesis, was elaborated and presented in the School Seminar of the School of History and Anthropology, Queen's University as part of the Sir Charles Wallace Fellowship, 2011–2012. I am thankful to the participants who gave their feedback on my presentation. Prof. Fiona Magowan, Director, School of History and Anthropology as my mentor deserves a special mention for her humbleness and enriching comments and her critical insights on my paper as also Dr Marina Roseman who invited me to be a part of her *River Lagan Writing Group* and gave her feedback. Thanks are due to Amelia, Evi, Esmourie, Theodore, Yuxing and many others who were part of this eclectic tribe of young academicians.
2. (a) Anatoly N. Khazanov (1984: 2) in his book *Nomads and the Outside World* has given examples from history and religious scriptures like Bible where nomads have been treated as a threat, scourge and a 'devil incarnate.' According to Khazanov, in China the Confucians despised the barbarian nomads, considering them incapable of following a civilised way of life. Further he says that from the times of Biblical prophets the view that the nomads were excessively savage and wild has often been associated with the view that they have a particular destiny, as a means through which God can chastise different peoples.

   (b) Peter Harrsion (2005) too has given examples from Bible to show that nomadism and peregrination was a cursed enterprise. He has given references and verses from Genesis to prove that nomads, wandering people and vagabonds were equated with infidels and heathens and akin to have an animal like existence.
3. Anatoly, N. Khazanov and Andre Wink (ed.) (2001): *Nomads in a Sedentary World*, Curzon Press, Surrey, UK. p. 3.

4. (a) Chris A. Bayly. (1983). *'Rulers, Townsmen and Bazaars: North Indian Society in the Age of British expansion, 1770–1870'*, Cambridge University Press, pp. 28–29.
   (b) According to Anand Yang (1979) the nature of official power and control in the nineteenth and early twentieth century can be described as *'Limited Raj'* system because landlords were the effective rulers and administrators for many of the day-to-day decisions in local society. As 'connections' or links to the local levels of society, they ensured the authority of British rule, and in return their position as local controllers was sustained and nourished by the powers of the state.
5. Khazanov (2001) maintains that nomads played a very important role as middlemen in various kinds of cultural exchange between different sedentary societies.
6. Casimir, Michael, J. and Rao, Aparna. (2003). 'Movements of peoples: nomads in India'in Veena Das (ed*) The Oxford India Companion to Sociology and Social Anthropology*, Oxford University Press, Delhi, p. 221.
7. Khazanov (2001), op. cit., p. 7.
8. (a) Casimir and Rao (2003), op. cit., p. 227.
   (b) These social and cultural exchanges between sedentary and nomadic communities find an interesting corollary between the 'conquerer and the conquered' as shown by Jean and John Comaroff's study of colonial evangelism and modernity in South Africa. In their second volume of a proposed three volume study, *'Of Revelation and Revolution,* Vol. 2: *The Dialectics of Modernity on a South African Frontier,'* the authors speak of a complex system of reciprocity between the conqueror and the conquered.
9. Casimir, op. cit., p. 227.
10. Ibid. Also in Neeladri Bhattacharya's (2003). 'Predicaments of Mobility: Peddlers and Itinerants in Nineteenth-century Northwestern India', in Claude Markovits et al., (ed.) *Society and Circulation: Mobile People and Itinerant Cultures in South Asia 1750–1950*, Permanent Black, New Delhi.
11. (a) Federici, Silvia (2004). *Caliban and the Witch*, Autonomedia, New York, p., 82.
    (b) The same scenario existed in India as well where large scale crimes against property was being effected as a ploy to fight against colonial policies and paupersiation.
12. Federici., ibid., p. 85.
13. Ibid., p. 83.
14. Relation between a travelling and a settled society still shows the same degree of conflict and antagonism as was witnessed in the 18th and 19th centuries. The best example can be had from the treatment meted out by the host society to the migrant population spread in different parts of the world as also within the national frontiers located in different provinces.
15. Federici., op. cit., p. 11
16. Ibid., p. 2
17. According to this thesis, which later attained the acclaim as a 'science of genetics,' people had either 'good genes' or 'bad genes' and those who had the latter like the vagrants, gypsies and nomads were made to undergo forced sterilisation and in some cases prosecution and banishment from the state. The popularity of eugenics led to the sprouting of many 'Eugene societies' in Europe and in England.
18. The 20th century witnessed the echoes of nomad problem in terms of racial politics and soon translated into Hitler's notion of a 'master race'. This led him to kill thousands of Roma gypsies and Jews as part of his 'Sterilisation and Euthanasia Programme' to cleanse the emergent German nation of biologically 'unfit' people or 'biological enemies' that threatened the German *Volk*.

19. Taking a Cohnian stance, this unwrapping and unfolding of the colonial state was done through the 'modalities of surveillance' by conducting studies in far flung areas of the Empire by the British administrator cum proto-ethnographers. This led to the production of voluminous compendiums, gazetteers, census, reports and government documents besides memoirs, letters and drawings. The *Blue Book of Sociology* was also the result of such a discursive endeavour which served as an epistemic guide and a referential handbook that contained all important information about the country and its people.
20. According to Bhangya Bhukya (2007), anthropometry was used as a means of identifying criminals in India which was later replaced by fingerprinting due to the former being an inaccurate, clumsy, costly and lengthy process, p., 200.
21. (a) Anand Yang however contests colonial historian's claim of an increasing crime rate in nineteenth century India. According to him, 'criminal statistics for British India are gross underestimations because there was little institutional representation at the local level.

    (b) Parama Roy (1998) has questioned colonial reports and documents relating to a sharp increase in cases of thuggee. Tom Lloyd (2006) too has raised concerns over the reliability of the confessions of the thugs and to prove his point cites the infamous case of Ghulam Hussain; an agricultural labourer who was one of the eight suspects to have been confessed. However, Hussain seemed to inflate the number of murders that he had committed with each subsequent interrogations led by Thomas Perry; the new district magistrate appointed by the East India Company during 1808–09.

    (c) Bhukya, op. cit., notes that cases of crime against property in India increased from 7939 in 1898 to 11,382 in 1900, p. 190.
22. It was a new kind of criminal activity whereby parents were killed in order to kidnap and traffic their children.
23. The thugs were called *'Phansigars'* or noose operators and stranglers. This also included *Shudgarshids* or the tribe of jugglers and fortune tellers described as 'notorious for kidnapping children' and for an 'abominable traffic' in the sale of sinews as charms against evil.
24. W.J. Hatch. (1976). *Land Pirates of India*, Concept Publishing Company, Delhi, p., 40.
25. K.S. Singh (ed.) (2001). *Tribal Society in India: 'Tribal Movements', Vol. II,* pp. 122, (New Delhi,). Famine was one of the prime reasons for 'dacoity' to have flourished in India during the colonial regime.
26. Arnold in Anand Yang's (ed.) (1995). p. 68.
27. Radhakrishna (2001), op. cit., p. 8.
28. Ibid. Also refer to Casimir et al. The introduction of railways in 1850 and a support by way of concessions given by the government encouraged a new sprout of wholesale 'railway traders' resulting in a virtual fleeing of the earlier traders. In this scenario, the only way out was to join the gang of dacoits, thugs or brigands. Radhakrishna gives the example of Koravas in South India was one such community of salt traders who lost their livelihood due to the introduction of railways.
29. Bhukya., op. cit., p. 203.
30. Ibid., p. 191. According to Bhukya, from 1916 to 1921, the number of criminal cases increased from 3,975 to 6,627.
31. Arnold (1995). op. cit., p. 68.
32. Radhika Singha. (2000). 'Settle, Mobilize, Verify: Identification Practices in Colonial India', *Studies in History,* 16, p., 152.
33. Bhukya (2007), op. cit., p. 188.

34. Nicholas B. Dirks (2001). *Castes of Mind: Colonialism and the Making of Modern India*, Princeton University Press, New Delhi.
35. (a) As Radhakrishna (2001) informs that the CTA 1911 had its origins in the report of the Indian Police Commission, p. 37.
36. Y.C, Simhadri, (1979). *The Ex-Criminal Tribes of India*, National Book Trust, p. 8
37. Bhukya (2007), op. cit., p. 179.
38. 'Zomia' is a geographical term coined by the Dutch historian Willem van Schendel in 2002 and is derived from the root word *Zo* in one of the Indian states Mizoram and means hill. The term refers to a huge mastiff of mainland South-East Asia that has historically been beyond the control of urban or low governments or low land bureaucracy. Scott has applied the notion of Zomia in his work 'The Art of Not Being Governed', which according to him includes the runaway, fugitive or maroon communities who have chosen' to stay away from modernist notions of progress and development and civilisational humdrums.
39. The term 'fourth world' was made popular by Manuel Castells for those who were on the fringes of civilisation, i.e. the sub-population socially excluded from the global society. This includes the nomadic, pastoral and hunting-gathering people living beyond the pale of industrial norms.
40. However, the collapsing of these tramping and itinerant groups into a single monolithic category called 'Nats' maintained subtle degrees of variation and difference within them.
41. Crooke, W. (1896), (Rep. 2005), *'The Tribes and Castes of the North-western Provinces and Oudh' Vol. IV,* D.K. Publishers Distributors (Pvt.) Limited, New Delhi, p., 57.
42. Markovits et al., (2003). *Society and Circulation: Mobile People and Itinerant Cultures in South Asia 1750–1950,* Permanent Black, New Delhi, pp., 2–3.
43. Markovits, op. cit., (2003), pp., 2–3.
44. (a) Yogendra Singh. (Rep., 2009). *'Modernization of Indian Tradition,'* Rawat Publications, Jaipur, pp., 13–16.

    (b) The twin concept of 'great tradition' and 'little tradition' was first used by Robert Redfield to analyse social change in his studies of the Mexican communities. Later Milton Singer and McKim Marriott utilised this conceptual framework to conduct studies on social change in India. It was also expanded by Yogendra Singh in his book *'Modernization in Indian Tradition'* for the Indian case.
45. Bhattacharya, Ibid., p, 168.
46. Op. cit., pp., 163–214.
47. Op. cit.
48. (a) D. Ibbetson. (1883). *'Punjab Castes'*, Government Printing Press, Lahore, 1916, pp., 284–288. According to Ibbetson, the term 'Nat' was used synonymously along with that of Bazigars in the Lahore Division. One can then presume that the Nats were found in Lahore what is now known as Pakistan.

    (b) In a loose sense, proto-ethnographers would mean those ethnographers who are non-academics and who do not have any academic training in that area.
49. Out of a total of 5,722 who were from the Depressed Class, J.H. Hutton who compiled the Census of India Report of 1931, Vol. I, Part I, says that the Nats comprised 227 in number. However, only 20 were found in Baluchistan states, while the remaining 5,702 being in the British territory. The enumerator is unable to say whether those 20 found in the Baluchistan States belonged to the Nat community as well.

50. The definition of an actor or *'nata'* is one who can apply the music of four kinds of instrument, and produce a play according to the meaning of the Sastra as well as his own reasoning.
51. The word *'nat'* had synonyms too like *'Bharata', 'Sailusa', 'Kusilava', 'Shaubhik'*, etc.
52. Jose Kalapura and Purushottam (2011) *Bihar ke Nat: Jeeney ki Baazigari*, Daanish Books, pp., 10–11.
53. Pandit Pandurang Vaman Kane. (1968). *Dharmashastra ka Itihaas, Part I,* Uttar Pradesh Hindi Sansthan, p., 125.

    (a) Elaborating on the notion of *Antyajya*, the word has been used for castes at the lowest rung of the caste hierarchy along with the Chandals. They were also referred to as 'Panchams' or the exterior castes and untouchables. Manu (8/279) has used it for Shudras as well. There are various typologies of 'antyajanya' found in the Smritis. Atri (199) has mentioned seven types of antyajanyas and includes *Rajaka* (washerman), *Charmakara* (leather-worker), Nats (also known as *Kolhatis* in the South). Vyas Smriti (1/12–13) has mentioned *Charmakaras, Mah, Bhilla, Rajaka, Pushkar, Nat, Virat, Bhed, Chandalas, Dasas, Shwapach, Kolik* as the twelve antyajanyas.
54. R.V.P. Unni. (1998) *Natyasastra: Text with Introduction, English Translation and Indices,* Vol. I, Nag Publishers, New Delhi, p., 19.
55. Mukherjee, K.K. et al., 2007. *'Girls and Women in Prostitution in India: A Report'*, Gram Niyojan Kendra, Ghaziabad, Uttar Pradesh, p., 4.
56. *The Asiatic Society of Bengal,* Vol. III, trans. H.S. Jarrett, 1948.
57. (a) Madhu Trivedi' (1999). Tradition and Transition: The Performing Arts in Medieval North India,' in *The Medieval History Journal*, 2, 1.

    (b) Tal according to Trivedi is a pair of brass cymbals like cups with broad mouth, p., 110.

    (c)*Duhul* was a drum; a Persian equivalent of ordinary *dhol* in Hindustani, p., 107.
58. Bhattacharya, op. cit.
59. H.A. Rose. (Rep., 2008), *A Glossary of the Tribes and Castes of the Punjab and NWFP*, Vol., III, p., 164.
60. This ritual continued in the colonial period when the British administrators would invite the Nats to sing, dance and perform acts of dare devilry in order to amuse and regale their guests.
61. It would be befitting to mention here that Levi Strauss in his renowned four volume work *Mythologiques* states that there is a similarity in myths of different cultures. According to him, mythical thought always progresses from the awareness of opposites towards their resolution. The origin myths are dealt with in detail by Casimir in Rao (ed.) (1987). *The Other Nomads: Peripatetic Minorities in Cross-cultural Perspective.* Kölner Ethnologische Mitteilungen.
62. According to this group, Gypsy is an abbreviated form of Egyptians.
63. (a) Judith Oakley (1983). *The Traveller Gypsies,* Cambridge University Press, UK

    (b) Slurs or derogatory terms to address non-Gypsy societies.
64. (a) Nord, Deborah Epstein (2006). *Gypsies and the British Imagination 1807–1930,* Columbia University Press, New York.

    (b) Rogue literature was a particular form of pamphleteering which dealt with rogues, beggars and vagabonds and dealt with the cozening tricks and their argot. A detailed exposition of this typology of literature has been assorted in the form of writings and pamphlets and titled *'Rogues, Vagabonds and Sturdy Beggars'* in Arthur F. Finney (ed.).
65. Johnson; as cited in Barrow.

66. As quoted in Ian Hancock's (2002) book *'We are the Romani People'.*
67. Op. cit.
68. Hancock, Ian (2002). We are the Romani people: Ames am e Rromane dzene, University of Hertfordshire Press, Great Britain, p. 9.
69. Ibid., p. 53.
70. Ibid., p. 51.

References

Achim, Viorel. 2004. *The Roma in Romanian history*. Bucharest: Central European University Press.

Barrow, George. 1907. *The Zincalis: An Account of the Gypsies of Spain*, London: John Murray.

Bauman, Zygmut. 2002. *Society under Siege*. John Wiley and Sons.

Bayly, Chris A. 1996. *Empire and Information: Intelligence Gathering and Social Communication in India, 1780–1870.* Cambridge: Cambridge University Press.

Bhukya, Bhangya. 2007. 'Delinquent Subjects: Dacoity and the Creation of a Surveillance Society in Hyderabad State', *Indian Economic and Social History Review,* Vol. 44, No. 2.

Casimir, Michael J., and Aparna Rao. 2003. 'Movements of Peoples: Nomads in India'. In *'The Oxford India Companion to Sociology and Social Anthropology'.* Edited by Veena Das. New Delhi: Oxford University Press.

Cohn, Bernard S. 1987. *An Anthropologist among Historians and Other Essays*, New Delhi: Oxford University Press.

Cole, Simon. 2001. *Suspect Identities: a history of fingerprinting and criminal identification*, Harward University Press, United States..

Comaroff, Jean, and John Comaroff. 1997. *Revelation and Revolution, Vol. II: The Dialectics of Modernity on a South African Frontier*. Chicago: The University of Chicago Press.

Crooke, W. (1896) 2005. *The Tribes and Castes of the North-western Provinces and Oudh, Vol. IV,*Reprint, New Delhi: D.K. Publishers Distributors.

Dirks, Nicholas B. 2001. *Castes of Mind: Colonialism and the Making of Modern India.* New Delhi: Princeton University Press.

Federici, Silvia. 2004. *Caliban and the Witch.* New York: Autonomedia.

Finney, K. Arthur (Ed). 1973. *Rogues, Vagabonds and Sturdy Beggars.* The University of Massachusetts Press.

Foucault, Michel. 1995. *Discipline and Punish: The Birth of the Prison*. New York: Knopf Doubleday Publishing Group.

Fraser, Angus. 1995. *The Gypsies.* USA: Blackwell.

Hancock, Ian. 2002. *We are the Romani People: Ames am e Rromane dzene*. Great Britain: University of Hertfordshire Press.

Harrison, Peter. 2005. 'Fill the Earth and Subdue it: Biblical Warrants for Colonization in Seventeenth Century England,' *Journal of Religious History*, Vol. 29, No. 1.

Hatch, W.J. 1976. *The Land Pirates of India*, New Delhi: Concept Publishing Company.

Hoyland, J. 1816. A Historial Survey of the Customs, Habits and Present State of the Gypsies. London: Darton, Harvey & Co.

Ibbetson, D. 1916. *Punjab Castes*. Lahore: Government Printing Press.

Kalapura, Jose, and Purushottam. 2012. *Bihar ke Nat: Jeeney ki Baazigari.*, New Delhi: Daanish Books.

Kane, Pandit Pandurang Vaman. 1968. *Dharmashastra ka itihaas, Part I* (in Hindi), Uttar Pradesh: Uttar Pradesh Hindi Sansthan.

Khazanov, A.M. 1984. *Nomads and the Outside World.* Cambridge: Cambridge University Press.

Khazanov, A.M., and A. Wink (eds.). 2001. *Nomads in the Sedentary World.* Surrey: Curzon Press.

Lloyd, Tom. 2006. 'Acting in the "Theatre of Anarchy": The Anti-thug Campaign and Elaborations of Colonial Rule in Early Nineteenth-century India', *Edinburgh Papers in South Asian Studies*, No. 19.

Markovits, C. et al., 2003. *Society and Circulation: Mobile People and Itinerant Cultures in South Asia, 1750–1950.*, New Delhi: Permanent Black.

Mukherjee, K.K. et al. 2007. 'Girls and Women in Prostitution in India: A Report'. Ghaziabad, Uttar Pradesh: Gram Niyojan Kendra.

Nord, Deborah Epstein. 2006. *Gypsies and the British Imagination: 1807–1930*, New York: Columbia University Press.

Oakely, Judith. 1983. *The Traveller – Gypsies.* Cambridge: Cambridge University Press.

Roy, Parama. 1998. 'Discovering India, Imagining Thuggee'. In *Indian Traffic: Identities in Question in Colonial and Postcolonial India.* Edited by Parama Roy. Berkeley: University of California Press.

Rao, Aparna (ed.). 1987. *The Other Nomads. Peripatetic Minorities in Cross-Cultural Perspective.* Kölner Ethnologische Mitteilungen, Bd. 8. Köln: Böhlau Verlag.

Radhakrishna, Meena. 2001. *Dishonoured by History: 'Criminal Tribes' and British colonial Policy.* New Delhi: Orient Longman.

Rana, Subir. 2011. 'Nomadism, Ambulation and the "Empire": Contextualising the Criminal Tribes Act, XXVII of 1871', *Transcience*, Vol. 2, Issue 2.

Richardson, Captain David. 1979. 'An Account of the Bazeegurs, A Sect Commonly Denominated as Nuts', *History and Antiquities, The Arts, Sciences, And Literature of Asia,* Vol. 7, Article 19 Edited by Sir William Jones. New Delhi: Cosmos Publications.

Rose, H.A. 1919. *Glossary of the Tribes and Castes of the Punjab and North-west Frontier Province.* Vol. III, Lahore: Government Press, Reprinted in 2008.

Scott, James. 2009. *The Art of not Being Governed: An Anarchist History of South-east Asia:* Yale University Press.

Sher, Singh Sher. 1965. *The Sansis of Punjab: A Gypsy and De-notified Tribe of Rajput Origin.* New Delhi: Munshiram Manoharlal.

Simhadri, Y.C. 1979. *The Ex-criminal Tribes of India.* New Delhi: National Book Trust.

Singh, Yogendra. 2009. *Modernization of Indian Tradition.* Jaipur: Rawat Publications.

Singha, Radhika. 2000. 'Settle, Mobilize, Verify: Identification Practices in Colonial India,' *Studies in History*, 16: pp. 151–198.

Trivedi, Madhu. 1999. 'Tradition and Transition: The Performing Arts in Medieval North India,' *The Medieval History Journal*, 2, 1.

Unni, R.V.P. 1998. *Natyasastra: Text with Introduction.* English translation and Indices, Vol. I. New Delhi: Nag Publishers.

Yang, Anand A. 1986. *Crime and Criminality in British India.* Association for Asian Studies, USA: University of Arizona press.

—— (ed). 1979. 'The Agrarian Origins of Crime: A Study of Riots in Saran District, India, 1886–1920', *Journal of Social History*, Vol. 13, No. 2.

CHAPTER 15

Tribal Entrepreneurial Growth

Drawing Comparative Inferences from Malaysia and India

RAJANITA DAS PURKAYASTHA

Introduction

Since the pre-Independence era, several tribes in India have remained crudely subjugated in their entrepreneurial initiatives. The economic pursuits of the poor tribal people, although diversified at varying lengths, could not establish them as successful entrepreneurs till date. Their historical advent through recurrent stages of stress and strain in quest of subsistence has turned them as mere objects of exploitation. While exposures could have helped them imbibe traits from other cultures through contact with external people and assimilation into a bigger space, these exposures otherwise resulted in their degradation in contrary. Till the pre-Independence era, the dual problems of economic isolation and socio-physiological confinements had resulted in their vulnerability. Following Independence, and subsequent rise of democratic form of political control, statutory provisions and welfare schemes for their protection and development were mandated by Indian government. Owing to their predominant rural presence, a series of remedial measures in the form of fund allocation, articles and schedules for entitlement and reservation to education, jobs, land and other facilities might have relieved these minority communities from the chronic maladies of segregation and isolation, but it has not been properly incorporated in their pervasive development. It is believed that there still exists considerable scope for rectification, and the actual beneficiaries are far from the reality of attaining self-sufficiency (Bhowmick 1994).

Tribes in India comprise nearly 8 per cent of the total population and by and large constitute the lowest strata of the informal economy. Their developmental challenges account for social, economic and geographical exclusion, with a perennial degradation of their livelihood base, reduced capacity, lack of awareness and motivation along with an absence of market-friendly approaches to skills and resource-building. All these are responsible for their vulnerability to exploitation, not only by the non-minorities but also the economically affluent ethnic minorities, out-migration from their natural habitats and vicious debt traps by unscrupulous moneylenders, loan sharks and middle-men (ILO-DWT 2005). Although agriculture remains the foundation for such communities, entrepreneurship has not grown sufficiently among them in keeping with up-to-date developments, which could provide scope for sustainable diversification. No serious efforts have so far been made to link livelihood to market, paving the way for growth of an innovative form of entrepreneurship, in tandem with their rich cultural embellishments (Bhowmick 1994).

The field of entrepreneurship is extremely important in boosting the socio-economic development of a community through human capital development and resolving social issues, apart from individual development. While an entrepreneur is prepared to seize every opportunity and face challenges around him/her and convert it into something new and productive, the field of entrepreneurship is influenced by the national economy, national mission and investment patterns (Othman et al. 2011). Entrepreneurship for tribal minorities has unfortunately become synonymous with small- and medium-scale enterprises (SMEs) that indulge in growing class consciousness and gender disparities whereas the projection should have been otherwise for the poor tribal people. Bhowmick (1994) also lays stress on the fact that although Indian government is spending good amount of money in developing these needy communities, nevertheless, there exists a serious lack of aptitude, learning and education along with the problems of ethnocentrism of traditional-based institutions and apathy of other groups abreast. Side by side, there are also lack of services like demonstration, exhibition, training and amenities of vocational and recreational curriculum in educating the tribal youth. The ownership of Scheduled Tribe (ST) run enterprises has shown a steady decline, which tend to be mostly smaller in size, located mostly in rural areas, with some exceptions in the case of tribal majorities of north-eastern (NE) states that are under-represented as compared to their share in state-wise populations. Interestingly, in NE states, female-owned and/or managed enterprises are significantly greater in number, indicating the fact that entrepreneurship is the key to social mobilisation among the backward business class and ST small business entrepreneurs (Despande and Sharma 2013).

When assimilation is the core target through enterprise formation and entrepreneurship, it is a pre-requisite for middle-income countries aspiring to become high-income nations. The variegated socio-cultural practices and linguistic specificities of the ethnic groups impart a distinctive demographic, economic and communicative identity to them. However, tribal and aboriginal minority populations, in different developing countries of South and South-Eastern Asia have been subjected to innumerable socio-economic hardships that have left these ethnic communities undeveloped and poverty-stricken. Tribal or ethnic minority entrepreneurship is conspicuously distinctive from other forms of entrepreneurship through their in-built socio-cultural dynamics that play a prominent part in building the solid foundation to such cultural entities. Mere economic return or business value is not the only motto of such enterprises. The realm of entrepreneurship has always been considered as a means of wealth-making, despite the fact that it is necessarily a context-dependent social process (Parker 2004; Lounsboury and Glynn 2001)

The traditional belief that an entrepreneur is not created but born and it is a western-stylised concept still thrives in the minds of the rural-based tribal poor. An entrepreneur's living experience influences his/her social reality as well as helps in shaping the entrepreneurial identity. For example, the Malaysian society is divided by intense ethnicity, religion, culture and to some extent by the rural-urban employment patterns including stake-holding, allowing the prominence of specific ethnic groups in leading positions in business and trade, i.e. the Chinese. On the other hand, as usual, the Malay holding superior positions of political power can restrain Chinese authority in various areas. Therefore, a collective symbiotic understanding of entrepreneurial experiences and joint participation of all ethnic races in this venture has been helpful in better positioning of business entrepreneurs. This is deliberated in the ethnic nationalism or 'malayness' in the business practices (Noor 2009).

As mentioned earlier, the roots of entrepreneurship might lie in the western capitalistic and industrialised economies, but, in the Indian context, a study of tribal entrepreneurship and assessing their prospects is extremely imperative for the betterment of this class of people. In the absence of an appropriate entrepreneurial climate for the development of entrepreneurs, grass-root innovations are practically not becoming feasible. Inspiring instances from a neighbouring country like Malaysia, with evidences of the development of entrepreneurial resources, have attracted the attention of policy-makers to develop entrepreneurship further in making Malaysia a high-income nation by the year 2020[2] (Fui 2003).

Using a thorough analysis of the literature and the argument presented herein, the rest of the present study makes an attempt to draw comparative inferences of the problems and the prospects of selected aboriginal and tribal enterprises in Malaysia and India, respectively. Two distinct lines of analogy are drawn first by describing the policy/planning of Scheduled Tribe entrepreneurship in India as well as Orang Asli entrepreneurship in peninsular Malaysia. The paper is concluded by outlining a functional comparison of these two and thereby proposing certain recommendations for improvising the scenario in Indian context.

The Scenario in India: Scheduled Tribe (ST) Entrepreneurship

Generally speaking, the Scheduled Caste (SC) and Scheduled Tribe (ST) people are among the most underprivileged and deprived section of the population. They are economically backward and have been subjugated by the landlords and rural gentry for a long period of time. The role of concerted efforts to improve the quality of life of SCs and STs have been mostly in the form of policy and planning undertaken by the government and involvement of civil societies that are contributing to rural development in the Indian economy (Bhowmick 1994)

Parker (2004), in his description on 'The Economics of Self-Employment and Entrepreneurship', has highlighted the discrimination hypothesis to be responsible for the under-representation of minorities from obtaining jobs in paid employment or restricting them to low-paid jobs. In other words, entrepreneurship may provide them with an escape-route from any form of employer discrimination and by ensuring greater participation in entrepreneurship these individuals will be capable to liberate themselves. In capitalistic markets, if lenders discriminate against minorities, the members find it difficult to borrow and become entrepreneurs.

Let us look at the economic census data (2005), which covered more than 42 million enterprises, employing 99 million workers with 39 per cent enterprise to be located in urban areas, employing about 49 per cent of all workers. Using data of smaller private firms from 19 large states of India, which account for 96 per cent of India's population and 95 per cent of all enterprises, it has emerged that the SCs and STs are under-represented in the ownership of enterprises. Since the majority of such enterprises are single-person enterprises, the measure of enterprise ownership is highly correlated with the extent of self-employment (Ghani et al. 2011). With no universally accepted definition of entrepreneurship, the STs constituting 7.7 per cent of the nation's population own only 3.7 per cent of non-farm enterprises, employing about 3.4 per cent of the non-farm force. The states with lower proportion of STs are also under-represented in entrepreneurship in comparison to SCs and Other Backward Castes (OBCs). In fact, the under-representation is not driven by pockets of under-development but is widespread within states. Despite the reformation of caste structures and the spill-over of political acceptance, the economics does not match up to the former two contexts. However, some ethnic groups are able to surmount the barriers of caste system, while some others find it difficult to overcome (Iyer et al. 2011).

Internationally, there is unsatisfactory evidence on why employers from non-ethnic backgrounds discriminate one ethnic group in comparison to another. Sometimes, minorities owning business establish themselves well in sectors that are above-failure, such as retail, transport, manufacturing, etc. Even if there is no discrimination on the basis of ethnicity, bank's lending rules reward high-collateral and safe-sector start-ups with loans, resulting in outcomes that resemble discrimination. In a competitive credit market, every marginal entrepreneur would be charged higher rates of interest than his no-marginal counterpart, which reflects his lower average probability of success. Human capital investment has a direct impact on paid-employment rather than on self-employment. Discrimination, on one hand, is the push factor, can on the other hand serve to be a pull factor in making entrepreneurship attractive among ethnic groups. Consumer discrimination could also push on the returns and the number of marginal entrepreneurs. There might be a parallel body of knowledge on the existence of credit associations or minority-owned banks but their coverage is mostly limited to smaller and failure prone businesses despite their ability to bootstrap impecunious businesses. More than three-quarter of firms in the survey were found to be non-registered or informal. They were not subject to government laws or environmental regulations and as a result could not access government/institutional sources of finance (Parker 2004).

In India, other than caste, financing constraints and lack of education could be attributed to expanding size of enterprises. These factors prevent the ST in venturing into industries that have significant economies of scale. The firms owned by them are smaller, significantly in the urban areas, in comparison to the non-minority ones. Inspired by Max Weber's (1930) 'protestant ethic'[3] thesis, entrepreneurship in minorities is determined by religious practices (Rafiq 1992). Again, empirical evidence has found religious variables to be insignificant (O'Farrell and Pickles 1989; de Wit and Winden 1989), though there are exceptions (Carroll and Mosakowski 1987; Clark and Drinkwater 2000). The absence of 'Role Models' on the other hand, can result in low self-employment averages among minority groups. From a geographical perspective, 'enclaves', create a self-supporting economic community information networks, sources of credit, 'niche' markets for the output of ethnic entrepreneurs and a steady supply of workers, possibly drawn from close-knit extended families that could increase opportunities for operation of minority-owned businesses despite the possibility that the scope of expansions in broader markets is difficult (Light and Bonacich 1988). However, the poor record of data in average private enterprise size amongst STs in rural or urban areas has been found to be in relation to single-person firms. By employing labour from within the family or clan, these firms limit the size of networks, more significantly in the rural areas. The sector-wise approaches in rural areas are more focussed on manufacturing rather than on other business services in the urban areas (ibid. 126–129).

The working paper by Iyer, Khanna and Varshney (2011) summarising the causative factors for this degraded scenario of ST and other minority business representation is indicative of some key findings. While discrimination exists, 'it cannot be the full answer' to the divide between caste-based stigma and expansion of the state of business dynamics by mediating disparities across varied caste and religious groups in India (Jodhka 2010: 47). The other factor could be the difference in physical and human capital which prevents these minorities to venture effective entrepreneurial sphere. There is a long-lasting difference in terms of land ownership (Iversen et al. 2011) to educational attainment (Desai and Dubey 2011). While dwelling on how entrepreneurship could flourish, it might be worthy enough to consider the experience of other minority groups from diverse parts of the world. The relationship between entrepreneurship and social structure and the experiences of overcoming the barriers would help validate the settings.

The Scenario in Peninsular Malaysia: Orang Asli Entrepreneurship

The *Orang Asli* is a heterogeneous community, comprising of 18 sub-ethnic groups living in various parts of peninsular Malaysia. The heterogeneous population consists of three main groups, 3 per cent Negrito, 54 per cent Senoi and 43 per cent Proto-Malays. Concerted efforts are being made since 1999 to reduce the incidence of poverty amongst the forest-dwelling communities with a significant decline to 7.5 per cent amongst a population of 22 million. Through the government's re-grouping and resettlement programmes, the aboriginals have benefitted in the form of a new form of agricultural development other than enjoying the basic facilities of roads, schools, clinics, water and electricity supplies (Lim 2003).

The New Economic Policy (NEP)[5] was institutionalised to redress the issue of *bumiputera* (son of the soil) dominance in economic share. It was hoped that by increasing the share of *bumi* ownership in business and linking up the small and medium enterprises to established corporations, the long-standing goal of 30 per cent bumiputera ownership would be realised by the Malay government. The Economic Transformation Programme (ETP)[6] has been introduced as a comprehensive effort to transform Malaysia as a high-income nation by 2020. Simultaneously, the government has introduced the New Economic Model (NEM)[7], which would be the driver for entrepreneurship for the upcoming decade and beyond. The entrepreneurial climate, with a special focus on marginalised groups, has dismantled the top-down regulatory barriers and adopted an action-oriented manifesto, to transform Malaysia as a fast growing economy. The rural industries are encouraged to join with the world markets through modernisation in production process, quality accreditation, market-linkage, etc. Additionally, *bumiputera* entrepreneurs get the opportunity to improve their business management skills through ICT, R&D and pragmatic interaction with non-bumiputera entrepreneurs (www.epu.gov.my)[8].

Among the programmes that were institutionalised to uplift the standard of *Orang Asli*, spearheaded by the Department of Aboriginal Affairs (JHEOA), involve *in-situ* development, re-groupment scheme and settlement in FELDA (Federal Land Development Authority) scheme. This developmental form could enhance productivity through modern agricultural farming techniques along with encouraging the setting up of enterprise and industries to widen the economic activities of the Orang Asli. The development of local institutions, cooperatives and entrepreneurship, especially among youths and providing guidance and support such as capital, place, training, advice, and management for entrepreneurial development also formed a core dimension of the developmental paradigm (Lim 2003).

Jamak et al. 2010, in a study on 'Assessing Entrepreneurship And Micro Business Enterprise of Orang Asli Aborigines In Pahang, Malaysia', confirmed that mixed blood aborigines in business are better than the achievement of the pure line, which can be seen from their higher median income of between RM1, 000 – RM2, 000, and also from their higher rates of business registrations. It was also found that they have strong desires to improve themselves, and as such are willing to participate or apply for any government projects as long as it benefits their livelihood and hence, impress standard of living. With education and exposure, many Orang Asli people have eventually moved out of their natural habitats to pursue desired jobs in towns and emulate urban culture through fashionable clothes, television sets, hand-phones, cars and motorcycles of the urban dweller. In a nutshell, the education, healthcare, telecommunications and the likes have improved the livelihood of the Orang Asli youth. In all these efforts, the government and other related organisations have made significant effort to improve and upgrade the living standards (ibid.: 12).

In an another study investigating the entrepreneurial behaviour (as a measure of their readiness to venture into business to ensure that they have the ability and determination to become successful entrepreneurs) among Orang Asli youth (N=6092) in the southern peninsular Malaysia, it was found that they possess high level of cognitive and non-cognitive entrepreneurial behaviours with the indication of a need for more information and knowledge regarding the function of entrepreneurship career (Othman et al. 2011). The Orang Asli youth nowadays are more willing to mix with outside people or other races, especially Chinese and Malays, when it comes to business dealings or working odd jobs with non-aborigine employers to earn a living.

It is indicative that over a period of time, the priority of Malaysian government has been in integration and socio-economic development of Orang Asli in their progress and development. In order to increase their productive capacities, the various land development and small holder betterment schemes have been devised from mid-1990 onwards. While modernisation has been a visionary of planning strategy, JHEOA has been particular of entrepreneurship development, along with a special focus on gearing up the Orang Asli cultural heritage and preserving traditions through sustainable tourism practices. Along with decent restructuring of the villages and fringe areas of settlement of the Orang Asli tribes, establishment of clusters like the small farmer association and cooperatives have been encouraged as growth centres for entrepreneurial incubation and inventory (Gomes 2007).

Conclusions

In the context of tribal entrepreneurship, the major reasons in getting the Indian government's efforts being wrongly placed are the dearth of planning approaches, miscalculated priorities and neglecting the imperative inter-ethnic variations. There is no shortage of efforts and institutional existence commissioned with the task of bringing the tribal communities in India into mainstream national life. The influence of modernity is not limited to mere influx of capitalism for social and economic transformation. The cultural traits and localisations need to be equally articulated. Despite the historic and cultural differences, an imposed limitation in capacity to participate will always hinder these minority groups from being involved in national development process. Malaysian government (JHEOA)'s initiatives of rural development along with the pro-entrepreneurial policies and programmes, such as the New Economic Policy, and the New Economic Model declaring entrepreneurship as the key driver of the economy for the next 10 years, are the examples to be cited here. A special focus on education and skill-development at primary and secondary levels of education along with inculcation of a desire for entrepreneurship through an effective form of development management would open doors of opportunities for the present day Malay aboriginals such as Orang Asli youth.

Modernism is synonymous with mobility and accordingly the Orang Asli youth of present times adopt livelihood less dependent on forest and agriculture and more open to outside people who can help enhance their productivity. They are fast replacing their traditional income generating tendencies with business and other contractual jobs that posit them outside the perimeter of their settlements for survival. In some other cases, a feeling of community belonging by being attached to their original habitats and being satisfied with present source of income, by relying excessively on Chinese middlemen, for drawing revenue or clients is in progression. The scarcity and inadequacy of agriculture and forest resources have forced them to find for alternative means of income generation and seeking employment from diverse jobs and income generating units. Although there has been dependency on middlemen to run businesses and enterprises for their tasks, it is presumed that over a period of time and with the induction of more flexible regulatory system for business operation, their desires of emerging as successful entrepreneurs would be able to make a break-through discovery as a success story for Malaysian government. A congenial policy and programme support system, along with access to credit facilities, technological innovation, business advisory services and an updated infrastructural support system, will ultimately prepare the ground for entrepreneurial growth of Malaysian economy.

In India, the environment for entrepreneurial development needs to assimilate the pre-requisites of culture, finance, community network and learning. The institutionalisation of National Innovation Council and the presence of other ministries like Tribal Affairs and Rural Development might have legitimised schemes and funds, but these have not been efficient enough in gauging the primary foundations for building the entrepreneurial mind-sets among the present-day tribal youths. A pro-poor policy directive for propagating the growth of tribal enterprises, along with ubiquitous credit facilities, hassle-free business regulations, technological drivers and an integrated platform for network and interaction is necessary for these laid-back enterprises to compete on a global scale. India may very well initiate the inception of an innovative research journey on this concept of tribal entrepreneurship by looking into unexplored areas of a distributed manufacturing, circular economy framework, efficient networking systems, public pooling of resources, capacity utilisation and a digital presence to indicate global visibility to spur the growth of entrepreneurship. It is necessary to bear in mind that for minorities and other underprivileged communities, entrepreneurship could devise means of escape from hardships of poverty and inequality but at the same time the policy-makers and planners along with the civic and private sector should formulate schemes and the welfare mechanisms that foster a competitive entrepreneurial growth in the economy and equip them with a self-confidence rather than cripple their psychology with a funder/donor dependency syndrome.

Most of entrepreneurial research lays stress on individual success patterns, behavioural characteristics and seem to consider wealth accumulation as the only yardstick to entrepreneurial success. In the context of community-based entrepreneurship, as small-scale business units/firms, in the case of tribal people, more and more research focus is required along the lines of forming an understanding of the successful institutional cultures and role models for enhancing their expertise and resource base. The principles of accounting, psychology, organisational behaviour, innovation and business management have contributed to the basics of entrepreneurship. However, a parallel investigation into the cultural dimensions of a successful tribal enterprise(s) is also indispensable to portray the story of a successful process trend of a unique entrepreneurial venture wherein the marginalised communities make an attempt to sustain, gain and maintain their distinct identity and legitimacy, if not authenticity.

Notes

1. A Pilot model project by ILO-DWT South Asia, January 2001–December 2005, to demonstrate praticipatory implementation modalities for tribal empowerment and community driven approaches to gender and culture sensitive employment and entrepreneurial initiatives.
2. Also known as Wawasan 2020 in Malay. Launched by the longest reigning Prime Minister, Tun Dr. Mahathir in the year 1990. It was pronounced when the New Economic Policy (NEP) was coming to an end. It is a long term goal for the nation to become a fully-developed country by the year 2020.
3. *Protestant Ethic and the Spirit of Capitalism* is a book written by Max Weber, a German Sociologist, economist and politician. It is considered as the founding text in economic sociology and sociology in general.
4. Surinder Jodhka, a sociologist at the Indian Institute of Dalit Studies, New Delhi, conducted an ethnographic study and discovered that the Dalit enterprise did not run fairly well, despite being a large and potentially productive segment of the population.
5. An affirmative action programme launched by the Malaysian Government in the year 1971 under Prime Minister, Tun Abdul Razak. The NEP ended in 1990 and was succeeded by National Development Policy of 1991. The NEP is referred to in the present tense because many of the tangible economic benefits it offered, are still continuing.
6. Economic Transformation Programme was launched on 25 September, 2010 as a part of Malaysia's National Transformation Programme to elevate the country to a developed the nation status by 2020, trageting a GNI per capita of US $15,000.
7. The New Economic Model was unveiled on 30 March, 2010 by Prime Minister Tun Razak and is intended to double the per capita income in Malaysia by 2020. From becoming ethnically based to need-based, the affirmative action programme would become more competitive, market and investor-friendly.
8. Official website of the Economic Planning Unit of the Prime Minister's office.
9. Jabatan Hal Ehwal Orang Asli, Department of Orang Asli Affairs, Malaysia.

References

AUSAID, CIDA, DANIDA, and MIGROS. 2005. Cooperative Federation of Switzerland. *Socio-Economic Empowerment of Tribal People through the Cluster Level Approach in Orissa*. ILO-DWT for South Asia and Country Office for India. New Delhi.

Bhowmick, P.K. 1994. *Rural and Tribal Developmental Practices in India*. New Delhi: MD Publications.

Carroll, G.R. and E. Mosakowaski. 1987. The Career Dynamics of Self-employment', *Administrative Science Quarterly*, 32(4): pp. 570–589.

Clark, K. and S. Drinkwater. 2000. 'Pushed out or Pulled in? Self-employment among Ethnic Minorities in England and Wales', *Labour Economics*, 7: pp. 603–28.

Desai, S. and A. Dubey. 2011. 'Caste in 21st Century India: Competing Narratives'. *Economic and Political Weekly*, 46(11), pp. 40–49.

Despande, A., and S. Sharma. 2013. *Entrepreneurship or Survival? Caste and Gender of Small Business in India*. Working Paper No. 228. Centre for Development Economics, Department of Economics, Delhi School of Economics.

deWit, G. and F. van Winder. 1989. 'An Empirical Analysis of Self Employment in the Netherlands'. *Economic Letters*, 32: pp. 97–100.

Fui, L.H. 2003. 'Economic Advancement and Poverty Eradication among the Aborigines in Malaysia', Paper submitted to the XII World Forestry Congress, Québec City, Canada.

Ghani, E., W.R. Kerr and S.D. O'Connel. 2001. 'Spatial Determinants of Enterpreneurship in India'. *Harvard Business School Working Paper*, pp. 12–27.

Gomes, G.A. 2007. *Modernity and Malaysia: Settling the Menraq Forest Nomads*. New York: Roultedge.

Iversen, V., A. Kalwij, A. Verschoor and A. Dubey. 2011. 'Caste Dominance and Economic Performance in Rural India'. Working Paper, Indian Statistical Institute, Kolkata.

Iyer, Lakshmi, T. Khanna., and T. Varshney. 2011. *Caste and Entrepreneurship in India*. Harvard Business School Working Paper, pp. 12–28.

Jamak, A., et al. 2010. 'Assessing Entrepreneurship and Micro Business Enterprise of Orang Asli Aborigines in Pahang, Malaysia', *Journal of Asia Entrepreneurship and Sustainability*, Vol. VI, Issue 1: pp. 53–68.

Jodhka, Surinder S. 2010. 'Dalits in Business: Self-Employed Scheduled Castes in Northwest India'. *Economic and Political Weekly*, 45(11).

Light, I. and E. Bonacich. 1988. 'Immigrant Entrepreneurs: Koreans in Los Angeles, 1965–82'. Berkeley and Los Angeles: University of California Press.

Lim., H.F. 2003. 'Economic Advancement and Poverty Eradication among the Aboriginals in Malaysia', Paper submitted to the XII World Forestry Congress, Quebec City, Canada.

Lounsbury, M., and A.M. Glynn. 2001. 'Cultural Entrepreneurship: Stories, Legitimacy and the Acquisition of Resources'. *Strategic Management Journal*, 22: pp. 545–564.

Noor, N.M. 2009. 'The Future of Malay-Chinese relations in Malaysia', *Peace Psychology in Asia*. London: Springer: pp. 161–172.

O'Farrell, P.N. and A.R. Pickles. 1989. 'Entrepreneurial Behaviour within Male Work Histories: A Sector Specific Analysis'. *Environment and Planning A*, 21: pp. 311–331.

Official Website of the Economic Planning Unit-Prime Minister's Department, accessed 1 February 2014, <www.epu.gov.my.>

Othman, Norasmah, Mohd Hasril Amiruddin, and Mazura Mansor. 2011. 'The Entrepreneurial Behavior of Orang Asli Youths in South Peninsular Malaysia', *International Journal of Education and Information Technologies* 5, no. 1: pp. 132–139.

Parker, C.S. 2004. *The Economics of Self-Employment and Entrepreneurship*. Cambridge: Cambridge University Press.

Rafiq, M. 1992. 'Ethinicity and Enterprise: A Comparison of Muslim and non-Muslim Asian Business in Britain'. *Journal of Ethnic and Migration Studies*, 19(1): pp. 43–60.

Index